Teaching Chinese Language in Singapore

Kay Cheng Soh
Editor

Teaching Chinese Language in Singapore

Efforts and Possibilities

Editor
Kay Cheng Soh
Singapore
Singapore

ISBN 978-981-10-8859-9   ISBN 978-981-10-8860-5 (eBook)
https://doi.org/10.1007/978-981-10-8860-5

Library of Congress Control Number: 2018937346

© Springer Nature Singapore Pte Ltd. 2018
This work is subject to copyright. All rights are reserved by the Publisher, whether the whole or part of the material is concerned, specifically the rights of translation, reprinting, reuse of illustrations, recitation, broadcasting, reproduction on microfilms or in any other physical way, and transmission or information storage and retrieval, electronic adaptation, computer software, or by similar or dissimilar methodology now known or hereafter developed.
The use of general descriptive names, registered names, trademarks, service marks, etc. in this publication does not imply, even in the absence of a specific statement, that such names are exempt from the relevant protective laws and regulations and therefore free for general use.
The publisher, the authors and the editors are safe to assume that the advice and information in this book are believed to be true and accurate at the date of publication. Neither the publisher nor the authors or the editors give a warranty, express or implied, with respect to the material contained herein or for any errors or omissions that may have been made. The publisher remains neutral with regard to jurisdictional claims in published maps and institutional affiliations.

Printed on acid-free paper

This Springer imprint is published by the registered company Springer Nature Singapore Pte Ltd. part of Springer Nature
The registered company address is: 152 Beach Road, #21-01/04 Gateway East, Singapore 189721, Singapore

Foreword

The Singapore Centre for Chinese Language (SCCL) was established in 2008 as Singapore's sole government-mandated research organization entrusted to study the teaching and learning of Chinese Language. It is endowed with the following mission:

> To provide quality training in pedagogy and research, to enhance the learning of Chinese Language and culture, and to establish Singapore's brand name in Chinese Language teaching.

And, with this mission, the Centre aspires to become:

> A Centre of Excellence for the learning, teaching, and educational research of the Chinese Language in a bilingual context.

Over the years since its establishment, the Centre has conducted numerous practice-oriented in-service courses for Chinese Language teachers to meet their updating needs in teaching methodologies. It also mounted master's and doctoral programs for the study of Chinese Language pedagogies in collaboration with The University of Hong Kong. Besides, the Centre published many series of research-based instructional materials for use by students in the classroom and monographs on teaching methodologies for teachers.

The research staff at the Centre has presented a large number of their research outputs at local and international conferences and has their papers published in conference proceedings and learned journals. Some of these have been reproduced together with pre-published ones in the monograph *Teaching Chinese Language in Singapore: Retrospect and Challenges* (Soh, 2016, Springer), to which the present monograph is a sequel.

The present monograph is titled *Teaching Chinese Language in Singapore: Efforts and Possibilities*. It is dedicated to the commemoration of SCCL's 10th anniversary and presents field-tested innovative ideas of curriculum and pedagogies which deserve larger-scale application and further verification in the schools. I hope it would serve as a meaningful reference for the Chinese Language education research fraternity and inspire young teachers and researchers to take pride in enhancing Chinese teaching and learning through bridging theory and practice.

I am thankful to my predecessor Dr. Chin Chee Kuen for molding the research tradition at the Centre, the researchers for their unrelenting efforts, and Dr. Soh Kay Cheng, our Research Consultant, for undertaking the task of compiling and editing the two monographs. I am confident that the ardent collaboration of them all will leave an impressive mark in the scene of innovative teaching and learning of Chinese Language, not only in Singapore but beyond.

Dr. Suan Fong Foo
Executive Director
Singapore Centre for Chinese Language
Nanyang Technological University
Singapore

Preface

The monograph *Teaching Chinese Language in Singapore: Retrospect and Challenges* (Springer, 2016), as the title implies, first provides a historic perspective and then looks into challenges ahead. The present monograph *Teaching Chinese Language in Singapore: Efforts and Possibilities* is a sequel to it. And, again, as the title implies, the new compilation presents results of recent efforts in solving some instructional problems of teaching Chinese Language and points to possible further developments.

The articles in this monograph are all written by the experienced researchers at the Singapore Centre for Chinese Language, Nanyang Technological University. As their responsibilities, the authors are constantly in search of innovative ideas for teaching Chinese Language more effectively and efficiently. This is a demanding task as Chinese Language is one of the most difficult, if not *the* most difficult, languages on earth. It is made doubly difficult by the complex language environment of the multilingual Singapore and the ever-changing trends in home languages.

The articles are organized into three parts. Part I: *Curriculum and Instructional Materials* includes a keynote speech delivered to international conference and deals with innovative ideas for Chinese Language curriculum, worthy of further empirical verification. There are also thoughts, based on experience and empirical evidence, regarding instructional materials such as textbooks qualities and Chinese characters, with consideration for the students' home language backgrounds.

Part II: *Teaching of Oral and Written Chinese* includes articles on the teaching of oral interaction (which has been emphasized by the most recent review of the Ministry of Education) and the teaching of narrative at the secondary school level. There are also reports on efforts to find effective and efficient methods of teaching written Chinese, a most challenging aspect of teaching the Chinese Language. Topics covered include computer-assisted essay writing, scaffolding, the use of First Language (English) in Second Language (Chinese) essay writing, and strategies used by secondary school students in writing Chinese essays, the use of dramatics and creative pedagogies in teaching Chinese.

Finally, Part III: *Assessment Literacy* presents two reports relevant to assessment literacy, a topic which has come to the fore in the recent years in Singapore. First is a report on a survey of primary school teachers, revealing how much they know and yet to know about this critical aspect of teaching. This is followed by a report on the development and validation of the *Assessment Literacy Scale* for use with teachers.

As for the Appendix, it reports a different kind of research—research into language research reports and ways to enhance the statistics. Data collection is time-consuming in language research; therefore, it cannot be over-emphasized that the usefulness of data should be enhanced and the results properly presented, for the benefits of both the researchers and their audiences.

Although all authors are on the payroll of the Centre, the views expressed in the articles are grounded in the empirical evidence available, within the methodological limitations of the research designs, and the views do not necessarily coincide with the official views of the Centre.

It is indeed a great pleasure for me to organize and edit my colleagues' research outputs into this monograph. I hope it will build a bridge between researchers at the Centre with researchers out there all over the world for the common goal of enhancing the teaching of Chinese Language to learners regardless of their language backgrounds. I must also admit that any errors left in the texts are my responsibility.

Singapore																						Kay Cheng Soh

Contents

Part I Curriculum and Instructional Materials

Chinese Language Curriculum in Singapore (1960–2000):
From Culture Transmission to Language Application 3
Chee Kuen Chin

Conceptualization of the Chinese Language Teaching Paradigm 25
Chee Kuen Chin

Chinese Language Teaching Paradigm: Case Study 37
Chee Kuen Chin, Cheng Gong and Boon Pei Tay

Mandarin Competence of Primary School Students in Singapore:
A Preliminary Comparison Across Academic Level and Home
Language Backgrounds 51
Hock Huan Goh, Chunsheng Zhao and Siew Hoon Kwek

Part II Teaching of Spoken and Written Chinese

Improving the Teaching of Chinese Speaking of Young Students from
English-Speaking Families: Teacher's Professional Development 65
Jing Yan, Hock Huan Goh and Hong Xia Zhou

Oral Interaction: Concept, Competence, and Assessment 83
Jinghua Fan

Teaching Oral Narrative Skills to Chinese
Children in Singapore 99
Li Li, Su Yee Au and Geok Hoon Tan

Effective Ways in Teaching Chinese Characters Without Phonetic
Clues 111
Jiaoyang Cui, Hock Huan Goh, Chunsheng Zhao and Kay Cheng Soh

Scaffolding Instruction of Chinese Essay Writing with Assessment as Learning 121
Cheng Gong, Chee Lay Tan and Chee Kuen Chin

Facilitating Creative Writing Instruction Using iPads in Secondary Schools: A School-Based Research 135
Chee Lay Tan, Lynn Dee Puah and Hee San Teoh

Effect of Phonological and Semantic Radicals on the Identification of Chinese Characters: Instructional and Research Possibilities 159
Limei Zhang and Suan Fong Foo

Part III Assessment Literacy

Investigating the Training Needs of Assessment Literacy among Singapore Primary Chinese Language Teachers 167
Limei Zhang

Teacher Assessment Literacy Scale: Design and Validation 179
Kay Cheng Soh and Limei Zhang

Epilogue. 193

Editor and Contributors

About the Editor

Kay Cheng Soh (苏启祯), Ph.D. (NUS, Singapore). He is currently Research Consultant at the Singapore Centre for Chinese Language. His academic interests include child bilingualism, creativity, world university rankings, and international achievement comparisons. His publications include books on the psychology of learning Chinese Language and various aspects of education.

Contributors

Su Yee Au Singapore Centre for Chinese Language, Nanyang Technological University, Singapore, Singapore

Chee Kuen Chin Singapore Centre for Chinese Language, Nanyang Technological University, Singapore, Singapore

Jiaoyang Cui Peking University, Beijing Shi, China; National University of Singapore, Singapore, Singapore

Jinghua Fan NUS, Singapore, Singapore

Suan Fong Foo Singapore Centre for Chinese Language, Nanyang Technological University, Singapore, Singapore

Hock Huan Goh Singapore Centre for Chinese Language, Nanyang Technological University, Singapore, Singapore

Cheng Gong Singapore Centre for Chinese Language, Nanyang Technological University, Singapore, Singapore

Siew Hoon Kwek Singapore Centre for Chinese Language, Nanyang Technological University, Singapore, Singapore; Academy of Singapore Teachers, Ministry of Education, Brisbane, Singapore

Li Li Singapore Centre for Chinese Language, Nanyang Technological University, Singapore, Singapore

Lynn Dee Puah Nanyang Technological University, Singapore, Singapore

Kay Cheng Soh Nanyang Technological University, Singapore, Singapore

Chee Lay Tan Cambridge University, Cambridge, UK; Singapore Centre for Chinese Language, Nanyang Technological University, Singapore, Singapore

Geok Hoon Tan Academy of Singapore Teachers, Ministry Of Education, Singapore, Singapore

Boon Pei Tay Singapore Centre for Chinese Language, Nanyang Technological University, Singapore, Singapore

Hee San Teoh National University of Singapore, Singapore, Singapore

Jing Yan Singapore Centre for Chinese Language, Nanyang Technological University, Singapore, Singapore

Limei Zhang Singapore Centre for Chinese Language, Nanyang Technological University, Singapore, Singapore

Chunsheng Zhao Singapore Centre for Chinese Language, Nanyang Technological University, Singapore, Singapore; Academy of Singapore Teachers, Ministry of Education, Brisbane, Singapore

Hong Xia Zhou Singapore Centre for Chinese Language, Nanyang Technological University, Singapore, Singapore

Part I
Curriculum and Instructional Materials

Chinese Language Curriculum in Singapore (1960–2000): From Culture Transmission to Language Application

Chee Kuen Chin

Abstract This article traces the development and modification of Chinese Language curriculum for Singapore schools during the period of 1960–2011. The curriculum modification was influenced by the changing conditions in the social environment and student proficiency in the language. The trend was shifted from culture transmission to language application. This article also reports later development in Chinese Language curriculum in Singapore. As a response to the changing socio-linguistic environment, the curriculum emphasizes clearly on language application in daily life, while paying attention to national and world trends in globalization.

This article discusses the development trail of the Chinese Language curriculum in Singapore since independence. It covers the post-independence period of 50 years (1965–2015). The development of the Chinese Language curriculum in Singapore can be divided into four stages, which include Chinese–English medium schools coexistence (1960s–70s), rigorous education streaming (1980s), complex and diversified curriculum (1990s), and differentiated curriculum (2000s–2010s).

In Singapore, the planning, designing, and implementation of the Chinese Language curriculum were closely associated with the prevailing social, political, and linguistic forces in each period of time. They were the responses to both internal and external driving forces. The curricula were centrally written and released by the relevant divisions in the nation's Ministry for Education.

The article is previously presented as keynote speech at the International Conference on "Heritage and Creativity: Deepening Language Education Innovation", Beijing Normal University in 2016 and has been revised since.

C. K. Chin (✉)
Singapore Centre for Chinese Language, Singapore, Singapore
e-mail: cheekuen.chin@sccl.sg

© Springer Nature Singapore Pte Ltd. 2018
K. C. Soh (ed.), *Teaching Chinese Language in Singapore*,
https://doi.org/10.1007/978-981-10-8860-5_1

The article will discuss the main objectives, structures, and language teaching at different stages and make appropriate reference to those driving forces. This article is a factual report on the Chinese Language curriculum implemented over the past five decades or so in Singapore.

Chinese–English Medium Schools Coexistence Stage (1960s–70s)

Singapore became an independent state in 1965. After independence, the government decided to implement a bilingual education policy which required all students to study two languages. In 1968, with the intent of retaining various ethnic groups' language and culture in a multi-racial and multi-cultural society, and to use each ethnic group's mother tongue as an effective channel for transmitting Asian values and traditions, the government made the mother tongue of three main ethnic groups (i.e., Chinese, Malay, and Indian) compulsory subjects in the school curriculum. The mother tongues were also required subjects in all national examinations for primary and secondary school students. The first primary school Chinese Language curriculum was released in 1971, and the first secondary school curriculum was released in 1973. It was the period when both Chinese Medium Schools (CMSs) and English Medium Schools (EMSs) coexisted with CMSs which used Chinese Language as the main medium of instruction while EMSs used English for the same purpose. The Chinese Language curriculum released during this period comprised two syllabuses, one catering for First Language learners in CMSs and the other for Second Language learners in EMSs. They shared several common characteristics elaborated on below.

Ethnic Exclusivity The learners of these two curricula were restricted to ethnic Chinese students. This was in line with the bilingual policy, that teaching in the mother tongue of three ethnic groups in schools was designed to preserve the roots of their cultures as well as to master language skills, irrespective of language courses. Both the 1971 and 1973 Chinese curriculum consisted of two syllabuses. One syllabus catered for Chinese for First Language (L1) learners while the other catered for Second Language (L2) learners. Both curricula arranged objectives into learning phases, with each phase covering two academic standards. The six standards in primary education were divided into three learning phases and the four standards in secondary education were divided into two learning phases. In total, there were five learning phases in the whole foundation of education in Chinese Language.

Use of Essential and Associate Objectives in Curriculum Planning The Ministry of Education (1971, 1973) used two sets of objectives in curriculum planning, the *essential objectives* and the *associate objectives*. The essential objectives were a series of progressive language objectives targeted at the development of three language skills in different learning phases. The three language skills were oral (listening and speaking), reading, and writing skills. The associate objectives were affective objectives which covered Chinese culture, national education, moral education, care for society, respect for cultures in different ethnic groups, understanding the region, and so on. The associate objectives also served as criteria for the selection of teaching materials. However, assessment of students' Chinese Language ability was only based on the essential objectives.

Use of Essential Objectives The difference between L1 and L2 curricula lay only in the essential objectives (i.e., language objectives). For instance, one of the Phase 3 (primary 5/6) reading objectives required students who learned Chinese as a L2 to be able to "*read short and simple reading materials*" while the comparable objective for L1 learners in the same learning phase required them to read simple story books, Chinese newspapers, and magazines independently (Ministry of Education 1971). For another example, one of the writing objectives for Phase 4 (secondary 3/4) L2 learners was to extract the main points in Chinese articles while the comparable objective for the L1 learners in the same learning phase was to write a summary of Chinese articles (Ministry of Education 1973). The L1 and L2 curriculum shared the same set of associate objectives (affective objectives) in the same learning phases.

Nurture National Consciousness and Promote Traditional Culture The curriculum developed in this stage used substantial amounts of text from various genres as teaching materials to fulfill the educational goal for Chinese Language teaching to nurture traditional culture and values of the East so as to facilitate nation-building in addition to developing language skills.

Teaching materials for the primary school were selected according to the associate objectives spelt out in the syllabus. They were chosen and arranged in a manner compatible with the life experience and psycho-linguistic developmental of primary students. The materials, written in age-appropriate genres like children's songs, poems, stories, fairy tales, were useful in preparing children's good moral and attitude toward life and, at the same time, cultivating their self-discipline and patriotism. It also educated children to respect fellow-Singaporeans' languages and cultures and to be aware of roles and responsibilities for all citizens in the new nation. There was, however, little difference in terms of language used between CMS and EMS teaching materials in lower primary in the 1971 curriculum. The teaching materials began to show differences in the language used at upper primary level, introducing greater complexity in sentence structures, and variety in vocabulary for L1 reading passages.

The teaching materials of the CMS syllabus in the 1973 curriculum were mainly modern Chinese literary works. The CMS teaching materials took the form of an anthology. The selected reading texts in the anthology were organized into two components, namely "*intensive reading materials*" (IRMs) and "*general reading materials*" (GRMs). The IRMs were mainly modern literary works produced by Chinese writers from the twentieth century and some classical literary works by writers or poets from ancient China. Students were introduced to the literary works to appreciate the beauty of the genre styles and the themes and values behind the literary works. They were also requested to master the linguistic elements of these literary works, including meaning of the vocabulary and word compounds and forms of expressions. The IRMs provided a comprehensive learning experience for students to help them master Chinese Language and understand Chinese culture deeply. The GRMs were more practical pieces used in daily life, commentaries, elementary modern Chinese Language grammars, articles on literature and art, and so on. At the upper secondary level, the GRMs also included *Guoxue*(国学) and basic classical Chinese Language grammars. Content from the GRMs was *not* used in examinations. The GRMs provided students with learning opportunities to broaden their horizon of the Chinese Language beyond examinations. The literary works for the EMS syllabus were rewritten to simplify the vocabulary that suits the language proficiency level of L2 learners.

Emphasize Improving Writing Capacity The 1970s' was a time when fostering Chinese oral skill was not emphasized in the Chinese curriculum. This was closely related to the socio-linguistic environment found in Singapore at that time. In the 70s, the main languages used in ethnic Chinese families were Mandarin or Chinese dialects or both. Mandarin or Chinese dialects were heard and spoken in most Chinese families. As students had already been exposed to their ethnic language at home, the provision of authentic contexts for them to use Chinese Language for interacting was deemed unnecessary. The 1971 and 1973 Chinese Language curricula hence paid more attention to developing students' written capacities.

In general, the main objective of the 1971 and 1973 Chinese Language curricula was to develop students' reading and writing abilities in the language. Both curricula introduced traditional Chinese culture, moral values, and the uniqueness of the local multi-racial and multi-cultural society through the teaching materials. In addition to written language abilities, the Chinese as L1 curriculum included elements of Chinese literature and *Guoxue* that reflected the very strong emphasis on mother tongue-oriented language teaching in the 1970s' curricula.

The overall objectives of Chinese Language curricula in the 1970s' were basically the same for both L1 and L2. However, language proficiency requirements for L1 and L2 were different. The language proficiency gap between L1 and L2 became wider with the increase in class levels. The main differences lay in the domains of reading and writing where writing varied the most.

Rigorous Education Streaming Stage (1980s)

The 1980s' of the twentieth century marked a critical stage in education development in Singapore. Singapore implemented an education streaming system (ESS) in the foundation stage of education (primary and secondary education). The ESS streamed students at two stages, primary 3 and primary 6. Students were streamed into different education tracks according to their streaming examination results in primary 3 and the Primary School Leaving Examination (PSLE) in primary 6. ESS required all students to study two languages irrespective of their tracks. They all studied English language at L1 level and their mother tongue at either L1 or L2 level, depending on the streams they were enrolled in.

In the primary education stage, students were streamed into Normal Stream (6 years to sit for PSLE) and Extended Stream (8 years to sit for PSLE). In the secondary education stage, based on the overall score they had obtained for PSLE, students were streamed into Special Stream (4 years to sit for Singapore-Cambridge General Certificate of Education (Ordinary level) Examination; GCE 'O' Level Examination), Express Stream (4 years to sit for GCE 'O' Level examination), and Normal Stream (5 years to sit for GCE 'O' Level examination). All streams studied English Language at the L1 level. Students in the Special Stream (overall score obtained in PSLE in top 8–12%) studied Chinese Language at the L1 level. Students in the Express Stream and students in the Normal Stream took Chinese Language at the L2 level. The most significant impact of the ESS on Chinese Language teaching was that students' Chinese Language proficiency were now decided by the education stream that he was enrolled in, not the language medium of the school that he was attending. Language streams that prevailed since independence now ceased and were replaced by education streams. There were a number of important features in the 1980s' curriculum.

Primary School Chinese Language Syllabus (1981) There are two main features in the 1981 primary school syllabus.

First, all education streams achieve the same curriculum goal, and the overall curriculum goal for the 1981 primary Chinese Language syllabus stated specifically that:

> The overall goal of Chinese Language teaching is to cultivate students' listening, speaking, reading and writing language capabilities, and instill in them the oriental values that would help in the work of nation building. Upon completion of primary Chinese Language syllabus, students will be able to listen and understand general topics of daily life, speak Chinese fluently, read ordinary children's literature books and local news in brief from Chinese newspaper and write short letters. (Ministry of Education 1981: 1)

In order to achieve this overall goal for students in different streams, the 1981 syllabus classified the curriculum objectives into *general objectives* and *additional objectives*. General objectives were the core objectives that should be achieved by all students irrespective of their education streams. The additional objectives were for students who were taking Chinese as L1, or who were taking Chinese as L2 but possessed a higher level of language proficiency. Both sets of objective were hierarchical in nature where the objectives of lower standards in upper streams could be the objectives of upper standards in lower streams. Table 1 lists some examples of these hierarchical curriculum objectives.

Secondly, it was the first time that a Chinese Language Syllabus included a Chinese Characters List. The rationale was to control the quantity of characters for each class level so that students would be able to acquire vocabularies in texts in a gradual and systematic manner (Ministry of Education 1981). The Chinese

Table 1 Curriculum objectives of primary school Chinese Language (1981)

Language skills	Curriculum objectives	General objectives in standard	Additional objectives in standard
Oral (speaking and listening)	• Use short sentences to converse • Describe a story of more than 100 words • Make a brief speech	Primary 2 (Normal Stream) Primary 6 (Normal Stream)	Primary 7 (Extended Stream)
Reading	• Understand the meanings of the idioms learned	Primary 4 (Normal Stream) Primary 6 (Extended Stream)	
	• Read the general local news		Primary 6 (Normal Stream) Primary 8 (Extended Stream)
Writing	• View the picture(s) provided and write an essay of about 70 words • Understand and apply learned words and phrases • Write an essay of about 200 words with the given topic	Primary 6 (Normal Stream) Primary 7 (Extended Stream)	Primary 3 (Normal Stream) Primary 8 (Extended Stream)

Characters List of the 1981 syllabus specified 1800 basic Chinese characters and another 200 additional characters. In their primary years, students learning Chinese as a L2 needed to master the forms and meanings of 1800 Chinese characters while students learning Chinese as a L1 a total of 2000 Chinese characters.

Secondary School Chinese Language Syllabus (1983) Four key features were observed in the secondary school CL syllabus developed in 1983.

Firstly, inclusion of moral education in language syllabus. The overall curriculum goal of the 1983 syllabus clearly articulated that Chinese Language teaching was to "*cultivate students' listening, speaking, reading and writing capacity while enabling them to recognize and absorb the valuable traditional oriental culture through the language learning*" (Ministry of Education 1983: 4). It was thus emphasized that the Chinese Language syllabus should inculcate awareness of patriotism, filial piety, love for others, spirit of serving the society, personal accomplishment, respect for labor, respect for lifestyles, custom and etiquette of different ethnic groups, and so on. The 1983 syllabus reflected the language education view of encompassing moral values in literary texts (文以载道).

Secondly, the use of modules instead of class levels in planning curriculum objectives. In the traditional Chinese curriculum, objectives were set in accordance with class levels. The 1983 syllabus changed the practice by using modules to set curriculum objectives. The whole syllabus for secondary school Chinese Language comprised a total of 60 teaching modules with different streams completing different numbers of modules within 4–5 years. Each module contained four lessons. The following table lists the number of modules prepared for different streams (Ministry of Education 1983) (Table 2).

The 1983 syllabus organized the 60 modules into three modular groups. There were 20 modules in each group. The curriculum objectives encompassing four language skills were set according to the modular groups and progressed spirally. Below are some of the examples:

Thirdly, the development of the Chinese Characters List. Following the practice of the primary school Chinese Language Syllabus, the 1983 syllabus also developed a Chinese Characters List to control the quantity of characters for different streams in secondary education. Students in Special and Express Streams learning Chinese as L1 were requested to master 3500 Chinese characters (including those learned in primary years). Students in Express Stream learning Chinese as L2 would have to master 3000 Chinese characters (including those learned in primary years).

Table 2 Modules by streams by class levels of secondary school Chinese Language Syllabus (1983)

Stream	Standard	Number of modules	
		Chinese as First language	Chinese as Second language
Special	Secondary 1	13	
	Secondary 2	13	
	Secondary 3	14	
	Secondary 4	10	
	Total	50[a]	
Express	Secondary 1	13	10
	Secondary 2	13	10
	Secondary 3	14	10
	Secondary 4	10	10
	Total	50	40
Normal	Secondary 1	10	7
	Secondary 2	10	8
	Secondary 3	10	8
	Secondary 4	10	7
	Secondary 5	10	10
	Total	50	40

[a]Excluding the first 10 modules of secondary 1 CL2 instructional materials. CL1 started with module 11 at the beginning of secondary 1 and completed with module 60 at the end of secondary 4 or 5

Table 3 Examples of curriculum objectives in secondary school Chinese Language Syllabus (1983)

Language skills	The first modular group (module 1–20)	The second modular group (module 21–40)	The third modular group (module 41–60)
Listening	Able to understand the local news in general	Able to understand the foreign news in general	Able to understand speeches and news in relation to social, political, and economic issues of Singapore
Speaking	Able to converse with others on topics related to daily life	Able to discuss with others about school work and career-related topics	Able to discuss issues related to economic, social, and culture of Singapore
Reading	Able to read and understand the local news, announcements, and simple passages in publications	Able to read and understand speeches of political leaders and community leaders in general, as well as articles in newspapers and magazines	Able to read and understand newspaper editorials and literary and artistic works
Writing	Able to write simple correspondences and proposition essays with not less than 220 words	Able to write covering letters, simple notices, and proposition essays with not less than 300 words	Able to write proposition essays with not less than 500 words

For students in Normal Stream, if they learned Chinese as L1, they would have to master 3000 Chinese characters at the end of secondary 4 and 3200 Chinese characters at the end of secondary 5. If they took Chinese as L2, they would learn 2400 and 2700 Chinese characters at the end of secondary 4 and secondary 5, respectively (Table 3).

The 1983 syllabus also compiled a Chinese Idioms List to control the number of idioms that each stream should master by the end of secondary education. Chinese as L1 learners in both Special and Express Streams would learn 250 idioms. Chinese as L2 learners in Express Stream would master 200 idioms. For Normal Stream, students would learn 200 idioms if they were L1 learners and 125 idioms if they were L2 learners.

Fourthly, more attention to oral and practical writing teaching. The 1983 syllabus included oral and practical writing in the instructional materials for the first time in any Chinese Language syllabus in Singapore. All modules began their first lessons with oral or practical writing materials. The oral materials included interviews, news broadcasts, dialogues on daily life issues, forums, debates. The practical writing materials included local news, short notes, notices, circulars, official correspondences.

Complex and Diversified Curriculum Stage (1990s)

Entering the 1990s, the Ministry of Education further divided the Normal Stream of secondary education into Normal (Academic) and Normal (Technical) Streams. Students in the Normal (Academic) Stream continued to learn Chinese as L2. A much easier new L2 subject called Foundation Chinese was developed to cater to students in the Normal (Technical) Stream. At the same time, the Ministry for Education revised the strict requirements for offering Higher Chinese in secondary education by allowing more capable students in the Express Stream to learn Chinese at L1 level. By definition, the capable students were those students whose PSLE score fell into the top 30% and obtained at least grade A in English Language and Mathematics in the same examination. At the same time, the Ministry for Education provided another channel to help students who performed very well in all subjects except Chinese Language with Chinese B curriculum

The Chinese Language curriculum thus became more diversified in the 1990s. New syllabuses for primary and secondary schools were implemented in 1993 with the features as described below.

Firstly, setting overall curriculum objectives from the language and culture domains. Both primary and secondary school syllabuses set overall objectives for the language and culture domains. The objectives in secondary school were the enhancement and deepening of primary school objectives. Table 4 compares some objectives given in the 1990s' primary and secondary school syllabuses.

As can be seen from Table 4, the secondary curriculum objectives were a continuation of the primary objectives but extended to become broader and deeper.

Secondly, inclusion of shared national values. The Singapore Government released a White Paper on national shared values in 1991. The five shared values were: (1) *nation before community and society above self,* (2) *family as the basic unit of society,* (3) *community support and respect for the individual,* (4) *consensus not conflict,* and (5) *racial and religious harmony* (Parliament 1991: 2). The Chinese Language curriculum developed in this stage infused these values into language teaching to enable students to understand the values that helped Singapore succeed in the journey toward nation-building. The inclusion of the shared national values highlighted the language education view of transmitting culture and traditional values through language teaching.

Thirdly, use of thematic approach to organize curriculum content. A thematic approach was used to organize curriculum content. There were eight major themes used to organize the curriculum module and in the selection of teaching materials. These eight themes were (1) *interpersonal relationships,* (2) *community and nation,* (3) *foreign cultures and artifacts,* (4) *Chinese traditional culture and values,* (5) *health and personal hygiene,* (6) *natural world,* (7) *technology,* and (8) *imagination and fantasy* (Ministry of Education 1993a, b). Each theme embraced various sub-themes to make the contents of Chinese Language teaching more varied and relevant to the changing environment. It is noted that among the themes, Chinese traditional culture and values seemed to have the most sub-themes. The proportion

Table 4 Overall objectives of 1990s primary and secondary school syllabuses (examples)

Domain	Primary school Chinese Language syllabus (1993)	Secondary school Chinese Language syllabus (1993)
Language	Nurture students' listening, speaking, reading, and writing capacities and increase their interest in learning Chinese • To enable students to understand general topics and reports relating to their daily lives	Strengthen students' listening, speaking, reading, and writing capacities and increase their interest in learning Chinese • To enable students to understand topics, news reports, and so on relating to their daily lives
	• To enable students to use Chinese to converse, discuss, and comment on general topics fluently and accurately	• To enable students to use Chinese to communicate, discuss, debate, comment, give impromptu speeches and so on expressively and accurately
	• To enable students to read general passages, children's literature books and short local news while enabling them to have a wider range of reading interests and be able to appreciate children's literature	• To enable students to read general news, reviews, popular literary works, and so on and at the same time cultivate their broad interests in reading and be able to appreciate literary works
	• To enable students to write short essays, personal letters, and reports	• To enable students to write various genres, formal letters, personal letters, reports, and so on
Culture	Students will know and absorb the Chinese culture and traditional values through the study of Chinese Language • To enable students to understand Chinese culture	Students will know more and absorb more about Chinese culture and traditional values through the study of Chinese Language • To enable students to understand Chinese culture more deeply
	• To enable students to absorb and reflect traditional values by putting them into practice in daily life	• To enable students to absorb and reflect traditional values by putting them into practice in daily life
	• To make students understand the importance of getting along in harmony with people in a multi-ethnic, multi-cultural, and multi-religious society	• To make students understand that we should get along in harmony with people in a multi-ethnic, multi-cultural, and multi-religious society
	• To help students understand and put into practice Singapore's 5 shared values	• To help students understand and put into practice Singapore's 5 shared values

of the teaching materials aligned with this particular theme was also the highest in the primary and secondary instructional packages. This feature again reaffirmed the language education view of transmitting culture and traditional values through language teaching.

Differentiated Curriculum Stage (2000s–2010s)

Entering the twenty-first century, English has become the living and working language for the majority of Singaporeans and has increasingly become the predominantly spoken language at home. Although the *2000 Census of Population* showed that 35% of the total of Chinese families used Chinese as the predominant home language over 23% used English, the gap narrowed for those below the age of 14 (Department of Statistics 2000). A survey conducted by the Ministry of Education in 2004 showed that the proportion of families from Chinese or English language backgrounds were comparable (Ministry of Education 2004). The Chinese Language curriculum therefore needed to address the learning needs of students from diverse family language backgrounds.

The diverse home language environment posed a new challenge for curriculum design and language teaching. The Chinese Language curriculum had undergone two rounds of major reform within the first 20 years of the twenty-first century. The first round paid greater attention to learners' learning differences, emphasizing that the Chinese Language curriculum should be tailored for learners from different language backgrounds. The second round of reforms emphasized that, besides learners' differences, nurturing learning interest and applying language learned to real-life situations were of equal importance. It aimed to nurture active learners and proficient users of the Chinese Language (Ministry of Education 2011a, b).

The Tailored Chinese Language Curriculum

Given the fact that language backgrounds of ethnic Chinese students were getting more and more complex, the Chinese Language curriculum in Singapore was reaching a critical point where it needed to be re-structured and re-designed. The Chinese Language curriculum needed to adopt a model that was different from the past to allow students with different abilities and needs to learn the language within their learning capacities. To that end, the Ministry of Education implemented a new Chinese Language Syllabus in 2007 and 2011, respectively. The Chinese Language curriculum developed in this period had several features.

Primary School Chinese Language Syllabus (2007)

Greater attention was paid to curriculum differentiation in the 2007 primary syllabus. This was achieved by adopting four strategies as described below.

Firstly, two-stage curriculum planning. In order to teach students from complex language backgrounds according to their ability, the 2007 syllabus divided the six-year primary Chinese Language teaching into two stages. Primary 1–4 were designated as the foundation stage and Primary 5–6 as the oriented stage. Two courses were provided, namely Chinese Language course and Higher Chinese Language course, with two sets of instructional materials developed to differentiated objectives as spelled out in the course syllabuses to meet the learning needs of students from different language backgrounds. Students were allowed to study Higher Chinese from primary 1. An additional course, Basic Chinese was offered in the oriented stage for students who were less academically oriented.

Secondly, setting the overall curriculum goals. The 2007 syllabus set the overall curriculum goals for three domains, namely *language ability, humanistic literacy,* and *universal capacity*. Language ability involved development of four language skills. Humanistic literacy involved core elements of Chinese culture and traditional Asian values. Universal capacity covered knowledge and skills that were needed in the twenty-first century.

Thirdly, setting the basic language attainments and encouraging students to achieve the best level they can. The modular approach was adopted in curriculum design. Under the modular approach, each CL instructional unit in primary 1 and 2 comprised three modules (i.e., *Introductory Module, Core Module,* and *Advanced Module*). The introductory module of each unit prepared students from English-speaking family background to learn the keywords and main sentence structures of the unit orally. Once they had achieved the learning objectives of the module, they would proceed to study the core module which focused on written skills. Students who had basic oral skills in Mandarin began their study with the core module in each unit. The core module was the compulsory module for all students. The core module set the basic language proficiency level all students must attain. The more capable students were given a chance to study the advanced module in each unit where they could further enhance their Chinese proficiency level.

In primary 3 and 4, most of the students began their study in the core module. For minority students who still faced difficulty in learning the language, a *Supplementary Module* was provided for them to receive additional coaching. In the Oriented Stage (primary 5 and 6), only core and advanced modules were provided in the CL course. For students who were less academically oriented, a Basic Chinese course was provided for them to reduce their learning burden.

The Higher Chinese Language course comprised only core and advanced modules throughout two stages of primary education, to encourage students with interest and ability to excel in the language from primary 1.

Fourthly, modules of each course focusing on different language skills. In conjunction with the differentiated curriculum design, Chinese Language, Higher Chinese Language, and Basic Chinese courses each focused on the development of different language skills for students. Table 5 summarizes the teaching foci of the three courses (Ministry of Education 2007: 15).

Table 5 Teaching foci of different courses in primary school Chinese Language syllabus (2007)

Foundation stage (primary 1–4)		
Courses	Module	Teaching focus
Chinese	Introductory (primary 1 and 2)	Listening and speaking Chinese character recognition
	Supplementary (primary 3 and 4)	Chinese character recognition
	Core (primary 1–4)	Listening and speaking Chinese character recognition and writing Reading
	Advanced (primary 1–4)	Increase the breadth and depth of reading
Higher Chinese	Core (primary 1–4)	Listening and speaking Chinese character recognition and writing Reading Increase the breadth and depth of reading
	Advanced (primary 1–4)	Writing
Oriented stage (primary 5–6)		
Basic Chinese	Core	Listening and speaking
Chinese	Core	Reading
	Advanced	Increase the breadth and depth of reading Writing
Higher Chinese	Core	Reading Increase the breadth and depth of reading Writing
	Advanced	Strengthening writing skills

Secondary School Chinese Language Syllabus (2011)

Firstly, variety of courses for students with different language abilities. In order to cater for the learning needs of students with different language backgrounds and abilities, the 2011 Chinese Language syllabus offered five different courses. Each course pitched at different language proficiency levels that needed to be achieved by students taking the course. Table 6 summarizes the overall objectives of these five courses (Ministry of Education 2011a: 13–15).

In addition to the above language objectives, the 2011 syllabus continued with the practice of the 2007 syllabus by including objectives for humanistic literacy and universal capacity in the curriculum. The humanistic literacy objectives were essentially identical to the 2007 syllabus. The universal capacity objectives raised the requirements and planned to develop students' twenty-first century skills further by infusing creative and critical thinking skills, self-directed inquiry skills, ICT skills, and collaborative skills into the language learning.

Table 6 Overall objectives of five Chinese courses in secondary school (2011)

Courses	Overall objectives
Basic Chinese (Normal Technical)	Strengthen students' oral interaction skills, nurture basic ability in reading and writing, eventually will achieve the following objectives: • Able to listen and understand narrative, persuasive, and practical speeches that suit their language ability • Able to express their views and feelings with regard to the general topics and interact with people • Able to read narrative and practical texts that suit their language ability and experience the thoughts and feelings behind the texts • Able to write simple narrative and practical correspondence • Able to recognize 1500–1600 commonly used Chinese characters and be able to write 1000–1100 of them
Chinese B	Strengthen students' oral interaction skills, nurture basic ability in reading and writing, eventually will achieve the following objectives: • Able to listen and understand narrative, persuasive, and practical speeches that suit their language ability • Able to express their views and feelings with regard to general topics and interact with people • Able to read narrative, persuasive, and practical texts that suit their language ability and be able to appreciate simple literary works at a preliminary level • Able to write narratives and practical correspondence that are within their language ability • Able to recognize 1600–1700 commonly used Chinese characters and be able to write 1100–1200 of them
Chinese (Normal Academic)	Strengthen students' four language skills, especially nurture their ability in reading and writing, eventually will achieve the following objectives: • Able to listen and understand narrative, persuasive, argumentative, and practical speech that suits their language ability • Able to respond to general topics with personal views and feelings and able to interact with people • Able to read narrative, persuasive, argumentative, and practical texts that suit their language ability and able to appreciate simple literary works at a preliminary level • Able to write narratives, persuasive essays, argumentative essays, and practical correspondences that are within their language ability • Able to recognize 2200–2300 commonly used Chinese characters and be able to write 1800–1900 of them
Chinese (Express)	Strengthen students' four language skills, especially nurture their ability in reading and writing, eventually will achieve the following objectives: • Able to listen and understand narrative, persuasive, argumentative, and practical speech that suits their language ability • Able to respond to more complicated topics with personal views and feelings and able to interact with people effectively • Able to read narrative, persuasive, argumentative, and practical texts that suit their language ability and able to appreciate literary works

(continued)

Table 6 (continued)

Courses	Overall objectives
	• Able to write narratives, persuasive essays, argumentative essays, and practical correspondence that are within their language ability and able to write simple literary works • Able to recognize 2400–2500 commonly used Chinese characters and be able to write 2000–2100 of them
Higher Chinese	Strengthen students' four language skills, especially nurture their ability in writing, eventually will achieve the following objectives: • Able to listen and understand narrative, persuasive, argumentative, and practical speeches that suit their language ability • Able to interact with people effectively on complicated topics and able to make a short speech on a given topic • Able to read narrative, persuasive, argumentative, and practical texts that suit their language ability and able to appreciate literary works in depth • Able to write narratives, persuasive essays, argumentative essays, and practical correspondence that are within their language ability and able to write simple literary works • Able to recognize and write 2700–2800 commonly used Chinese characters

Table 7 Proportion of language skills in five secondary school Chinese Language courses

Language skills	Basic Chinese (%)	Chinese B (%)	Chinese (normal academic) (%)	Chinese (express) (%)	High Chinese (%)
Listening and speaking	65	50	40	35	25
Reading	25	30	30	35	30
Writing	10	20	30	30	45

Secondly, each course with different emphasis on language skills. In view of the differences in the overall objectives of the five courses, though all the four language skills would be taught in all courses, the proportion of each skill in terms of curriculum hours for each course was different. Table 7 lists the proportion of each skill in each course (Ministry of Education 2011a, b: 7).

Graded Curriculum Objectives According to Domains

The 2007 and 2011 syllabuses adopted a grading concept to set curriculum objectives. There were five language domains for setting objectives in the 2007 primary school syllabus. These five domains were (1) oral (listening/speaking), (2) recognize and write Chinese characters, (3) reading, (4) writing, and (5) comprehensive language applications. Each domain arranged the objectives into three levels (two standards in one level starting from primary 1). In addition to the five language domains, there were four humanistic literacy domains (values, Chinese culture, love and care, and aesthetic) and four universal capacity domains (thinking skills, self-learning skills, ICT-based learning skills, and social and emotional management skills). Humanistic literacy and universal capacity objectives were not divided into levels.

There were four language domains in the 2011 secondary school syllabus, namely (1) *listening,* (2) *speaking,* (3) *reading,* and (4) *writing.* The curriculum objectives in the domains were arranged into five levels, starting at level 3 and ending at level 7. Table 8 shows the corresponding arrangements for language domains, levels, and courses for easy reference.

Table 8 Level structure for 2011 Chinese Language syllabus (secondary)

Level / Course	3 L	3 S	3 R	3 W	4 L	4 S	4 R	4 W	5 L	5 S	5 R	5 W	6 L	6 S	6 R	6 W	7 L	7 S	7 R	7 W
Basic Chinese																				
Sec 1	✓	✓	✓	✓	✓	✓														
Sec 2	✓	✓	✓	✓	✓	✓														
Sec 3			✓	✓																
Sec 4			✓	✓																
CL B																				
Sec 1	✓	✓	✓	✓	✓	✓														
Sec 2	✓	✓	✓	✓	✓	✓														
Sec 3							✓	✓												
Sec 4							✓	✓												
CL (Normal Academic)																				
Sec 1					✓	✓	✓	✓												
Sec 2					✓	✓	✓	✓												
Sec 3									✓	✓	✓	✓								
Sec 4									✓	✓	✓	✓								
Sec 5													✓	✓	✓	✓				
CL (Express)																				
Sec 1					✓	✓	✓	✓												
Sec 2					✓	✓	✓	✓												
Sec 3									✓	✓	✓	✓								
Sec 4													✓	✓	✓	✓				
HCL																				
Sec 1					✓	✓	✓	✓												
Sec 2									✓	✓	✓	✓								
Sec 3													✓	✓	✓	✓				
Sec 4																	✓	✓	✓	✓

Note L Listening, S Speaking, R Reading, W Writing

In addition to language domains, the 2011 syllabus also embraced four humanistic literacy domains and four universal capacity domains, both were identical to the 2007 syllabus.

The School-Based Curriculum Formed an Integral Part of the Curriculum

The Chinese curriculum developed in this stage included school-based curriculum (SBC) as an integral part of the curriculum framework. It was the first time that the SBC became a key component of the Chinese Language curriculum in Singapore. It was hoped that the SBC would supplement the central curriculum to better suit students with different language abilities, learning interests, and educational needs, so that their potential in Chinese Language could be developed to the highest possible level.

The 2007 syllabus suggested that SBC could represent 20–30% of curriculum hours in primary education (Ministry of Education 2007). It was suggested that the SBC at primary school could take the form of enrichment studies or extended studies in the core module. At the Oriented Stage, schools could consider the learning needs of students and use SBC as a supplementary or enhancement learning module to improve the teaching efficiency of Chinese Language (Ministry of Education 2007).

The 2011 syllabus suggested that SBC could represent 10–15% of curriculum hours in secondary education (Ministry of Education 2011a). It was suggested that the SBC could be a simplified, extended, or deepened version of the central curriculum. It also encouraged schools to use authentic materials or supplementary readers available in the market to assist students in learning. If resources were available, schools could develop a brand new SBC to enhance students' learning experience (Ministry of Education 2011a).

However, the SBCs of both the primary and secondary schools should be guided by the overall objective of the central curriculum. SBC was an integral component of the central curriculum and it should not become a separate module from the central curriculum.

Nurturing Active Learners and Proficient Users

With the arrival of the knowledge-based economy resulting from the information era in the twenty-first century, the trend of globalization has been accelerating in many countries. More and more countries are aware that in a highly competitive global environment, a nation's workforce that is multilingual will have an advantage as the world is moving away from a single dominant economic language and moving toward the direction of plural language. Singapore is an open economy and, in order to guarantee sustainable competitiveness, being able to master more than one language is a survival skill for its citizens, not the privilege of a small number of elites

With the growth of Asia in the twenty-first century, citizens of Singapore who can master their mother tongues well will not only be able to retain their traditional cultures and values, but also use their languages to communicate and connect with people who use the same languages with the same cultural background in the region and beyond. Hence, *communication, culture,* and *connection,* the so-called 3C components become the curriculum goals for the new round of mother tongue language curriculum reform in 2010 (Ministry for Education 2011b).

A new mission has been entrusted to the Chinese Language curriculum of Singapore in the twenty-first century. In addition to the transmission of Chinese culture to younger generations, the Chinese Language curriculum needs to strengthen the students' ability and skill in communicating and connecting with people using the same language and sharing the same culture. To do so, Chinese Language teaching should try to engage students in using the language in their daily lives. Chinese Language teaching must provide students opportunities to apply language skills in authentic tasks in various real-life scenarios. The ultimate goals of Chinese Language teaching are, therefore, to nurture active learners and proficient users in the language. The Chinese Language curriculum should provide students with enjoyable learning experiences and useful language skills so that they can continue to use the language after they have left school.

The Ministry for Education released a report, *Nurturing Active Learners and Proficient Users* (Ministry of Education 2011b) which was submitted by the Mother Tongue Languages Review Committee in 2011. The report proposed a new direction for the Chinese Language curriculum. As a matter of follow up, the new Chinese Language syllabus for primary schools was launched in 2015, marking the commencement of a new round of Chinese Language instructional development. The 2015 syllabus has the following four unique features.

Closely Aligned With 3C Curriculum Goals and Twenty-first Century Skills

The 2015 primary school syllabus set the general objectives from three curriculum domains: (1) language ability, (2) humanistic literacy, and (3) universal capacity. Table 9 shows how the general objectives of these three domains are aligned with the 3C curriculum goals for the twenty-first century skills.

As shown in Table 9, the overall objectives of the language ability and humanistic literacy domains are well aligned with the 3C curriculum goals. The overall objectives of the universal capacity domain focus on development of twenty-first century skills as required in the context of a contemporary global education.

Table 9 Domains and objectives of the 2015 primary school Chinese Language curriculum

Domain	General objectives [Cn represents different 3C curriculum goals] C1: communication; C2: culture; C3: connection
Language ability	• Able to understand information on general topics in various types of media (print media, radio, new media, etc.) that suit the language proficiency level of students (C3) • Able to state own experiences, feelings, and ideas clearly (C1) • Able to read the reading material that suits the language proficiency level of students independently and able to access knowledge and information (C2/C3) • Able to use common writing methods to express emotion and points of view according to needs (C1) • Able to interact with people, both orally and in writing, to share feelings, exchange information, and disseminate points of view (C1) • Able to communicate with people using comprehensive language skills (i.e., combination of listening, speaking, reading, and writing skills) (C1)
Humanistic literacy	• Cultivate moral accomplishments and positive values, promotes one's all-round development (C2) • Attend, love, appreciate, and transmit profound Chinese culture (C2) • Possess general living knowledge and awareness of local affairs and customs (C2/C3) • Love family, concern for society, loyal to our country, and care for the world (C2) • Cultivate global awareness, understanding, and respect for different cultures for the sake of cross-cultural communication (C1)
Universal capacity	• Nurture capacity of imagination, creativity, and critical thinking to analyze and solve problems • Develop independent learning, be able to engage in enquiry-based study to lay the foundations for life-long learning • Develop social and emotional management skills to handle interpersonal relationships, be able to collaborate with others and to make contributions in a team • Use information technology as a means of effective communication orally and in writing (C1) • Use information technology as a learning tool to search for and process information, acquire knowledge, and enhance learning effectiveness

Note Compiled and modified from: Ministry of Education (Singapore) (2015) Syllabus Chinese Language (Primary)

Continuation of Differentiated Curriculum Model Operate on the idea, "*set the basic language attainments and encourage to achieve to the best level possible,*" the modular curriculum model was retained. Teaching foci for different courses at the foundation stage and oriented stage are also identical with the 2007 syllabus in general.

Stress on Training of Communication Skills The 2015 primary school syllabus stresses further the development of students' communication skills in the context of daily life. Besides setting the objectives of the traditional four language skills, the 2015 syllabus includes objectives for two interactive language skills, namely "oral interaction" and "written interaction." Under each objective, the syllabus lists a set of knowledge or skills that need to be taught in the six years of primary education. It is worth noting that the stress put on students' language interaction skills requests Chinese Language teaching to go beyond the classroom and to integrate the language learning into students' daily life experiences. Family, neighborhood, community, and society can all provide students with authentic contexts to learn the language. Chinese Language teaching is moving toward the direction of authentic learning.

Conclusions

By way of summary, the developmental trail of the Chinese Language curriculum in Singapore from the 1960s' to 2010s' displayed the following 10 characteristics:

(1) Curriculum goals have been transformed from a twin goals model to that of a multi-domain model.
(2) Curriculum composition has been changed from solely one central curriculum to that of one central curriculum supplemented by a number of school-based curricula.
(3) The development of the curriculum has been changed from language streaming to education streaming.
(4) Curriculum structure has been changed from an anthological approach to that of a modular approach.
(5) Course content organization has been changed from a non-thematic approach to that of a thematic approach.
(6) Course levels have been moved from simple bi-level (First or Second language) composition to a multi-level multi-standard structure.
(7) Background of learners has changed from mainly Chinese speaking family to multi-language speaking family.
(8) Perception of teaching Chinese has changed from developing language abilities, understanding traditional culture, cultivating Asian values and national identity to nurturing communicative language ability, enhancing humanistic literacy, and applying language skills in daily life.
(9) The learning path adopted by the curriculum has been changed from developing students' four language skills simultaneously to that of stressing different skills in accordance with students' language backgrounds and learning abilities.
(10) The nature of the curriculum has been transformed from mother tongue language teaching to that of non-mother tongue language teaching.

References

Department of Statistics (Singapore). (2000). *Census of Population 2000*. Retrieved from http://www.singstat.gov.sg/publications/publications_and_papers/cop2000/census10_stat_release1.html on 20 April 2015.
Ministry of Education (Singapore). (1971). *Chinese Language Syllabus and Teaching Guide for Primary Schools*.
Ministry of Education (Singapore). (1973). *Syllabus for Chinese Language in Chinese and English Secondary Schools*.
Ministry of Education (Singapore). (1981). *Chinese Language Syllabus for Primary Schools*.
Ministry of Education (Singapore). (1983). *Chinese Language Syllabus for Secondary Schools*.
Ministry of Education (Singapore). (1993a). *Chinese Language Syllabus (Primary)*.
Ministry of Education (Singapore). (1993b). *Chinese Language Syllabus (Secondary)*.
Ministry of Education (Singapore). (2004). Report of the Chinese Language curriculum and Pedagogy Review Committee.
Ministry of Education (Singapore). (2007). *Syllabus Chinese Language (Primary)*.
Ministry of Education (Singapore). (2011a). *Syllabus Chinese Language (Secondary)*.
Ministry of Education (Singapore). (2011b). *Nurturing active learners and proficient users: 2010 mother tongue languages review committee report (MTLRC)*. Singapore: Ministry of Education.
Ministry of Education (Singapore). (2015). Syllabus Chinese Language (Primary).
Parliament (Singapore). (1991). *Shared Value*. Retrieved from: https://www.academia.edu/1740666/White_paper_on_shared_values_1991_ on 21 April 2017.

Chee Kuen Chin (陈之权) received Ph.D. from the Central China Normal University, China. He was an immediate past Executive Director and is currently Academic Consultant cum Distinguished Principal Lecturer at SCCL. His academic interests include Chinese as a Second Language, curriculum development, Chinese Language pedagogies, ICT-mediated in teaching and learning of Chinese Language and cultural studies. He has published five scholarly books on Chinese Language research and a university textbook. He has more than 100 journal articles, book chapters, keynote speeches, and conference papers to his credit.

Conceptualization of the Chinese Language Teaching Paradigm

Chee Kuen Chin

Abstract Chinese Language curriculum in Singapore has undergone several major reforms since the nation's independence. This article analyses the characteristics and language education views of Chinese Language curricula and discusses a paradigmatic shift needed for Chinese Language curriculum which takes into consideration various trends and conditions in Singapore, with an emphasis of affording students to use the language in real-life situations with specific purposes.

The bilingual education policy of Singapore has been implemented since Independence (University of Singapore Students' Union 1980). In the late 70s of the twentieth century, the government decided in the policy to use English as the first language for all students and the main teaching medium, whilst Mother Tongue is the second language which is made compulsory for all students to learn (Goh and The Education Study Team 1978). Later, the Mother Tongue was designated as a key subject for cultural inheritance and more students were encouraged to study it close to the level of first language (Lianhe Zaobao 1999). The government hoped that traditional, moral, and culture values could be transmitted from generation to generation through Mother Tongue so that the Asian social qualities in Singapore society would be preserved and further enhanced. This bilingual–bicultural policy has indeed nurtured a group of bilingual talents in the Chinese community who can use two languages fluently to communicate with the West and the East. The success of the implementation of the bilingual education has also made an impact on the language learning environment. The most obvious influence is the decrease in the number of Chinese who speak Chinese as their main home language. The number of Chinese who speak English as their only or main home language has increased

---

The article is previously presented as invited speech at the Symposium on "Rhetoric and Chinese Language Teaching", Kaohsiung Normal University in 2013 and has been revised since.

C. K. Chin (✉)
Singapore Centre for Chinese Language, Singapore, Singapore
e-mail: cheekuen.chin@sccl.sg

© Springer Nature Singapore Pte Ltd. 2018
K. C. Soh (ed.), *Teaching Chinese Language in Singapore*,
https://doi.org/10.1007/978-981-10-8860-5_2

yearly. The official data show that there were about 20% of the ethnic Chinese students admitted to Primary One in 1988 came from English-speaking families (Cheah 2001); In 2010, ethnic Chinese Primary One students who came from such families increased to 59% (Ministry of Education, Singapore 2011).

In spite of the shift in home language, Chinese Language remains a language commonly used in the community and Singapore is still a multilingual society providing much room for the practice of Chinese Language. There are opportunities to input and output Chinese Language everywhere in the daily life in Singapore. The key concern here is how we should utilize these social resources to serve the purpose of Chinese Language teaching and learning. If we look at these kind of social resources squarely, and if we really believe that teaching which integrates social resources will have a positive effect on students' motivation and learning outcome, we must change the thoughts and concepts of teaching with regard to Chinese Language. We need to change the existing paradigm for teaching Chinese Language and look for a new paradigm which is congruent to the needs of language learning. Chinese Language teaching in Singapore has reached the critical point for paradigmatic change awaiting our exploration and development.

Paradigms for Chinese Language Teaching in Singapore

In the past 20 years, a paradigm shift has taken place in Chinese Language teaching in Singapore, in both theory and practice. The change can mainly be seen in the aspects of teaching methods and learning approach.

From Artistic to Integrated Paradigm

Since the 1980s, Chinese Language teaching has undergone several reforms in Singapore. Although the impact of home language on Chinese Language learning was highlighted in each reform, the orientation of the curriculum has all along been set at the level of transmitting traditional Asian culture and values and training the language skills of students. Therefore, the promotion of traditional (Confucian) Chinese and Asian culture and values has been the backbone of the Chinese Language curriculum. Teaching materials selected on the basis of such purpose inevitably bear the sense of transmitting morals through texts as a natural consequence. The difference between Chinese Language curricula (e.g. higher Chinese and normal Chinese) is usually shown through the levels of language while the themes of the curricula remain the same.

With such a curriculum, the language proficiency and cultural literacy of Chinese Language teachers become very important. Chinese Language teachers do not only need to have excellent language ability, they also need to have sufficient knowledge of Chinese culture to teach effectively. Chinese Language teachers are required to have solid professional knowledge as well as enthusiasm in teaching. This kind of paradigm is referred to artistic paradigm by scholars. Its teaching effect varies with teachers.

At the turn of the century, the older generation of Chinese Language teachers who graduated from traditional Chinese schools began to retire because of age. The succeeding younger local Chinese Language teachers were educated in the new curriculum with emphasis on English Language. Save for a minority, the language proficiency cultural literacy of the young generation of local Chinese Language teachers was understandably not as good as those of the older generation. Therefore, Chinese Language teaching can no longer rely on the personal qualities of the teachers. Chinese Language teaching began to emphasize procedures, rules, and systems. Chinese Language teaching has then follows the scientific paradigm. It has to adopt the scientific paradigm to build the four basic elements (teacher, student, content, method) in language teaching. It also has to adopt the introspective paradigm to value the self-reflection of teachers in order to improve the teaching ability through introspection. Action research and lesson study, which encourage teachers to review their own teaching, are typical examples of the introspective paradigm. Chinese Language teaching in Singapore now can no longer rely on the artistic paradigm as the only thought of teaching. It has to adopt multiple paradigms. Therefore, Chinese Language teachers must use a dynamic insight from the angle of multiple and integrated paradigms in order to understand teaching from different levels and multiple perspectives (Sang 2008: 96).

From Acceptance to Instructional Paradigm

In Chinese Language lessons in the old paradigm, the teaching basically focused on the preaching cultural values and teaching linguistic skills. Teachers are the demonstrators of high standard of language and are also the source of cultural knowledge. Teachers must first have their own buckets of water before they can provide water for the students' needs; teachers must reserve sufficient water before they can fill up the containers of students for the acceptance of knowledge (Li 2006a, b). This learning method, from the perspective of the relationship between teachers and students, is regarded as Receiving Paradigm.

The arrival of the Internet era has changed the learning in schools. Students changed from passive absorption to active participation. They build up knowledge through discovery and exploration. They also make use of the networks to learn by themselves. Students start to become the owner of learning. Situational creation, problem inquiry, collaborative learning, and meaning construction have gradually become the new ways of learning. Facing the massive flow of modern educational technology, teachers must play change role as instructors as well. They have to guide student learning through organizing and monitoring. Students behave increasingly like actors and teachers increasingly like directors. Directors are coaches who coordinate with actors to procure a successful acting (Li 2006a, b).

Teaching and learning of Chinese Language in Singapore have to change with times. The way to unify teaching and learning effectively for the improvement of teaching effect is directly related to the change of thoughts and perspectives of teaching and that is the paradigmatic shift in teaching.

Needs of the Twenty-First Century

In January, the Ministry of Education released the *2010 Mother Tongue Languages Review Committee Report* (hereinafter "the Report"). The committee made a historical summary of the curricula and teaching of Chinese Language in Singapore in the past 20 years. They then suggested a forward-looking objective, Active Learners and Proficient Users. The Report clearly points to the next stage of Chinese Language teaching to focus on nurturing students' skills in applying the language in their daily lives and to enable students to communicate with people in Chinese Language with confidence in real-life situations. The Report suggested that Mother Tongue Language teaching should integrate with the daily lives and interests of students and to guide them learn their Mother Tongue Languages effectively through different strategies. To be consistent with the changing language environment, the Mother Tongue Language teaching must move away from the paradigm of cultural transmission. It has to emphasize more on students' ability to practically applying the language. Chinese Language teaching must adopt the objective of nurturing active learners and proficient users, and language learning should be in real-life contexts.

The objective of nurturing active learners and proficient users is consistent with the current direction of international language education. Contemporary language teaching focuses on a learner-centred approach (Tarone and Yule 1999). It emphasizes nurturing students' ability to use the language in real situations and scholars believe that effective language learning must enable students to apply what they have learned. Language knowledge and skills taught in classrooms have to be consolidated through application in real-life situations (Benson 2001; Tarone and Yule 1999; Nunan 1988).

Information technology is an indispensable part of contemporary teaching (Zhong 2006). In fact, over the past 20 years or so, we experienced the use of the computer as a tutor and as a learning tool, and ICT as a learning system. This has a great impact on the methods of learning. The task-oriented approach of language learning can enhance the development of interpersonal communication skills. The availability of information technology also provides the convenience of real-time interaction needed for effective language learning.

However, it is not easy to attain the objective of nurturing active learners and proficient users, as advocated in the Report, especially when learning the language as a Second Language. Language teaching needs general planning by setting spontaneous curricular combining content and extra-curricular resources. We need to consciously build up a relationship between teachers, students, content, and materials. Chinese Language teaching has to enhance students' interests by providing vibrant and diversified learning experiences. Learning of Chinese Language has to be related to daily lives to promote effective learning. There should be a variety of the design of teaching Chinese Language in Singapore to put forward a paradigm suited to the local language reality. Chinese Language teachers should take cognizance of the change in the home language environment and understand the shift in the status of teachers. There is also a need to re-look at the teacher–student relationship afresh to establish a practical and effective integrated paradigm.

In the following, the present author first states the key elements of the integrated paradigm and then elaborates on the features of each key element as well as the thoughts for its embodiment. In the subsequent chapter, he then discusses a school-based research project at the Singapore Centre for Chinese Language as an example to illustrate the teaching process and its effects from the implementation of the paradigm advocated hitherto.

Chinese Language Teaching Paradigm

From the above analysis, for the effective implementation of the objective of nurturing active learners and proficient users, it is proposed that the paradigm for the next stage of Chinese Language teaching in Singapore should have four key elements:

(I) Learning-centred
(II) Tasks as principle axis
(III) Interaction as principle
(IV) Technology as means.

An integrated teaching paradigm that consists of these four key elements can properly differentiate Chinese Language teaching in Singapore from that in other regions and thereby highlights the features of Chinese Language teaching in Singapore. These four key elements are further elaborated below.

Learning-Centred

Active learning involves the design of the learning process and the ways in which teachers make effective treatments of the students' language. Language learning unavoidably involves input, shift, and output, which respectively represent the three stages of language learning, namely acceptance, guidance, and communication. The three stages circulate repeatedly during language learning. Here, the teachers play important but different roles in the process and gradually raise the demand based on what the students have achieved.

Acceptance

At this stage, the main activity is teaching by teachers and accepting by students. First, teachers make language input through explaining linguistic knowledge. Here, teachers are the *active subject* (actor) and the students are the *passive object* (acted on). The teacher–student relationship is a "*subject–object relationship*". To enable students to easily understand the language input from the teachers, more examples are used during the process of explanation.

Guidance

At this stage, the main activity is to make use of scaffolding, to imitate, and apply. Teachers, acting as the guide of learning, have to provide the suitable scaffoldings to enable students learn actively and grasp the content. Here, the students are the *active subject* and teachers the *passive object* that provide the scaffoldings required. In language teaching, teachers have to help students grasp what they have to learn. For the teaching of a Second Language, teachers have to provide more opportunities for imitation and application so that students can have something to follow and imitate and can learn by themselves according to the procedures, steps, forms, and methods provided by teachers.

Communication

At this stage, the main activity is to participate equally and to express actively. Here, the teachers are no longer coaches. They are the learning partners of students. Both teachers and students become the *active subjects*. The teacher–student relationship and the student–student relationship are all inter-subject relationship. There should be multi-directional dialogues, communications, and multi-directional participation between teachers and students and among students. Through active communication, learning opportunities are created. Language practice can be done in different learning contexts to enhance the language ability in expression.

Tasks as Principle Axis

Chinese Language teaching in Singapore can use the task-based learning approach based on the input–output hypothesis of the language acquisition (Krashen 1982), the interaction hypothesis of the cognitive psychology theory (Swain 1985), and the core theory of constructivist theory (Bruner 2009) as its principle axis. It emphasizes on learning and grasping language through practical application.

Task-based learning is divided into three segments: pre-task, task cycle, and post-task. In the pre-task segment, teachers bring in the task and introduce the knowledge related to the learning theme and task to students. In the task cycle segment, teachers set the task, decide the form for the completion of the task (pair-up, small group, or large group), guide students to plan for the task and provide the necessary support (e.g. scaffolding). Students execute the task and report the results after completing the task. Then, in the post-task segment, teachers guide students to analyse the situation in the completion of the task. Teachers now sum up the language issues and errors which students have committed and provide remedies and reinforcement according to the needs.

Task-based language learning requires the interaction and cooperation of the social environment to assist learners to understand the speakers' expressions in the contexts, and guide learners to form expressions appropriately (Liu 2011; Deng and Cheng 2010; Zhu 2007; Chen 2004; Wei 2005). Students can have better understanding of the target language in the process of using the language to finish the task. In this process, the students experience and understand the language and make timely self-adjustments of their language mistakes. It is a process of making and verifying hypothesis which has a positive effect on language learning.

To achieve the objective of applying the knowledge, Chinese Language teaching in Singapore needs to ensure students learn and apply the language in a natural environment. Thus, providing real or quasi-real settings that are related to students' daily lives is good for meaning construction and this can also promote the connection among language knowledge, language skills, and language experience (Cheng 2006).

In the multilingual social environment of Singapore today, it is suitable to use tasks as the mainline in Chinese Language teaching, as this allows students to accomplish a number of tasks relevant to their daily lives and to grasp language when completing the tasks, so that they gradually develop the habit of thinking and expressing in Chinese Language. Chinese Language teaching should let student have the feeling of "learning is living, living is also learning" (Liu 2011: 121).

Before getting students to complete the tasks in, the teachers have to set the language focus relevant to the tasks. Zhang (2008) suggests two ways of setting language focus that match the tasks:

1. *Structure-oriented*. Teachers set the tasks according to the learning objectives and preset the language focus based on the requirements for the accomplishment of the tasks. This is a kind of "structure-oriented" approach. Students must and can only use the prescribed form of language in the process of completing the tasks. Its advantage is that students must use their best effort to apply the specific language focus. Its drawback is that it causes the loss of naturalness in the use of language.
2. *Social-driven*. Teachers do not provide specific language focus but assign tasks to students directly and let the tasks create the need for variations in language so that students can use the language under a natural condition. This approach allows a natural use of language. Its disadvantage is that there is no guarantee that language learning will happen consequentially.

Structure-oriented approach can be used in the initial stage of task-based learning. In the true kind of task-based learning, there must be a balance between "structure-oriented" and "social-driven". That is to strengthen the naturalness and at the same time enhance the certainty and completion of tasks under real or quasi-real settings.

Interaction as Principle

One of the purposes of learning a Second Language is to communicate with people. The aim of nurturing active learners and proficient users is to use it with the hope of being able to actively socialize and interact with people in Chinese Language in different real-life situations. In the teaching of Chinese Language as a Second Language, it is very important to create settings for training the verbal and written interaction skills of students (Ministry of Education, Singapore 2011).

The form of social interaction can be broadly categorized into four types (Soller and Lesgold 2010):

1. *Construction*: During the process of interaction, learners ask questions and give responses to construct new knowledge. Through asking questions and giving responses, learners have acquisition, exchange, absorption, complementarity, and construction of knowledge.
2. *Criticism*: During the process of interaction, learners challenge the arguments of their partners and point out their deficiencies, contradictions, and omissions. Learners experience the process of questioning, defending, refatting, and arguing.
3. *Accumulation*: During the process of interaction, learners trace, absorb, and accumulate important knowledge. Once they have accumulated sufficient knowledge, learners will publicize the knowledge and share it with people. Learning is a process of tracing, absorbing, accumulating and publicizing knowledge.
4. *Motivation*: During the process of interaction, learners provide explicit encouragement to each other. Members of the team work together and encourage each other to make learning successful.

In teaching Chinese Language that takes interaction as its principle, the teachers should be concerned about the social activities of students. If the students have restricted or even wrong perception, concept, or point of view, they should be reminded and guided to look for the correct knowledge or knowledge chains (accumulation). Through asking questions and giving responses to each other, they should have better understanding of the concept (construction). They can then share with others. If teachers see a certain small group of students relying on a few students' interpretation on the text all along, they should encourage them to challenge the point of view, to raise questions, and be brave to express different points of view (criticism). Then, through exchange of ideas and discussion, a viewpoint which is acceptable to most classmates can be formed and can also be further explained (construction). Furthermore, the teachers can encourage students to acknowledge and express appreciation of the performance of their peers (motivation).

Learning models such as cooperative learning, collaborative learning, inquiry-based learning and task-based learning can all promote the development of language interaction. In the teaching of Second Language, the designers of teaching always combine these activities with their teaching strategies for complementarity to serve the objective of language teaching.

Technology as Means

Chinese Language teaching in Singapore should be congruent to the students' proficiency in and frequent use of information technology to stimulate their interests and enthusiasm in learning Mother Tongue language (Ministry of Education Singapore 2011). For the purpose of achieving the objective of nurturing active learners and proficient users, the educational information technology cannot stop at the level of providing knowledge or information. It should actively promote learning. We should fully utilize information technology, which students love, to nurture different kinds of learning styles and communication skills. Teaching based on information technology should make effort to achieve the goal of "learning style of today is the living style of tomorrow" (Lu 2005: 46).

As a means, information technology can provide timely and flexible support to the acquisition of information (input), conversion of information (collaboration and construction) as well as production of information (output) in the process of learning. In the process of guiding students to learn, teachers have to provide scaffolding to guide students' learning. Teachers can utilize the platform of learning network and, according to the needs of learning and students' level and ability, provide students with three types of learning scaffolding:

(1) *Acceptance Scaffolding*: Acceptance scaffolding provides the necessary resources to learners to assist them in redeploying knowledge they possess and helps them carry out learning activities, including, for example, online tools (dictionaries, terminologies, translation, reading machines and search engines etc.), collaboration techniques guidelines, tasks timetable and webpages which are related to the theme of learning etc.
(2) *Conversion Scaffolding*: Conversion scaffolding guides learners to process the information they obtained into new forms. It can assist them to carry out knowledge integration, conversion and construction, for example problem-posing, thinking maps, mind-maps, tables, etc.
(3) *Output Scaffolding*: Output scaffolding assists learners to organize and present the end products clearly and orderly, for example, end-product samples,

templates, application software, multimedia source materials (e.g. image library, audio library).

Students are different in their language proficiency. Their learning progress, talent in learning language, and home language environment are all different. Thus, information technology can help to develop differentiated Chinese Language teaching to meet different learning needs according to their ability. Teachers can, based on the aim of teaching and the objective of training, provide activities for synchronous learning or asynchronous learning. Scholars think that the Web-based differentiated teaching has the following advantages (Zhong 2006; Li 2006a, b; Leng 2006):

(1) Provide abundant learning resources.
(2) Free to choose learning styles.
(3) Not restricted by time and space.
(4) The virtual space in the learning platform promotes multi-directional exchange and communications. Information and thoughts can be exchanged, checked, and corrected timely and quickly.
(5) The learning situations and progress of students can be monitored and managed effectively.
(6) Timely comments and instructions can be provided.

Educational information technology provides an irreplaceable leverage in today's learning. It makes learning proactive, cooperation-oriented, realistic, and constructive. It also enhances meaningful learning.

Conclusion

In the conceptualization of the Chinese Language Teaching Paradigm, we consider the language shift in Singapore where Chinese Language is concerned, the contemporary theories of language learning, and the prevalence of educational technology which affects the way young students learn. We also strongly believe that for the students to learn Chinese Language efficiently, they should be afforded the opportunities of using the language in real-life situations with specific purposes. By integrating these trends, the paradigm was conceptualized. It was field tested in an experiment and showed great promise (see next chapter).

References

Scholarly Books

Benson, P. (2001). *Teaching and researching autonomy in language learning.* London: Pearson Education Limited.
Bruner, J. S. (2009). *The process of education.* Cambridge, MA: Harvard University Press.
Krashen, S. (1982). *Principles and practice in second language acquisition.* New York: Pergamon Press.
Li, C. (2006a). *Language teaching paradigms.* Beijing: Hua Ling Press.
Li, M. (2006b). *Information learning.* Beijing: Beijing Normal University Press.
Lu, S. (2005). *The change of new curriculum learning mode.* Beijing: China Personnel Publishing House.
Nunan, D. (1988). *The learner-centred curriculum: a study in second language teaching.* Cambridge: Cambridge University Press.
Tarone, E., & Yule, G. (1999). *Focus on the language learner.* Oxford: Oxford University Press.
University of Singapore Students' Union. (1980). *New education system and Singapore.* Singapore: University of Singapore Students' Union.
Zhong, Z. (2006). *Information teaching models.* Beijing: Beijing Normal University Press.

Book Chapter

Cheah, C. M. (2001). Bilingual education and Chinese Language teaching. In Y. S. Goh & C. H. Neo (Eds.), *Anthology of Chinese language teaching* (Vol. 2, pp. 1–12). Singapore: Chinese Language Society (Singapore).

Articles

Chen, X. (2004). Study of contemporary teaching paradigms. *Journal of Shan'xi Normal University, 33*(5), 113–118.
Cheng, K. (2006). Reflections on the reform of foreign language teaching in China. *Journal of the Chinese Society of Education, 2,* 55–58.
Deng Y., & Cheng, K. (2010). Activity: The basic characteristic of task—Based language learning. *Education Review, 1,* 84–87.
Leng, B. (2006). The differentiated teaching and learning resources design in network environment. *Journal of Yanbian University (Natural Science Edition), 32*(4), 308–311.
Liu, W. (2011). Tasks design in task-based teaching. *New Curriculum (High School), 2,* 121.
Sang, Y. (2008). Effective foreign language teaching: Perspectives based on teaching paradigm. *Journal of Xi'an International Studies University, 16*(2), 87–96.
Soller, A., & Lesgold, A. (2010). Modeling the process of collaborative learning. In H. U. Hoppe, H. Ogata, & A. Soller (Eds.), *The role of technology in CSCL: Studies in technology enhanced collaborative learning* (pp. 63–86). New York: Springer.
Swain, M. (1985). Communicative competence: Some roles of comprehensible input and comprehensible output in its development. In S. Gass & C. Madden (Eds.), *Input in second language acquisition* (pp. 235–253). Rowley, MA: Newbury House.
Wei, Y. (2005). Interpretations on task-based teaching principles. *Global Education, 33*(6), 54–57.

Zhang, S. (2008). Complex between accuracy and fluency: Task-based guidelines for balanced development. *Journal of Sichuan Normal University (Social Sciences Edition), 35*(5), 82–90.

Zhu, Y. (2007). Task-based language teaching series. *Forum on Contemporary Education, 14*, 130–131.

Government Documents

Goh, K. S., & The Education Study Team. (1978). *Report on the Ministry of Education.* Singapore: Ministry of Education.

Ministry of Education. (2011). *Nurturing active learners and proficient users: 2010 mother tongue languages review committee report (MTLRC).* Singapore: Ministry of Education.

Newspaper

Lianhe Zaobao. (1999, January 21). Deputy Prime Minister Lee Hsien Loong policy statement (full text).

Chee Kuen Chin (陈之权) received Ph.D. from the Central China Normal University, China. He was immediate past Executive Director and is currently Academic Consultant cum Distinguished Principal Lecturer at SCCL. His academic interests include Chinese as a second language, curriculum development, Chinese Language pedagogies, ICT mediated in teaching and learning of Chinese Language and cultural studies. He has published five scholarly books on Chinese Language research and a university textbook. He has more than 100 journal articles, chapters, keynote speeches, and conference papers to his credit.

Chinese Language Teaching Paradigm: Case Study

Chee Kuen Chin, Cheng Gong and Boon Pei Tay

Abstract This chapter reports an experimental study based on the theoretical framework for Chinese Language teaching in Singapore based on the paradigm propounded in the previous chapter. Experimental and control students were compared on oral and composition skills, with sizable gain in both measures favouring the former group. Stages of implementation and variables involved are detailed.

A school-based research project completed by Singapore Centre for Chinese Language is used here to show the thoughts, organization, process and effect of teaching which is based on the Chinese Language teaching paradigm. The case study demonstrates the elements of the paradigm but not to do a detailed data analysis.

Pedagogical Thoughts

The paradigm shift from the transmission model to an integrated model calls for a pedagogical rethinking of Chinese Language teaching in Singapore. As discussed in the previous chapter, the integrated model could effectively enhance Chinese Language teaching by combining four key elements of the model, namely learning centred, tasks, interaction and technology.

One of the important goals of education today is to help students understand the complex global society in which they are living. Students need to be competent in

---

C. K. Chin (✉) · C. Gong · B. P. Tay
Singapore Centre for Chinese Language, Nanyang Technological University, Singapore, Singapore
e-mail: cheekuen.chin@sccl.sg

C. Gong
e-mail: cheng.gong@sccl.sg

B. P. Tay
e-mail: boonpei.tay@sccl.sg

© Springer Nature Singapore Pte Ltd. 2018
K. C. Soh (ed.), *Teaching Chinese Language in Singapore*,
https://doi.org/10.1007/978-981-10-8860-5_3

examining complex situations and defining solvable problems with multiple sources and media (Bruce and Bishop 2002). They need to become active learners and be able to identify problems and find workable solutions themselves. They need to learn how to learn, find problems, investigate the problems, find creative ways to solve them and share their perspectives with others. They need to fulfil their learning tasks through collaboration so that they could develop cognitive skills at a higher level. Learning today should aim to develop skills of inquiry, communication, construction and expression. In other words, the four primary interests of the learner as described by Dewey (1956) are still applicable to learning today (Bruce and Bishop 2002).

In terms of second language teaching, language educators in the last two decades have been calling for connecting the language learned in the classroom with its practical use in daily lives. Krashen and Terrell (1983) indicated that second language learning needs to be linked with the outside world. They opined that second language teaching should encourage students to interact with native speakers outside the classroom (p. 181). Pegrum (2000) urged that exposing foreign or second language students to the outside world could provide them with opportunities for realistic language input in a dynamic and meaningful context and thus increase their motivation. He believed that natural communication in authentic situations would help in the transition of a classroom language to a contextual language. Ozverir and Herrington (2011) pointed out that maintaining essential contextual conditions have been important in second or foreign language teaching. They hold the view that language learning should involve students more in real-life tasks so that the knowledge and skills acquired would not become inert. All these scholars are supportive of using the outside world or authentic situations as resources for second or foreign language learning. Their views are relevant to the teaching of Chinese as a second language in Singapore. The integrated model as proposed in the previous chapter is constructed based on the concept of authentic learning whereby students will be exposed to real-world contexts to complete authentic language tasks. The model takes the form of an inquiry-based learning process. In the process, students are requested to identify real-world problems and find workable solutions through inquiry-based projects on their own. They will be using Chinese Language to communicate with native speakers and peers to gather information they need. They will construct solutions after having analysed and interpreted the information and then report back to the classroom to make a presentation and defend their views.

Inquiry is an active learning process. Inquiry-based learning views learners as inquirers whereby they learn through work on meaningful problems in real situations (Bruce and Bishop 2002). Inquiry learning provides learners with opportunities of asking, investigating, creating, discussing and reflecting when working on any question or problem (Bruce and Davidson 1996). Scholars in the field of language education in China opined that, through their researches, inquiry-based learning could improve students' language performance. Jin (2008) argued that inquiry-based language learning helped in stimulating students' interest in learning the language, enhanced their abilities in analysing and solving problems, and nurtured their creative thinking. Yang (2009) found that inquiry-based learning facilitated active participation in language learning. Huang (2008) argued that inquiry-based learning would promote collaborative learning as students needed to complete their inquiry tasks using team effort to solve the meaningful problems. The studies of these scholars from both West and East have echoed the common stand that inquiry-based learning does help in language learning. Below is the detailed description of an inquiry-based project that was designed based on the integrated model linking language learning with the outside world.

In the project, the teachers embedded learning in real-life situations of students. They requested students to form small groups and plunge into the thick of life to explore the themes relevant to their daily lives to accomplish the inquiry-based tasks. In the process of exploration, students needed to use different methods to collect opinions from the public to understand public's thoughts on a selected topic according to the theme of inquiry.

After they collected the opinions, students organized and sorted out the data and conducted oral presentation in Chinese Language in the classroom. They answered questions from teacher and classmates extemporaneously. After the oral presentation, students further consolidated the opinions of different groups to complete the written assignments. Teachers made use of information technology to provide assignment instructions and scaffolding in each of the inquiry-based learning activity.

Organization of Teaching

Table 1 is the yearly scheme of work of this task-oriented inquiry-based learning. Each of the tasks is aligned with the secondary 1 and 2 instructional materials developed by the curriculum branch in the Ministry of Education of Singapore (Ministry of Education 2011, 2012) or school-based teaching materials developed by the experimenting school.

The design of these six tasks follows the principle of starting from simple to complex, from easy to difficult, and from familiar to unfamiliar. Teachers let students first interact with people and things that they were more familiar with (i.e. environment and people of the school) to complete simpler tasks in order to nurture their confidence in using Chinese Language. Students then entered the real-life situation to carry out more complicated and challenging tasks. In the design of teaching, it followed the sequence of language usage in daily lives, i.e. input first and then output, listening and reading first and then speaking and writing. Students first read and understood the materials to grasp the language (vocabularies and sentence patterns or chunks) needed for the tasks. Then, they used the language to communicate with people in real-life situations to obtain information and integrate the information input together. In group presentation, they verbally expressed their thoughts first and then listen to opinions of other students and gave their own response. After that, they revised their thoughts with reference to the classmates' opinions and consolidated the output.

Table 1 Yearly scheme of work for task-oriented inquiry-based learning

Teaching materials	Task theme	Setting	Form
Central teaching material: "between opening and closing" (《开关之间》)/Little thoughts arose from the conflict between bus passengers	Survey of students' behaviour in school canteen	Quasi-real (preset)	Interview involving school canteen operators, teachers, students and janitors
Central teaching material: "Making rice dumplings" 《包粽子》 /the process of making rice dumplings with family	Writing Singapore food guide	Quasi-real (preset)	Interviewing food experts from the four main Chinese dialect groups—role-played by non-Chinese Language school teachers who speak fluent Chinese Language
Central teaching material: "say sorry" 《说声对不起》/small dispute between father and child	Survey of parent-child relationship of students	Real (a small number of interviewees)	Questionnaire for parents of classmates, schoolmates of other classes
School-based teaching material: "everyone is responsible for civilized mass rapid system, MRT" 《人文地铁, 人人有责》 /MRT passengers' behaviour and reflection	Code of conduct of train passengers	Real, in MRT station	Street interview by random-pick of MRT passengers
News from Chinese newspaper: "students run a business in shopping mall stall" 《学生商场摆摊做生意》 /the process of learning to start a business and the experience gained by students	Start-up business proposal of neighbourhood store—understand the requirements first before proposing a plan	Real neighbourhood shopping mall near the school	Questionnaire for owners of neighbourhood stores
School-based teaching material: "the winter of Jiangnan" (《江南的冬季》)/what the author saw and heard when he travelled with family	Holiday travel package	Quasi-real simulated situation	Telephone enquiry—call a customer service officer of one travel agency to learn about information of different kinds of travel packages. The customer service officer was role-played by a researcher

Teaching Flow

This inquiry-based learning started from the second semester of Secondary one and ended at the second semester of Secondary two, lasting for one and a half academic year. The whole flow of teaching is divided into three stages.

First Stage

The stage commenced in the second semester of Secondary one. This was for training of basic ability. Before starting the inquiry-based learning, students have to grasp the usual procedures and skills of inquiry-based learning. Students need to know things such as design of questionnaires, interview questions, data collection and presentation and possess the basic skills to be able to carry out the tasks in an efficient way. Teachers and researchers, through setting a few small topics, allow students to try designing simple questionnaires and interview questions and to learn the basic methods of presenting data (such as using excel spreadsheet to input data and convert data into statistic charts). These built up in the students a good technical foundation for the inquiry-based tasks. Starting the preparation work half a year earlier helps to reduce the anxiety of students when facing the tasks and to enhance students' enthusiasm in learning.

Second Stage

The stage started from the first semester of Secondary two. At the stage, Mini Quest is a kind of simple Web-based learning mode. Its framework is relatively short, divided into three parts: the situation, the task and the result. It can usually be finished within 2–3 class hours. Teachers and researchers set simple and easy tasks for students through Mini Quest Website. Students finished the tasks on campus or in class. To help students adapt to the inquiry-based learning under real-life situations more quickly, teachers and researchers arranged two real-life situations and one quasi-real situation in the three activities. These three simulated situations included interviewing interested parties of school canteen (real-life situation), interviewing food experts role-played by school teachers of different Chinese dialect groups (quasi-real situation) and doing questionnaire survey with their own parents (real-life situation). The people and things in these three situations are the most familiar ones to students. The purpose is to let students finish these three simple tasks comfortably under less pressure and to gain inquiry-based learning experience. These three Mini Quest activities integrated with the content of the central teaching materials. Students were also required to use the vocabularies, sentence patterns and chucks from the text. It is a structure-oriented language setting.

Third Stage

The stage commenced in the second semester of Secondary two. At this stage, WebQuest was used. WebQuest is an inquiry-based learning mode which is Web-based and is widely used in many countries. Its framework is more complicated, divided into six parts in total: introduction, task, process, resources, evaluation and conclusion. Topics explored in the WebQuest are more complex, and the research process is also comparatively longer. At this stage, the tasks set by teachers and researchers required students to go out of the campus and get into the real-life settings to interact using Chinese Language with strangers they encountered. These tasks were quite demanding. Teachers and researchers set up three settings, namely MRT station, neighbourhood mall and travel agency. Students finished a street interview, a questionnaire survey and a telephone enquiry in these three settings. A set of code of public conduct, a start-up business proposal and a travel package were produced for the tasks. After finishing the tasks, students first did oral presentations and then they finished the written assignments. This series of inquiry-based tasks was basically designed according to the theme of the school-based teaching materials. However, it imposes no restriction on students regarding the use of vocabularies, sentence patterns and chunks so that there is more naturalness in the use of language. It is a language setting of social-driven approach. Since teachers and researchers consciously adopted the keywords and important sentence patterns which were needed for the tasks in the teaching materials, it was structure-oriented.

Teaching Effect

To objectively review the efficacy of inquiry-based learning based on social resources on the standard of oral and written expression of students involved in the project, the research team did a comparative analysis on the performance of the experiment group of students ($N = 31$) and the control group of students ($N = 29$) before and after the experiment. The results of the comparisons are shown in Table 2.

Oral Examination

The pretest results of oral examination of the experiment group students before the experiment were lower than that of the control group students, indicating lack of group equivalence prior to the experiment. The mean difference of the oral examination is −1.68 in favour of the control group, and the effect size is a small but near medium Cohen's $d = -0.47$. The results after the experiment show that, for oral examination, both the performance of the experiment group and control

Table 2 Oral and composition results of experiment and control groups

	Experiment group (N = 31)		Control group (N = 29)		Mean difference	Effect size
	Mean	Standard deviation	Mean	Standard deviation		
Pretest						
Oral examination	22.69	5.62	24.37	3.56	−1.68	−0.47
Oral examination	26.47	2.91	26.66	2.01	−0.19	−0.09
Gained score	3.78	4.48	2.29	2.89	1.49	0.52
Post-test						
Composition	56.21	10.92	58.39	6.39	−2.18	−0.34
Composition	64.42	5.94	58.02	7.67	6.40	0.83
Gained score	8.21	8.79	−0.37	7.06	8.58	1.22

group students improved. The mean difference was reduced to −0.19, still in favour of the control group.

However, the gain score mean is 3.78 for the experiment group and 2.29 for the control group. The gain score means show a difference of 1.49, and the effect size is 0.52 in favour of the experimental group. Thus, in spite of the initial disadvantage, the experimental group did benefit more from being involved in the study.

Written Composition

The pretest results of written composition of the experiment group students before the experiment were lower than that of the control group students, indicating lack of group equivalence prior to the experiment. The mean difference of the written composition is −2.18 in favour of the control group, and the effect size is a small Cohen's $d = -0.34$. The post-test results show that the performance of the experiment group improved (by 8.21), while the performance of the control remains unchanged (ignoring the minute difference of −0.37).

The gain score mean is 8.58 in favour of the experiment group with a corresponding $d = 1.22$, which is a very large effect size. This shows that the experimental group has gained a lot from being involved in the project.

We have also conducted focused group discussions with students. Students who participated in inquiry-based learning generally reflected that their confidence in communicating with others and oral presentations using Chinese Language has improved, and their interest in learning Chinese Language has also become stronger. We believe that the personal experience and sense of achievement they obtained in the process of completing the inquiry tasks would bring about a gradual change of their attitudes towards Chinese Language.

The preliminary results of this experiment (as a case study) show that the inquiry-based learning activities which have been designed and carried out based on the proposed Chinese Language teaching paradigm can effectively enhance and consolidate students' curricular knowledge and extracurricular knowledge spontaneously through the active interaction with people in an environment similar to real-life situation and the experience of solving problems and accomplishing tasks in the activities. It can improve students' ability in language expression under the condition of natural application of the language. Details of this project can be found in the relevant reference articles (Gong et al. 2012).

Elements of Teaching Paradigm

The teaching paradigm suggested in Chap. 2 places emphasis on consolidating four key elements in second language teaching and enhances spontaneous integration of the elements through effective organization of teaching. The integrated teaching paradigm formed by these four key elements aims at providing learners with opportunities of applying Chinese Language to communicate with people, developing self-directed learning ability through the accomplishment of tasks and nurturing the lifelong learning ability which is required with the assistance of information technology. Diagram 1 shows the relationship of the key elements of the integrated teaching paradigm.

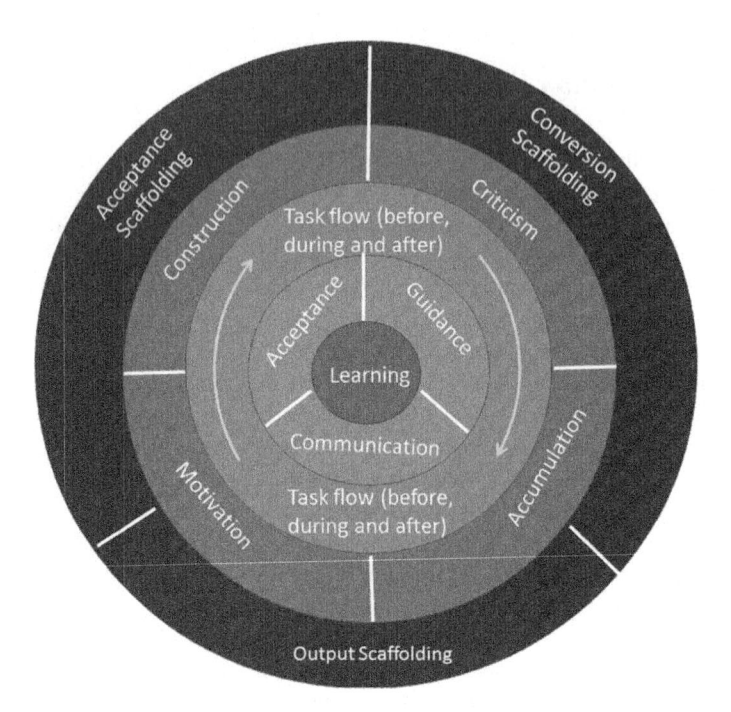

Diagram 1 Relationship among the four key elements of integrated teaching paradigm

This concentric circle model is a four-ring disc which can be turned around flexibly. Designer of the teaching turns the sections of each ring according to the needs to form different permutations and combinations to meet the teaching requirements.

Learning Centred

Every language lesson is a complete language learning process. Teachers ensure that students have grasped certain content of learning and certain language focus. Students go through the stages of acceptance (language input), guidance (language conversion) and communication (language output). Teachers first carry out language input for students. They then guide students to imitate, apply and grasp the language focus. Through multi-directional conversation and communication, students' application of the language can be promoted and their ability to express can be improved.

In inquiry-based learning in lower secondary level based on social resources, before teachers ask students to do the tasks, they teach students the relevant content of the texts as well as the vocabularies and sentence patterns covered therein during lessons. Teachers teach vocabularies and sentence patterns according to the content of the texts. Teachers follow the three-step cycle flow of acceptance-guidance-communication in the teaching of every applicable vocabulary and sentence pattern to ensure that students can grasp every language focus.

Tasks as Principle Axis

After students have grasped certain language knowledge, vocabularies and sentence patterns, teachers start to set tasks for students and request them to complete the tasks according to certain requirements within the given time. According to the students' language ability and task requirements, teachers should not only set up the structure-oriented or social-driven language setting but should also introduce to students the relevant knowledge which is related to the learning theme and the tasks in the pre-task section to get them well prepared. In the task cycle (or in-task) section, teachers start to set up tasks and decide the form of tasks (set for individuals or small group). They also assist students to make the necessary tools for the task and tell students clearly the expected outcomes of the tasks. If necessary, teachers let students practise in class (e.g. previewing survey or interview). After finishing the tasks, students report the results in different forms and answer questions from teachers and students. In the post-task section, teachers review the learning process together with students to analyse students' performance. They also draw conclusions on the language problems which have arisen in the process of completing the tasks or prepare reinforcement exercises.

The task of the inquiry-based learning in lower secondary level based on social resources, for example, required students to go to the MRT station to do street interviews. Before students entered the station to complete the interview task (i.e. survey on the conduct of passengers), teacher used social-driven and structure-oriented language to guide students in setting interview questions for the rehearsal of street interview to strengthen the confidence and adaptability of students. Teacher also told students the expected outcome of the task before the beginning of the task—developing code of conduct of train passengers. At the same time, teacher provided sample code of conduct for students' reference. After that, students were divided into groups to start the action. They determined the targets of the interviews and made sound recordings and written records of the interviews. After task completion, the teachers organized presentation in class. The groups took turn to report their first drafts of the code and listened to the comments from teacher and students to improve their drafts. After the presentation, teacher guided students to review again to re-examine the areas that they had done well and areas that could be improved and then summed up the experience. Teacher also did correction teaching for common mistakes found in the presentation to correct the wrong language expressions of students timely.

Interaction as Principle

Interaction is an important way of learning language. The interaction situation should, however, be combined with the real-life application situation as much as possible. As said, the long-term bilingual education policy has created a living social environment that uses Chinese Language in Singapore. If this is well utilized, it can improve the learning Chinese Language. Teachers should consciously create real-life interactive environment to provide opportunities for students to apply the language. Interaction can take place at any stage of the flow of the task-based learning. The four types of interaction can be adopted flexibly by teachers according to the learning situations. For example, teachers can enhance students' construction of new knowledge, the development of self-evaluation and peer-assessment ability of students can be improved through criticism, students can search and share knowledge with one another through accumulation, and students' motive in learning and their teamwork can be improved through motivation. Chinese Language teaching should provide situations which are similar to real-life situations as far as practicable to improve students' ability to communicate and enhance students' confidence through different types of interaction.

In the process of inquiry-based learning in lower secondary level based on social resources, teachers and researchers let the groups finished tasks in real or quasi-real situations for many times through construction. Students also obtained deep understanding of the topic of inquiry. In the many group discussions in relation to the tasks, group members, through criticism, gave opinion on their members' viewpoints and even started debates and disputations. They reached consensus and presented the outcome in the end. In the process of monitoring the task, teachers did not only provide scaffolding to help students understand the flow and procedures of the task, and the necessary tools or samples for the completion of the tasks, they also met with different groups of students regularly to check their understanding of the knowledge or concepts. If any mistake of knowledge has been found, teachers would utilize the interaction of accumulation to request students to look into the knowledge and to openly present the knowledge they have acquired at the end of the task cycle. In the process when the groups were completing the tasks, teachers would encourage group members to give encouragement to each other. Teachers also gave a lot of acknowledgement and appreciation to the groups for motivation. Using various types of interaction appropriately can develop students' learning initiative and strengthen their learning motive.

Technology as Means

Information technology has become indispensable for improving learning, increasing interest and enhancing motivation. While the third generation of network technology has been increasingly well developed, information technology will definitely play an increasingly important role in the near future. Among the Chinese Language teaching paradigms suggested in Chap. 2, information technology exists as a learning support system for providing detailed learning instructions, activities procedures and online resources to learners. It also provides the necessary scaffolding in their learning process. It takes care of the individual differences in learning and develops students' self-directed learning ability through scaffolding.

As in the inquiry-based learning in lower secondary level based on social resources, teachers provided a lot of acceptance scaffolding to students, including online translation, reading machine, task flowchart and timetable as well as online resources. These assist students to handle the difficulties they faced in absorbing information or the uncertainty in scheduling the task progress due to lack of experience. Teachers also provided conversion scaffolding to students, including questions which can assist their thinking and mind maps, sample questions of interview and survey, customized excel files for the analysis of data, etc., to help them effectively organize the collected data, and sum up and sort out the data. Teachers also provided the conversion scaffolding to give product samples, templates (e.g. customized power point files), etc. This made students more confident in presentation. Using technology can effectively provide different kinds of support in different learning stages to meet the learning needs of students. Information technology will play a more and more important role in Chinese Language learning in Singapore.

Conclusion

To implement the curricular reform objective of nurturing active learners and proficient users, Chinese Language teaching in Singapore must integrate with real life and fully utilize the high-quality teaching resources (including hardware and software resources) and the advantageous social environment to promote the learning. Through a case study, we found that the Chinese Language teaching paradigm integrating resources from everyday life is suitable for the learning of Chinese Language as a second language in Singapore.

Chinese Language teaching has to go beyond the home and classroom and thereby allows practice in the wider world outside. Chinese Language teachers should fully utilize social resources to let students use Chinese Language to communicate in real-life environment so that they can improve their language ability and confidence. The findings of the project echo the views of Krashen and Terrell (1983), Pegrum (2000), Ozverir and Herrington (2011), Yang (2009) and Huang (2008). Chinese Language teaching in Singapore needs to fully utilize the bilingual society. Chinese Language teaching should also learn from the successful experience of contemporary language teaching and the educational technology.

Changing teaching paradigm is the first imperative of Chinese Language teaching in Singapore while the integrated paradigm is an important option for the curriculum and teaching of Chinese Language in the future.

References

Bruce, B. C., & Bishop, A. P. (2002). Using the Web to support inquiry-based literacy devel-opment. *Journal of Adolescent and Adult Literacy, 45*(8), 706–714.
Bruce, B. C., & Davidson, J. (1996). An inquiry model for literacy across the curriculum. *Journal of Curriculum Studies, 28,* 281–300.
Dewey, J. (1956). *The child and the curriculum: And the school and society*. Chicago: University of Chicago Press.
Gong, C., Chin, C. K., & Tay, B. P. (2012). A preliminary study on enhancing students' communicative competency in Singapore. In W. S. He (Ed.), *Facing pluralistic linguistic contexts: Reflections on Chinese language education* (pp. 196–203). Suzhou: Suzhou University Press.
Huang, X. (2008). Change the way of study to promote students' active development. *Science Educator, 08*(4), 75.
Jin, G. (2008). On the role of inquiry learning in Chinese language teaching. *China Education Innovation Herald, 08*(9), 22.
Krashen, S., & Terrell, T. (1983). *The natural approach: Language acquisition in the classroom*. Oxford: Pergamon.
Ministry of Education. (2011). *Chinese language for secondary schools (Higher Chinese)(1A/1B)*. Singapore: Marshall Cavendish Education.
Ministry of Education. (2012). *Chinese language for secondary schools (Higher Chinese)(2A/2B)*. Singapore: Marshall Cavendish Education.
Ozverir, I., Herrington, J. (2011). Authentic activities in language learning: Bringing real world relevance to classroom activities. In *World Conference on Educational Multimedia,*

Hypermedia and Telecommunications (EDMEDIA) 2011, 27 June–1 July 2011, Lisbon, Portugal (pp. 1423–1428).

Pegrum, M. A. (2000). The outside world as an extension of the EFL/ESL classroom. *The Internet TESL Journal, 4*(8). Retrieved on April 28, 2015: http://iteslj.org/Lessons/Pegrum-OutsideWorld.html.

Yang, L. (2009). The application of inquiry learning in Chinese language teaching. *Shan'xi Education, 09*(3), 101.

Chee Kuen Chin (陈之权) received Ph.D. from the Central China Normal University, China. He was an immediate past Executive Director and currently Academic Consultant cum Distinguished Principal Lecturer at SCCL. His academic interests include Chinese as a second language, curriculum development, Chinese Language pedagogies, ICT mediated in teaching and learning of Chinese Language and cultural studies. He has published five scholarly books on Chinese Language research and a university textbook. He has more than 100 journal articles, book chapters, keynote speeches and conference papers to his credit.

Cheng Gong (龚成) completed M.A. at the Nanyang Technological University, Singapore. She is currently a teaching fellow at the Singapore Centre for Chinese Language, Nanyang Technological University. Her academic interests include teaching of writing with self-directed learning, theories and pedagogies of second language acquisition, and ICT-assisted language teaching. Her publications include one scholarly book, five teaching toolkits and a number of conference papers and journal articles.

Boon Pei Tay (郑文佩) completed M.A. at the University of Hong Kong, Hong Kong. She is currently a research associate at the Singapore Centre for Chinese Language. Her research interests include teaching of writing with self-directed learning, exploratory learning, second language writing and ICT-assisted language learning. She has published a scholarly book, three sets of teaching toolkit, and a number of journal articles and conference papers.

Mandarin Competence of Primary School Students in Singapore: A Preliminary Comparison Across Academic Level and Home Language Backgrounds

Hock Huan Goh, Chunsheng Zhao and Siew Hoon Kwek

Abstract This study investigates Chinese language competence of Primary 1, Primary 3, and Primary 6 students in Singapore schools. A total of 720 students were involved. Their Chinese language productions were classified into 15 parts of speech and six sentence patterns. Students of the three class levels show similar profiles for word types but divergent sentence patterns, albeit with different levels of competence. The same findings were observed when the students were compared in terms of home language background.

Singapore's multiculturalism creates its uniquely diverse language environment. Since the 1970s, it has influenced Singapore's language policy in view of the social, economic, and political needs of Singapore (Cheah 2003; Wu 2010; Zhao and Liu 2010). In the early years of Singapore, to eliminate the language barriers of different Chinese dialect groups, the Speak Mandarin Campaign was launched to promote the use of Mandarin among dialect group (Gupta 1997; Wu 2008). Concurrently, to integrate with the Western world, Singapore adopted English as its administrative language (Dixon 2005; Goh 2004). These policies eventually led to changes in the language environment of Singapore. One obvious change is the imbalanced development of languages, i.e. English and Mandarin. The unique feature is that the vast majority of the Chinese population, in the past 20 years, chose to give up dialect and Mandarin as their home language and switched to English for communication (Guo 2004; Goh 2017).

H. H. Goh (✉) · C. Zhao · S. H. Kwek
Singapore Centre for Chinese Language, Nanyang Technological University, Singapore, Singapore
e-mail: Hockhuan.goh@sccl.sg

C. Zhao · S. H. Kwek
Academy of Singapore Teachers, Ministry of Education, Brisbane, Singapore

The teaching of CL in such an environment faced many challenges, one of which is the lowering of CL competence among Chinese children (Li 2005). The home language environment has been gradually taken over by the English Language (Department of Statistics 2001). The two earlier CL reviews and the latest review pointed out that the need to preserve the use of Mother Tongue Languages.

In 1999, the review committee acknowledged the drastic change of the home language environment and pointed out that the then CL syllabus was no longer compatible with the students' CL competence. Therefore, it was necessary to simplify the teaching materials to facilitate students' learning of CL (Chinese Language Review Committee 1999). The 2004 review acknowledged that learning Chinese language is difficult and the review committee reiterated that the teaching of CL should take into account students' home language backgrounds and learning ability (Chinese Language Curriculum and Pedagogy Review Committee 2004). The most recent report on the teaching of Mother Tongue Language puts forward guidelines which emphasized that the aim of Mother Tongue teaching should be relevant to functions in daily life (Mother Tongue Language Review Committee 2010). These three reviews showed that the Chinese language in Singapore has gradually shifted its role from the culture and knowledge carrier to a mere language skill to fulfil daily communication. In such a non-supporting language environment, the direction of CL teaching has become a concern among Singapore CL educators (Li 2005). To help students with different language abilities and home language backgrounds, The Ministry of Education launched a new primary school Chinese language curriculum in 2007 adopting the modular approach. With a core module, the new curriculum provided a bridging module for the weaker students so that they would catch up on the core module. As the same time, the more competent students were provided an enrichment module so that they would enhance their ability beyond the core module (CLCPRC 2004).

With the implementation of the new curriculum, the overall Chinese language performance of students and the performance of children from different home language backgrounds need to be evaluated. For these, in 2011, the Singapore Centre for Chinese Language was funded by the Ministry of Education to embark on a systematic evaluation to enable an understanding the differences in Chinese language competence and compare children of different age groups and also to identify the differences in language abilities among children of different home language backgrounds.

This evaluation, therefore, aims to identify the gaps in Chinese language learning among different age groups and home language groups, so as to determine the contents of future CL curriculum. This article is a report on the preliminary results of this evaluation.

Method

Data

To carry out the above-mentioned evaluation, the Singapore Centre for Chinese Language built the Singapore Primary School Children Spoken Chinese Corpus (hereafter, Corpus) to find out the basic vocabulary and sentence pattern of children of different ages and from different home language backgrounds. The construction of this Corpus underwent three stages, i.e. language data collection, corpus building, and corpus-based analysis. This section will focus on the language data collection to outline the data basis of this analysis. For a fuller description of corpus building, refer to Goh et al. (2016).

The language data collection for the Corpus was indeed complex. Firstly, the corpus identified three school types which corresponded to children of different home language backgrounds. The three school types are Special Aided Programme (SAP) schools which are mainly populated by children from Chinese-speaking homes, the government schools which are mainly populated by children from bilingual-speaking homes, and the Traditional English schools which are mainly populated by children from English-speaking homes. This corpus collected three types of data to best capture the Mandarin-speaking abilities of primary school children. The three types of data were gathered through one-on-one interview, classroom talks, and home talks.

The interview mainly gathered language data of individual child through elicitation by researchers. This approach was a direct and simple way to gather a large amount of language data, but the data gathered will be less natural and hence is regarded as unnatural data. Classroom talks were gathered with the help of teachers; they conducted two 30-min oral activities for students to freely talk about a topic of their interest in Mandarin. This provided relatively natural language data as classroom interaction is the situation whereby children learn, use, and practise their oral skills. This type of data can hence be regarded as semi-natural data. Home talks were gathered with the help of parents whereby they recorded two 30-min home dialogues of daily activities (e.g. during dinner or outing in a car) using Mandarin. This type of data is considered as most natural, as children were in their most familiar interactional atmosphere and they used Mandarin as and when they felt the need. Table 1 shows the arrangements for data collection for the Corpus.

As shown in Table 1, for the Corpus, it was intended to collect one-on-one interview data from 720 children, but due to absence and loss of data caused by faulty equipment, the final gathered interview data was from 699 children. As for classroom talk and home talks, data of all the 48 classes, and the 72 families was collected as planned.

Moreover, before data collection, two questionnaire surveys were conducted. One of the surveys solicited the home language exposure and language use of the children. This survey was used to compute Chinese Exposure Index (CEI) which

Table 1 Distribution of data gathered for the SPSCSC corpus

	School type	P1	P3	P6	Total	Hours of records
Interview No. of students	SAP	60	60	60	180	90
	English	60	60	60	180	90
	Government	120	120	120	360	180
	Total	240	240	240	720	360
Classroom talks No. of classes	SAP	4	4	4	12	12
	English	4	4	4	12	12
	Government	8	8	8	24	24
	Total	16	16	16	48	48
Home talks No. of families	SAP	6	6	6	18	18
	English	6	6	6	18	18
	Government	12	12	12	36	36
	Total	24	24	24	72	72

represents the home language background of each child. This index forms a continuum from −1 to +1. However, for ease of description, this has been divided into continuum of four parts to form four typical home language groups, i.e. Predominantly Mandarin-Speaking Homes (PMSH; CEI 1.0–0.6), More Mandarin-Speaking Homes (MMSH; CEI 0.5–0.0), More English-Speaking Homes (MESH; CEI 0.0 to −0.5), and Predominantly English-Speaking Homes (PESH; CEI: −0.6 to −1.0). The other questionnaire mainly surveyed on the favourite topics of children to identify the topics for eliciting language data in the interview and classroom talks. The identified topic of interest ensured that children could express and elaborate on content they were familiar with and interested into best assess their Chinese language abilities.

All collected data were fully transcribed and processed to build the Corpus. The completed Corpus contains 1,285,096 word tokens with 8371-word types. These word types consist of 7358 common words (that are used in standard Mandarin), 164 idioms and phrases, and 849 names of person and places. Besides common words, 290 special words that are specifically used in Singapore, Malaysia, Hong Kong, and Taiwan were also found. These words can be seen as unstandardized words which should be reviewed for preservation or elimination from the education perspective.

Analysis and Results

As for sentence types and sentence patterns, the entire Corpus contained 299,394 sentences, of which most sentences are declarative sentences, forming 91.0% of the Corpus. The corpus has 6.9% of interrogative sentences, 2.2% of exclamation sentences, and 0.4% of imperative sentences. In terms of simple sentences, verb predicate sentences, elliptical sentences, and single-word sentences are the most commonly found sentence patterns, representing 28.6, 22.8, and 9.7%, respectively, of the simple sentence. As for complex sentences, the three most common sentence patents are "因为……所以…… (Because…hence…)" of the causal relation complexes, "……然后…… (…and then…)" in the successive relation complexes, and "如果……就…… (if…then…)" of the hypothetical complexes which occupy 3.2, 1.0, and 0.8% of the sentences, respectively.

Comparisons by Grades On the basis of the above, this study attempted to uncover the vocabulary and sentence pattern of students with reference to their academic grade and family background. As the classroom talks could not be tracked to individual child and the topic of home talk are not comparable, the following data description and analysis will only be based on the 699 students of the one-on-one interviews.

Table 2 above shows the proportions of word types covered by children in the 15 parts of speech (POS) in the Corpus. Generally, in most cases (such as adjectives, nouns, verbs, locatives, time, prepositions, adverbs, conjunctions, and pronouns), the lower grade students covered less proportions of word types in each POS, whereas students of higher academic grade covered more word types. Generally, word-type coverage in each POS increases in correspondence to the grade levels. In other words, older children covered a larger vocabulary while younger children covered less vocabulary. This is in line with the assumption of language development overage.

Although the coverage of POS aligns with the assumption of language development, children of Primary 1 and Primary 3 did not cover more than half of the

Table 2 Word-type coverage on parts of speech among students of different grades

Parts of speech	Word-type N	Primary 1%	Primary 3%	Primary 6%
Adjective	726	30.4	40.6	63.4
Noun	3384	31.5	42.6	63.6
Verb	2062	35.5	49.8	74.4
Locative	47	40.4	61.7	68.1
Time	109	45.0	55.1	72.5
Preposition	39	46.2	61.5	74.4
Adverb	268	47.8	57.8	76.1
Conjunction	66	48.5	59.1	81.8
Onomatopoeia	49	30.6	20.4	24.5
Quantifier	135	50.4	68.9	79.3
Position words	62	56.5	75.8	77.4
Interjection	32	65.6	59.4	65.6
Particle	21	66.7	61.9	85.7
Pronoun	94	71.3	73.4	87.2
Modals	27	77.8	74.1	70.4

word types for POS of the content words, i.e. nouns, verbs, and adjectives. In these POS, the children cover only between 30 and 49% of the word types. In addition, the POS less covered by Primary 1 children includes locatives, time words, prepositions, adverbs, and conjunctions. Although Primary 3 and Primary 6 children covered more than half of the word types in most POS, their coverage was usually around 70% of the word types. And, Primary 6 children cover 80% or more of the word types only in three POS, i.e. conjunctions, auxiliary words, and pronouns. Among the 15 POS, onomatopoeia is the least covered by children of all academic levels, as the word-type coverage of onomatopoeia among all children less than 25%. These differences among the grade levels are shown clearly in Fig. 1, where onomatopoeia takes a dip for all levels.

In terms of sentence patterns, the ratio of simple sentences and complex sentences is slightly different across the three grades (Table 3 and Fig. 2). The proportion of simple sentence produced by children of the three grades are more or less comparable, around 35% of the total number of simple sentences they produced. As for complex sentences, there is an obvious trend of progressive growth over the three grades. Primary 1 children produced the least complex sentences of about 20% of the total number of complex sentences produced. Primary 3 children produced a higher proportion of complex sentences, about 30%. And, Primary 6 children produced the greatest proportions of complex sentences, nearly 50% of the total number of complex sentences produced.

In terms of special sentence construction, pivotal construction (兼语句), serial-verb construction (连动句), *ba*-construction (把字句), and *bei*-construction (被字句) displayed a progressive growth among the children across the three grades. That is, Primary 1 children produced least of these four constructions, ranging from 9 to 22% of their total number of sentences produced, whereas

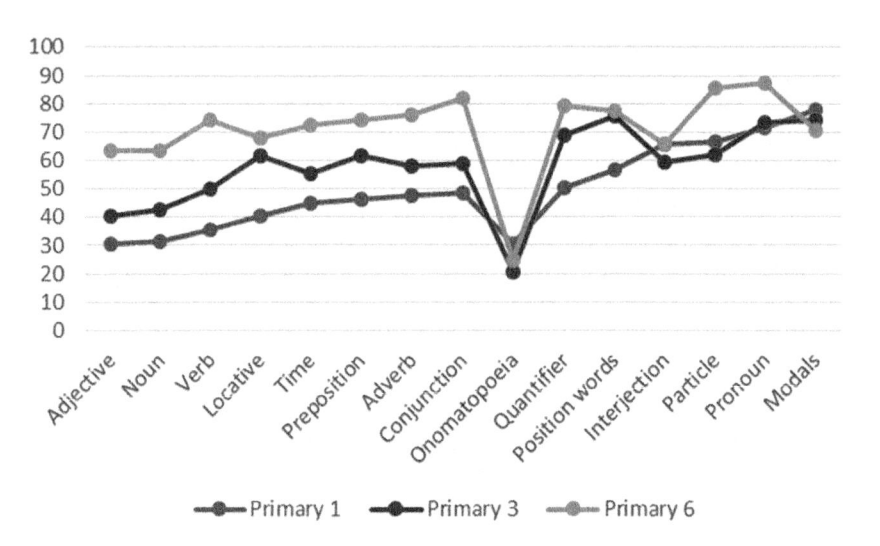

Fig. 1 Profiles of parts of speech by grades

Table 3 Sentence-pattern coverage across academic grade

	N	Primary 1%	Primary 3%	Primary 6%
Simple sentence	53,801	33.0	30.8	36.2
Complex sentences	11,890	20.0	30.6	49.4
Pivotal construction	2090	22.4	32.8	44.8
Serial-verb construction	54	13.0	27.8	59.3
ba-construction	586	9.4	30.7	59.9
bei-construction	311	9.0	26.7	64.3

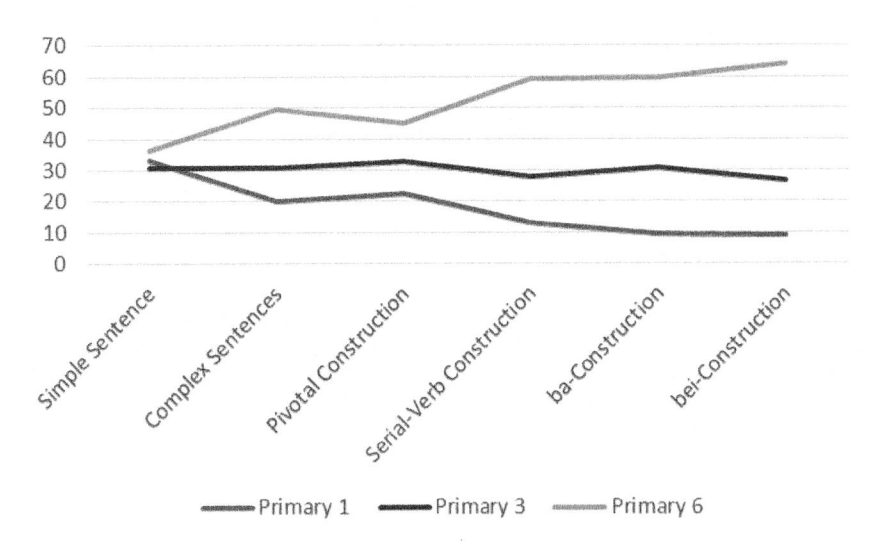

Fig. 2 Profiles of sentence structures by grades

Primary 3 children produced more sentences of these four constructions, ranging from 26 to 32% of their total number of sentences produced, and Primary 6 students producing the most sentence of these four constructions, ranging from 44 to 64% of t their total number of sentences produced.

Summing up these trends, children of all three grades have mastered the simple sentence patterns, but not all of the three grades mastered the complex sentence and the four special sentence constructions; only elder children were found to have mastered them. This is in line with the assumption of language development overage; i.e. the language use of young age learners tends to be simpler, while older ones tend to produce more complex sentences as their thoughts become more complex overage.

Comparison by Home Language Backgrounds After differentiating children via the computation of the CEI, it was found that the number of children identified as coming from predominantly Mandarin-speaking homes (PMSH) is rare, numbering only nine children in the entire sample. As the language database formed by these nine children is extremely small, their computed word-type coverage for the POS and the sentence patterns are rather low. This makes it hard to compare this group with the other three groups. This being the case, this article only compares the word-type coverage and sentence pattern results from children of the predominantly English-speaking homes (PESH), more English-speaking homes (MESH), and more Mandarin-speaking homes (MMSH) in the following analysis to give a preliminary understanding of the vocabulary and sentence pattern differences among children of different home language backgrounds.

Table 4 presents the word-type coverage in the 15 POS among children from different home language backgrounds. Generally, word-type coverage of seven POS (i.e. nouns, adjectives, verbs, quantifiers, adverbs, conjunctions, prepositions) shows a progressive trend across the three home language groups; children from predominant English-speaking homes covered fewer word types in the seven POS, whereas children from more Mandarin-speaking homes covered more word types in these seven POS. It is observed that the word-type coverage of six other POS did not show the progressive trend across home language groups; for locatives, time, position, particle, interjections, and modals, PESH children covered the least of these six POS whereas MESH children covered the most of these POS, and the MMSH children covered slightly fewer word types for these six POS. Furthermore, it was observed that two POS (i.e. onomatopoeia and pronoun) are rarely covered by PESH children, but are equally covered by MESH and MMSH children. These can be seen clearly in Fig. 3.

Table 4 Word-type coverage on part of speech among students of different home language background

No. of children	Word type	PESH	MESH	MMSH	PMSH
		−1 to −0.51	−0.5 to 0	0–0.5	0.51–1
		N = 98%	N = 256%	N = 173%	N = 9%
Noun	3384	22.9	49.0	50.5	12.9
Adjective	726	28.9	46.1	54.6	15.0
Locative	47	44.9	72.3	48.9	19.2
Verb	2062	30.7	57.0	61.5	18.1
Quantifier	135	37.0	69.6	70.4	25.9
Adverb	268	37.7	61.6	69.0	27.1
Time	109	39.5	66.1	58.7	22.0
Conjunction	66	43.9	71.2	72.7	25.8
Preposition	39	46	66.7	74.4	43.6
Onomatopoeia	49	10.2	28.8	28.6	2.0
Positions	62	50.0	67.7	66.1	35.5
Particle	21	57.1	76.2	71.4	42.9
Interjection	32	62	68.8	62.5	25.0
Pronoun	94	66.0	80.9	80.9	50.0
Modal	27	66.7	81.5	70.4	48.2

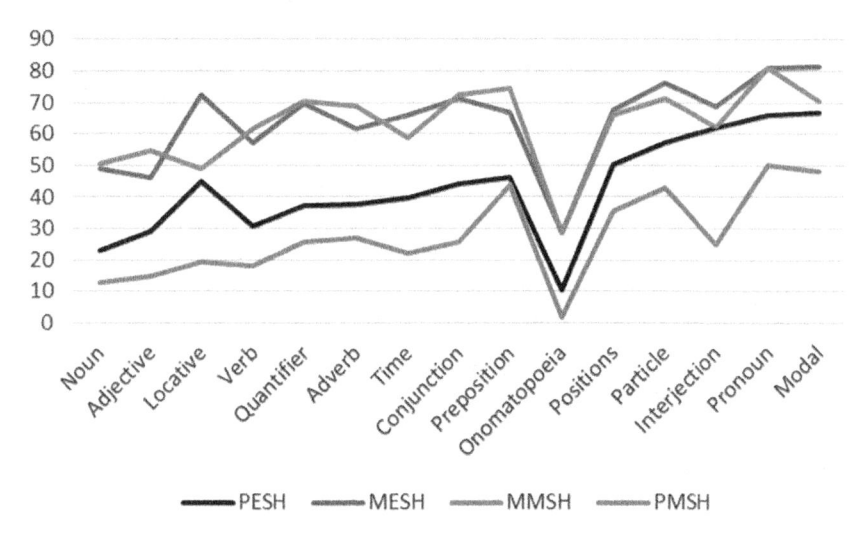

Fig. 3 Profiles of parts of speech by home language backgrounds

From the observations above, it is obvious that the word-type coverage of each POS is low among PESH children. But the children who are from bilingual families (MESH and MMSH) displayed a complex situation. Although both MESH and MMSH children generally displayed a higher coverage of word types in most POS, they did not show a specific pattern or trend. MESH children have a higher coverage for some POS but the word-type coverage of MESH and MMSH is almost the same.

Similar to the results on grade differences, for some of the POS in Table 4, children from PESH and MESH did not surpass half of the word types (i.e. nouns, adjectives, and locatives). Among these POS, PESH and MESH children only cover between 10 and 49% of the word types. Table 5 also shows that PESH children covered least of most POS, which includes verb, quantifier, adverb, time, conjunction, and preposition. The word-type coverage for these POS ranges between 30 and 46%. Also similar to the findings across grades, it is noted that onomatopoeia is rarely covered by children of all three home language groups, as their coverage of onomatopoeia word types is less than 30%.

With regard to sentence patterns, the proportion of simple sentences and complex sentences among the three home language groups did not display a progressive trend. That is, PESH children produced the least simple and complex sentences (17.3 and 12.7%, respectively). MESH children produced the most simple and complex sentences (47.4 and 46.9%, respectively). And, the MMSH children produced slightly less simple and complex sentences as compared to the MESH children (33.3 and 38.2%, respectively).

As for the four special sentence constructions, three of the constructions did not display a progressive trend as well (i.e. pivotal construction, serial-verb construction, and *ba*-construction). PESH children produced the least pivotal construction,

Table 5 Sentence-pattern coverage across home language background

	Total	PESH	MESH	MMSH	PMSH
		−1 to −0.51	−0.5 to 0	0–0.5	0.51–1
		N = 98%	N = 256%	N = 173%	N = 9%
Simple sentence	53,801	17.3	47.4	33.3	2.0
Complex sentences	11,890	12.7	46.9	38.2	2.2
Pivotal construction	2090	11.3	47.4	39.3	2.0
Serial-verb construction	54	11.1	50.0	35.2	3.7
ba-construction	586	9.4	48.5	38.4	3.8
bei-construction	311	9.0	36.0	52.1	2.9

serial-verb construction, and *ba*-construction with 11.4, 11.1, and 9.4%, respectively. MESH children produced the most pivotal construction, serial-verb construction, and *ba*-construction with 47.4, 46.9, and 47.4%, respectively. And MMSH children produced slightly lesser pivotal construction, serial-verb construction, and *ba*-construction as compared to the MESH children (33.3, 38.2, and 39.3%, respectively). Interestingly, the *bei*-construction shows a progressive trend across the three home language groups, where PESH children produced the least of such construction (9.0%), the MESH children produced more of such construction (36.0%), and the MMSH children produced the most of such construction (52.1%). The trends are clearly depicted in Fig. 4.

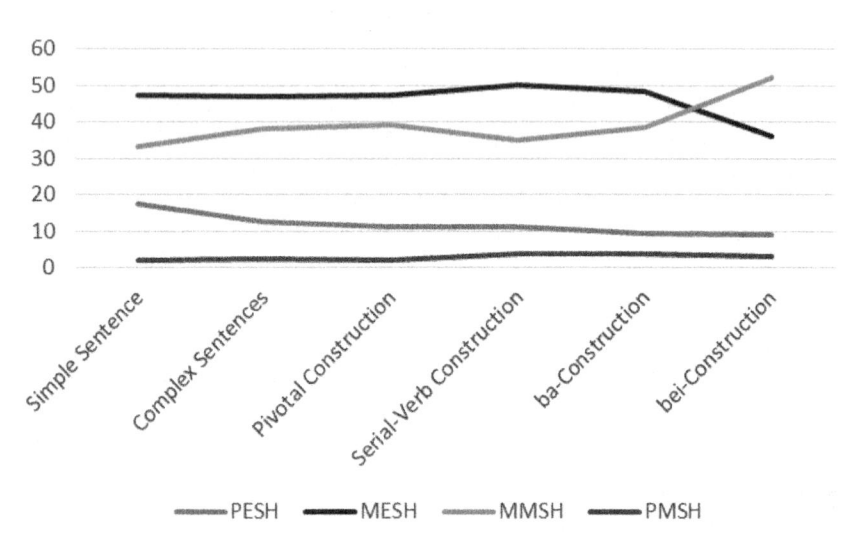

Fig. 4 Profiles of sentence structures by home language background

Conclusion

In summary, in terms of vocabulary, the word-type coverage of the parts of speech (POS) increases over the grades of the students and this is consistent with the principles of language development overage. However, it is noted that, while reaching Primary 6, the children only cover between 60 and 70% of word types in each POS. The curriculum developers may need to review if the uncovered word type is necessary for CL learning and then incorporate these word types into upcoming syllabuses.

With regard to home language backgrounds, the word-type coverage of children from the English-speaking homes is relatively low. Although this is not unexpected in view of their language experience, CL teachers will need to pay more attention to students from the English-speaking homes and help them expand their vocabulary.

As for the sentence patterns, the students of different grades also present a progressive trend whereby higher grade children covered more sentence patterns than lower academic grade children. This progressive trend was observed in children with different home language backgrounds as well where children from Mandarin-speaking homes covers more sentence patterns as compared to their English-speaking counterparts. Coverage of the *ba*-construction and the *bei*-construction by English-speaking children is similar to the coverage of the two constructions found in primary one child. This suggests that CL teachers need to find ways to help English-speaking children master the *ba*- and *bei*-construction.

As the results in this study are based on the computation of the Chinese Exposure Index, the number of children in each home language group is quite different, with the PESH group having the greatest number of children, followed by MMSH, PESH, and PMSH. This may have resulted in the non-progressive trend observed on some of the parts of speech and sentence patterns when viewed across home language groups. A more meaningful analysis could be conducted by reviewing the CEI computation and sampling an equal number of children from each home language group after the confirmed CEI, after which comparison can then be made. This shall ensure a more comparable set of data and result in more implicative findings.

References

Cheah, C. M. (2003). *Jiaoxue yu ceshi [Teaching and testing]*. Singapore: Singapore Chinese Teachers' Union.
CLCPRC (Chinese Language Curriculum and Pedagogy Review Committee). (2004). *Report of the Chinese language curriculum and Pedagogy Review Committee*. Singapore: Chinese Language Curriculum and Pedagogy Review Committee.
CLRC (Chinese Language Review Committee). (1999). *Report of Chinese language teaching & learning in Singapore*. Singapore: Ministry of Education.
Department of Statistics. (2001). *Census of population 2000, statistics release 2—education, language and religion*. Singapore.

Dixon, L. Q. (2005). Bilingual education policy in Singapore: An analysis of its sociohistorical roots and current academic outcome. *International Journal of Bilingual Education and Bilingualism, 8*(2), 25–47.
Goh, H. H. (2017). *Mandarin competence of Chinese-English bilingual preschoolers: A corpus-based analysis of Singaporean children's speech*. Singapore: Springer.
Goh, H. H., Lin, J., & Zhou, H. (2016). Xinjiapo jiaoyu zhuanyong yuliaoku de jianshe yu yunyoong [Construction and application of education-specific corpora in Singapore]. *Huawen Jiaoyu yu Yanjiu (TCSOL Studies), 63*(3), 36–45.
Goh, Y. H. (2004). *Huayuwen zai Xinjiapo de xianzhuang yu qianjing* [The current practice and prospect of Chinese language education in Singapore]. Singapore: Chuangyiquan Chubanshe [Candid Creation Publishing].
Guo, X. (2004). Haiwai huaren shehui hanyu (huayu) jiaoxue de ruogan wenti: Yi Xinjiapo weili [Some questions concerning the teaching of Chinese in overseas Chinese communities: With the status in Singapore as an example]. *Shijie Hanyu Jiaoxue [Teaching Chinese Language in the World], 72*(3), 79–88.
Gupta, A. F. (1997). When mother-tongue education is not preferred. *Journal of Multilingual and Multicultural Development1 8*(6): 496–506.
Li, Z. (2005). Xinjiaposhi Huayu [Singaporean Chinese language]. *Lianhe Zaobao*, June 10.
MTLRC (Mother Tongue Language Review Committee). (2010). *Nurturing active learners and proficient users*. Singapore: Ministry of Education.
Wu, Y. C. (2010). *Hanyu guoji chuanbo: Xinjiapo shijiao [Chinese international communication: Singapore perspective]*. Beijing: The commercial Press.
Wu, Y. H. (2008). *Wushi de juece: Xinjiapo zhengfu huayuwen zhengce yanjiu [Pragmatic decision-making: A study on the Chinese language policy of Singapore government]*. Beijing: Dangdai shijie chubanshe (Contemporary World Press).
Zhao, S., & Liu, Y. (2010). Chinese education in Singapore: Constraints of bilingual policy from the perspectives of status and prestige planning. *Language Problems & Language Planning, 34* (3), 236–258.

Hock Huan Goh (吴福焕) He received Ph.D. from NTU, Singapore. He is the Chair of Research and Ethics Committee and Research Scientist at the Singapore Centre for Chinese Language. His academic interests include Chinese language teaching in multi/bilingual context, child Mandarin competence, curriculum evaluation, and corpus-based application development. He has compiled and co-compiled a few frequency dictionaries of Singapore Chinese, published more than 10 co-authored articles, and did over 20 paper presentations. He has recently published a book on Mandarin competence of Singaporean Chinese preschoolers.

Chunsheng Zhao (赵春生) He completed his MA in Applied Linguistics (NTU, Singapore). He is currently a Research Associate at the Singapore Centre for Chinese Language. His academic interests include teaching of Chinese language as a second language, corpus-based language teaching, and Chinese etymology. He has co-compiled three frequency dictionaries of Singapore Chinese words and syntaxes and published journal articles.

Siew Hoon Kwek (郭秀芬) She completed his MEd (University of Queensland). She is a Master Teacher for Chinese language (Academy of Singapore Teachers/Singapore Centre for Chinese Language). She conducted training courses on Chinese language, pedagogy, and assessment. Her research interest is in Chinese language curriculum design, pedagogy, and assessment.

Part II
Teaching of Spoken and Written Chinese

Improving the Teaching of Chinese Speaking of Young Students from English-Speaking Families: Teacher's Professional Development

Jing Yan, Hock Huan Goh and Hong Xia Zhou

Abstract This article highlights the recent shift in the teaching of Chinese Language in Singapore from its traditional emphasis on oral communication. It looks into the Chinese Language teachers' beliefs, teaching strategies, and difficulties encountered in implementing the change. The research team design lessons plans which were implemented by purposively selected teachers in five schools. Teachers were observed and interviewed, and multiple case studies were reported.

In Singapore, there has been a shift in home language from Chinese to English for the last three decades (Singapore Department of Statistics 2000). According to the Report of Chinese Language Review Committee (2004), 50% of Primary 1 Chinese students and 59% Primary 2 Chinese students were found to come from English-speaking families. They are deemed to be less competence in Chinese language, similar to second-language (L2) speakers. This situation had exaggerated over the years and has led to great challenge in Chinese language teaching and learning since home language plays an important role in children's language acquisition and development. This change gives rise to the revision of the Chinese curriculum which shifts its emphasis to oral communication for early primary schooling.

The emphasis on oral communication is evident in the curriculum revisions. Firstly, the 2004 Chinese Language Review Committee (2004) stated that teaching speaking should be promoted, and the Committee suggested a series of teaching strategies for speaking, such as introducing a word list for oral communication, using songs and verses. Secondly, the 2010 report (Mother Tongue Language

---

J. Yan (✉) · H. H. Goh · H. X. Zhou
Singapore Centre for Chinese Language,
Nanyang Technological University, Singapore, Singapore
e-mail: jing.yan@sccl.sg

H. H. Goh
e-mail: Hockhuan.goh@sccl.sg

Review Committee 2010) further stresses the importance of fostering students' interactive communication skills.

Following the trend of the current Chinese curriculum, the research team first designed suitable teaching strategies within the framework of Communicative Language Teaching (CLT) for developing Chinese oral competence of English-speaking primary students. After that, the research team provided trainings to teachers, and then the teachers implemented these teaching strategies into practice. With a focus on teachers' professional development, this study explored the changes in teachers' perceptions and practices before and after the intervention.

More specifically, this study addresses the following research questions:

(1) What are the Chinese Language teachers' beliefs and perceptions of teaching oral Chinese to young students?
(2) What are the oral Chinese teaching strategies used by the teachers?
(3) What are the changes in the teachers' perceptions and practices after they have learned the newly designed strategies?
(4) What are the difficulties and challenges for implementing CLT in young students?

In this study, we first introduced the theoretical basis of CLT and relevant empirical studies and then the specific features of CLT. After that, certain components of CLT that serve as the framework for designing teaching strategies are clarified.

Communicative Language Teaching

Based on Canale and Swain (1980), communicative competence refers to, firstly, L2 speakers, in order to communicate effectively, have to grasp a certain amount of vocabulary and internalize the grammatical structures of that language for communicative purposes. Secondly, L2 speakers have to show an awareness of communication strategies to overcome difficulties they may encounter in a conversation. Thirdly, L2 speakers need to understand sociocultural knowledge of the society or communities in which the target language is used. CLT has communicative competence as the ultimate goal of language teaching, which differentiates it from some traditional teaching approaches, such as translation and audio-lingual method—two teaching approaches based on the concept of language being a system consisting of grammatical rules and vocabulary.

Communicative language teaching has been supported by theories of second-language acquisition such as comprehensible input hypothesis (Krashen 1977, 1985) and interaction hypothesis (Long 1985). According to Krashen (1977, 1985), second-language learners would acquire a second language if they were exposed to sufficient comprehensible input. Long's (1985, 1998) interaction hypothesis confirms the role of comprehensible input and, moreover, puts forward the role of interaction in producing comprehensible input. He stated that the input can be, through interaction, modified to the learner's current language proficiency level. Moreover, the interactional features such as comprehension checks, clarification requests, and negotiation of meaning have also been demonstrated positively to be contributing to second-language acquisition (Doughty and Pica 1986). The benefits of learner–learner interactions were emphasized and demonstrated by several studies; these benefits include reducing learning anxiety; increasing learners' talk amount, and opportunities to produce various speech acts (Pica and Doughty 1985; Porter 1986). Based on the above theories, CLT emphasize the following two principles:

- Information gap is a key factor in generating authentic communications that will facilitate language acquisition.
- Language is learnt through interaction and negotiation of meaning.

In general, CLT is an approach for designing and organizing language activities which is not specific to any language. Therefore, CLT has not only become prevalent in English language teaching in East Asia since the 1980s based on Ho et al. (2002) survey, but also been widely applied in teaching Chinese as a second/foreign language. For instance, some Chinese textbooks designed for foreign language learners have embedded principles of CLT (Yang 2003). According to Ding's survey (2006), teachers had perceived CLT as an effective approach in teaching Chinese as a second language. Gao's (2015) and Gu's (2006) studies found that task-based language teaching as a branch of CLT (Littlewood 2004), can be implemented in oral classes of teaching Chinese as a foreign language in enhancing students' Chinese learning motivation and communicative competence.

In Singapore context, CLT has also been applied in Chinese language teaching. For example, Liu and Sim (2013) conducted a research project on developing resources for task-based language teaching with iMTL portal in students who study Chinese language "B" syllabus. They found that after the intervention, students' oral competence improved. Therefore, this study made efforts in applying the framework of CLT in teaching Chinese speaking to primary students.

Teaching Strategies

A framework for designing teaching strategies has been proposed for following the above principles. The framework includes three components: vocabulary teaching strategies, teacher–learner interaction, and learner–learner interaction.

Vocabulary Teaching Strategies Games are designed for vocabulary learning. Vocabulary is students' language resources for interaction. However, traditionally teachers tend to use drills when teaching vocabulary, which is neither sufficient for vocabulary learning nor oral interactive competence. In the process of playing games, students need to listen carefully and respond to the teacher's or peers' oral language as quickly as possible to keep games going. Through participating in games, students are forced to strengthen the link between pronunciations and meanings in the short-term memory, which creates conditions for knowledge to transfer from short-term memory to long-term memory. In addition, playing games enhances young students' learning motivation. There are three principles for designing the games. First, the games are aimed for practising and exercising vocabulary only, without requirements of using other language skills, such as reading and writing. Second, the games are meaningful, which means students use vocabulary to achieve some goals rather than simply practising. Third, the games are interactive. Students are required to work in a group to play the games.

Teacher–Learner Interaction Questioning and responding strategies are designed for creating authentic communications. During authentic interaction, learners can comprehend teachers' discourse, abstract grammatical rules from context, and use language for communicative purposes. The principles for creating authentic teacher–learner interaction include providing unpredictable information, using genuine requests, and reacting to messages (Spada and Fröhlich 1995; Spada 2007). First, a teacher should provide unpredictable information, which means the information is new to students. Second, teachers' strategies of asking questioning and providing feedback have to be taken into consideration. There are two kinds of questions, namely pseudo request and genuine request. The difference between these lies in information exchange. Pseudo-requests refer to questions the answers of which are already known to both teachers and students. Therefore, asking a pseudo question is to provide an opportunity for practicing certain linguistic forms rather than exchanging information. Genuine requests refer to the questions which require answers that are unknown to the teacher. The purpose of asking this kind of questions is to gain information from the students. For CLT, teachers are encouraged to increase the number of genuine requests to make meaningful interaction. related to questions are the forms of feedback. Teachers' feedback can be responses to linguistic forms or to messages of students' responses, or both (Spada 2007). Response to message will be more likely to involve students in a conversation than to linguistic forms. Besides, response to message is coherent with the nature of interaction. For CLT, response to message is encouraged.

Learner–Learner Interaction Learner–learner interaction activities are designed for providing students chances to negotiate for meaning. During interaction, students can resort to their linguistic knowledge and use language for communicative purposes. During this process, they will notice the gap between what they can express and what they intend to express, which helps them internalize grammatical rules. There are two principles for designing the learner–learner interaction activities. First, the content of the activities is of students' interest and relevant to their life in order to get students focusing on completing a task. Second, for the purpose of getting students to interact in Chinese as young students are likely to code switch to their first language (English), the difficulty level in terms of linguistic knowledge and cognitive demanding is carefully controlled. In addition, formats of activities are structured by assigning roles of individual student.

The three components are designed to reflect the essential principles of CLT. The research team designed eight oral lesson plans within this framework with details of teaching steps, structures of activities, and worksheets. All the lesson plans were given to the participating teachers before the intervention. As the extent to which a class is communicative is mainly reflected in teacher–learner interaction and learner–learner interaction, this study, therefore, focused on the teachers' implementations of these two components.

Method

Research Approach

With the purpose of developing a set of Chinese speaking teaching strategies that are suitable for young students as well as to enhance teachers' professional development, design research is chosen as the research approach for this study. The main goal of design research is to design for implementation, featured in exploring the gap between designers and enactors so as to provide guidance on implementation (Collins et al. 2004). Interviews and class observations are frequent data collection instruments for this research methodology.

Procedure

The research team first conducted an environmental scan by making classroom observations of the teachers' regular teaching practice. Upon the design of lesson plans, the team trialled the designed lessons with two schools in a pilot study, after which the lesson plans were fine-tuned and delivered to teachers in the first training session. The research team provided all the eight lesson plans to the teachers. However, the teachers were required to make power-point slides based on the lesson plans on their own. This requirement aims to help the teachers internalize the lesson plans.

After this training, the research team commenced its main study whereby teachers of the five participating schools embarked on the use of the revised lesson plans. A final refinement of the lesson plans was made, and a second training was provided to teachers of the five schools.

Main study lasted for five months. Two research assistants were assigned to observe each class. Field notes were made during the observations. All classes were audio- and video-recorded except the sixth class of one school because it was video-recorded by the Ministry of Education for other purposes.

Table 1 Participating schools and the number of students

Schools	Modular classification	No. of students
School 1	Core	35
School 2	Core	27
School 3	Bridging	9
School 4	Bridging	12
School 5	Core	28

Participants

Five schools were purposively selected from the traditional English-background schools through discussions with Chinese master teachers. One teacher from each school who taught Primary 2 was chosen as the experimental teacher. Primary 2 students were our target student participants. Considering the key concern of design research being the collaborations between designers and enactors, experimental teachers were chosen based on their willingness in participating in the study. As such, their classes became the experimental classes. Thus, a total of five experimental teachers and classes were chosen for the study. By interviewing the teachers, some information of the five classes are shown in Table 1. The students were from English-speaking families, weak in Chinese due to Primary 1 Chinese Language results, with some of them coming from the Philippines, Thailand, Indonesia, and Europe. There are three core classes and two bridging classes. The primary Chinese curriculum uses the modular approach. Each unit of the Primary 2 textbook consists of three modules, i.e., bridging module, core module, and enrichment module. All students have to study the core module, whereas students of the bridging class have to study both the bridging and core modules. The bridging module was designed to equip low proficient students with vocabulary and sentence structures used in the core module.

Data Collection

Pre- and Post-Interview The team conducted pre- and post-intervention interviews with teachers to understand their perceptions of oral competence, use of teaching strategies, concerns and problems in teaching oral Chinese, and changes in perceptions and practice after the intervention. A set of predetermined questions were drawn up to elicit the information, such as "*What is your definition of oral competence?*" and "*What are your frequent teaching strategies?*" Each pre-intervention interviews lasted for half an hour and the post-intervention interview one hour.

Classroom Observation To understand how teachers apply the designed teaching strategies and to assist them in fine-tuning their oral Chinese lessons, the team made on-site observations. The observations were recorded in the field notes based on the lesson plans designed by the team. The purpose is to uncover to what extent the teachers implemented the lesson plans and what adaptations they made for the lessons. Thus, if the teacher follows the lesson plan, the observer confirmed it in the field notes. If the teacher reduced or added questions or activities, the observer detailed the adaptations made by the teachers. Two researchers observed the class for every lesson so that the field notes taken reflected consented observations.

Tracked Recording of One Teacher's Output To understand the extent of implementation and changes in the strategies, the team recorded one teacher's classroom output as a case study. The record was analyzed using Spada's and Fröhlich (1995) coding scheme consisting features of teacher–learner interaction within the framework of communicative approach. Comparison of their speech output provided rich quantitative evidence on the suitability of our designed teaching strategies.

Data Analysis

This part first presents the interview data. Teachers' beliefs and perceptions are compared before and after the research. Second, teachers' self-reported teaching strategies were compared with their responses to the designed teaching strategies. In addition, a case study of one of the experimental schools is presented with the purpose of providing insightful details on the implementation of CLT. (Note: the abbreviation, T1, T2, T3, T4, and T5 refer to the five experimental teachers, respectively.)

Teachers' Belief and Perceptions of Speaking Ability

Before the study, four out of the five teachers were aware of the communicative aspect of speaking. However, the grammatical aspect was highly regarded as important component of speaking skills. The necessary connection between what should been taught in class and applied in daily life seems unrealized by most teachers. The Excerpt 1 shows teachers' responses.

T1, T2, T4, and T5 believed that speaking ability involved the ability of listening comprehension and responding to what interlocutors have said. T3 however believed that speaking ability merely comprises of tone, pronunciation, and grammar, whereby the communicative aspect was unimportant. T4 emphasized that students should be able to produce complete sentences. T1 had an awareness of that there was a gap between classroom teaching and daily life communication. From

Excerpt 1 Teachers' perceptions in of speaking ability before the research

Speaker	Utterances
T1:	… two aspects, one is to answer teachers' questions, and the other one is for application in real life
T2:	I think in daily life, they should be able to … listen and speak, speaking means that they understand what I am talking, even they cannot understand the whole sentence, but he can grasp some words to answer
T3:	Pronunciation, intonation, grammar
T4:	Can speak complete sentences, can understand other people's talking, can answer
T5:	They can use some sentence structures to communicate with me, or communicate with other people

her point of view, there were different requirements of speaking in class and communication in daily lives.

After the research, there are changes in teachers' understanding of what is speaking ability. Take T3 for example, before the research, he emphasized on the grammatical aspect of speaking. The communicative aspect was completely neglected. After the research, he realized he should play the role of facilitator, motivated his students to speak and then scaffold the students to communicate better. T1 also realized that there were no absolute right or wrong answers when communication concerned since the ultimate purpose is to convey the message. Besides, T1 became to be aware of the connection between teaching in class and application in life. This can be seen from the Excerpt 2.

Excerpt 2 Teachers' perceptions of speaking ability after the research

Speaker	Utterances
T1:	Speaking is close to content of life. Teaching speaking can teach the content of life, can be used outside class. there is no right or wrong answers in speaking, ask open questions
T2:	… Is the students' ability to communicate
T3:	We shouldn't teach speaking on purpose, it is part of students [ability]. We need to elicit their speaking motivation, then we use theories to summarise sentence structures, let them speak the right sentences. The speaking ability is there, we play the roles of facilitator
T4:	Can speak, can listen. speaking is important, because speaking is for communication

Reported Teaching Strategies

Before the research, oral classes were oriented by certain syntactic structures and vocabulary set in the textbooks. The objectives of oral lessons were to learn the specific syntactic structures and vocabulary. And hence, the teaching of oral skills was only conducted at the syntactic level rather than at the discourse level. The teachers did not take into consideration how students could apply those syntactic structure and vocabulary in their daily communication. In other words, the communicative functions of the syntactic structure and vocabulary were not explicitly taught. This can be concluded from Excerpt 3.

Teachers reported that repetition and making sentences were frequently used teaching approaches. T3 reported that he mostly used repetition in oral lessons, and he would require his students to make sentences. He mentioned that his approach was oriented by the oral exam format. T1, however, was aware of the limitations in making sentences during oral lessons, but she has no other choices.

However, these two teaching strategies are not sufficient for training communicative language teaching as verbal communication is not just simply repetition or the arrangement of words into grammatical utterances but the orchestra of linguistic items with reference to context and discourse.

Teachers also reported that learner–learner interaction was seldom employed in oral lessons. There were many concerns about deploying learner–learner interaction activities. Firstly, teachers doubted that all students were able to engage in such activities. Secondly, students were likely to use English during such interaction. Thirdly, teachers were not confident in peer evaluation with regards to the young age of their students, and lastly, they are worried that students would be negatively influenced by their peers' mistakes. The Excerpt 4 illustrates these concerns of teachers.

Based on the interviews, we can see that though the participating teachers were aware of communicative aspect of speaking ability, the grammatical aspect was highly regarded. The oral lessons were oriented by syntactic structures and vocabulary in the textbooks. Repetition and sentence-making were reported as most frequently used teaching strategies. Learner–learner interaction was seldom used in oral lessons.

Excerpt 3 Teachers' reported speaking teaching strategies (1)

Speaker	Utterance
T4:	Usually learn to recognize some words, learn how to write characters, and sentence structures, sentence structures are in the textbook, for example "changchang", "… zhi hou"
T3:	Repeatedly do something
T1:	Sometimes some words, have to ask them to make sentences, or some words may be used in daily life, I will let them [use the words] to make a sentence

Excerpt 4 Teachers' perceptions of learner–learner interaction activities

Speaker	Utterance
T1:	I think it is better for me to listen [and evaluate], because they are too young [to do it] at the age of 7, 8. So, I don't think peers can evaluate what is wrong. That is why I don't consider of arranging them to talk in groups or evaluate. Usually I listen [and evaluate]
T2:	Actually I don't like group work unless there is any appropriate one. Because I often find that only the group leader or those who are more proficient do the work while the others just remain silent in the group

After the research, there were changes in the ways teachers provided feedbacks. The Excerpts 5 and 6 show the evidence that the teacher began to have the awareness of expanding students' oral production so as to sustain the topic in interaction. T2 noted that interaction was indeed mutual as interaction does not only mean teachers providing more opportunities for students to speak up, but students' responses also motivated teachers' responses and feedbacks. In addition, she tries to be a good listener, which is a premise for authentic communication.

From Excerpt 6, T3 realized that the grammar of speaking was different from the grammar of writing. Complete sentences are not often obligatory in speaking as in writing. T3 believed that she should not deny her students' anxiety to speak though they used improper expression or even used English sometimes. She made use of the opportunity to restate the students' expression in Chinese. She also came to understand that using standard sentence structure was not often the case in verbal communication, and the use of standard sentence structure was indeed an unnatural communication style.

Though there are many concerns for conducting learner–learner interaction, teachers reported that students performed better than they have expected. If the structure of the activities, students' roles, and task difficulty are carefully designed, beginner learners can successfully complete interaction task (Excerpt 7).

Excerpt 5 Teachers' strategies of providing feedback (1)

Speaker	Utterance
T2:	Students are very active, making me feel greatly encouraged. Interaction is more than giving students chances to talk. Students' responses are also encouraging to the teacher

Excerpt 6 Teachers' strategies of providing feedback (2)

Speaker	Utterance
T3:	In authentic communication, we don't talk with standard sentences each time. For example, when asked "Have you eaten?", deliberately, I should reply "yes, I have eaten." [But] this sounds unnatural in communication

Improving the Teaching of Chinese Speaking of Young Students ...

Excerpt 7 Teachers' responses to learner–learner interaction activities after the research

Speaker	Utterance
T2:	Students performed much better than I have expected in "Fan" activity, I thought they were not able to do it at the beginning. Make some changes on details and structure of activity, so that the students wouldn't become lazy, let them feel fresh

The use of CLT oral lessons has made substantial changes in the participating classes, the following changes were observed in general. During the research, all the experimental teachers have implemented new teaching strategies in their classes, though to different extents. The focus of their oral lessons has shifted from producing grammatically correct sentences to interactive communication. We observed that the teachers generally encouraged students to expand on topics of discussion and most teachers minimized their habit to immediately correct students' grammatical mistakes. In terms of vocabulary teaching, the games introduced by the research team were used in the participating classes and were well received by both teachers and students. The teachers have accepted to conduct more learner–learner interaction activities in their speaking lessons. By scaffolding what students need in the interaction tasks, controlling the tasks' difficulty, and employing highly structured activities, the learner–learner interaction was conducted successfully beyond the teachers' expectations.

A Case Study

To illustrate practice of CLT implementation, we chose T3 for a case study. First, we present the coding of four lessons in "Providing unpredictable information," "genuine request," and "reaction to message." The coding results indicate the extent to which the lessons are communicative. The first lesson (L1) is pre-class observation, while the other three lessons (L2, L3, L4) took place in the main study. The topics of these four lessons are "Chinese New Year", "I like … /don't like …", "Football" and "Fast Food Restaurant". Second, we present some excerpts of class talk to show T3's strategies of conducting interaction and providing feedback.

Providing Unpredictable Information

Figure 1 shows the amounts of providing unpredictable information of the four lessons, which are 65, 90.3, 47.2, and 55.4%, respectively. For a communicative class, the information should be unpredictable for both teachers and students so that authentic communication can occur.

T3 provided the highest amount of unpredictable information in the first intervention lesson. Then, it decreased in the second intervention lesson and raised up in

Provding unpredictable information

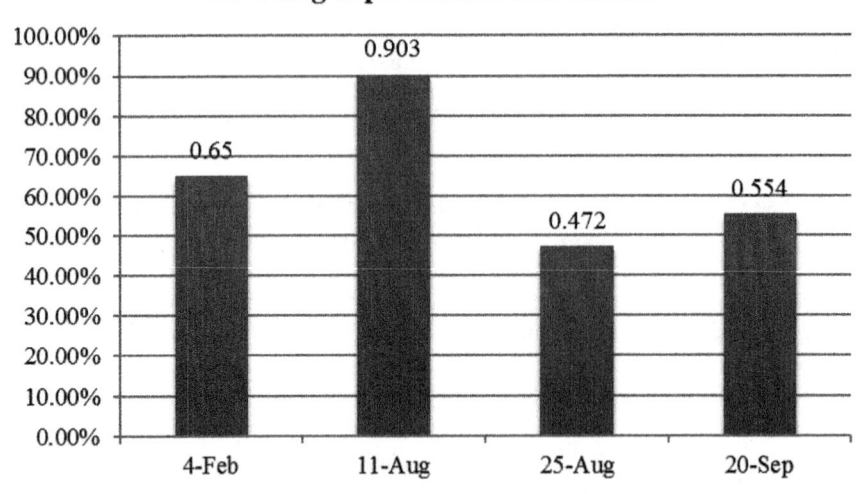

Fig. 1 Providing unpredictable information

the third one. Based on fieldnotes, the lowest amount of unpredictable information in Lesson 3 may be attributed to the following reasons: First, the topic of the third lesson is "Football Match", which the students are very familiar with. This led to less unexpected information communicated between the teacher and students. Second, the teacher focused teaching new vocabulary related to the topic, which constitutes to greater shared/predictable information during the classroom interaction. Another reason is that the teacher may return to his old habit, paying attention to students' use of certain syntactic pattern and ignored the exchange of unpredictable information.

The data of this category show that the effects of teachers' training are immediate and obvious on teacher's first lesson but did not sustain. However, the percentage increased afterward, indicating that teachers may take some time to sustainably apply the principles.

Genuine Request

Genuine requests also make authentic communication occur. Figure 2 indicates that the percentage of genuine request increases from Lesson 1 (26%) to Lesson 4 (53.4%) except Lesson 3. To some extent, T3 has improved on his questioning strategies. Again, based on fieldnotes, T3 focused on introducing a large amount of vocabulary related to the topic. He asked questions that required students to produce the new words repeatedly and hence led to the high amount of pseudo-requests which aimed at practising certain vocabulary.

Genuine request

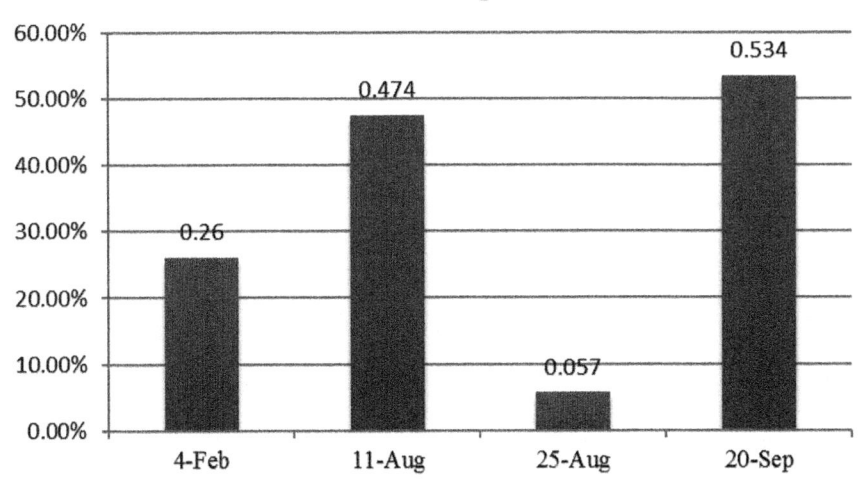

Fig. 2 Genuine request

Reaction to Message

Teacher's feedback is categorized into "reaction to form," "reaction to message," or reaction to both. For communicative class, reaction to message is encouraged. Figure 3 shows that the percentage of teacher's reaction to message increases first, then decreases, and increases again.

In general, the percentage of "Reaction to Message" in the three intervention lessons outperformed the lesson before the intervention, which indicates T3's improvement on providing feedback. The lowest percentage is in Lesson 3. As explained earlier, Lesson 3 was focused on teaching vocabulary, and the teacher's feedback was on whether the students have orally produced the new words correctly.

In addition to the above coding results, we selected some excerpts for demonstrating T3's strategies of asking questions and providing feedback. In the Excerpt 8, the teacher gave evaluative feedback to the student's answer, after which he guided the students to the correct answer by providing more information through expanding. In his last utterance, he gave a hint for the correct answer of the targeted word. This expansion facilitated learners' comprehending of the new word.

In this Excerpt 9, the teacher tolerated students' branching off and took advantage of this opportunity to keep the conversation going. By asking students to provide information about the consequences of playing soccer at home, the teacher created further opportunity for students to communicate in the target language. As a result, students became motivated in exchanging their own life experience with their teacher. Furthermore, the interaction was enhanced and students' language output increased in the process.

Reaction to message

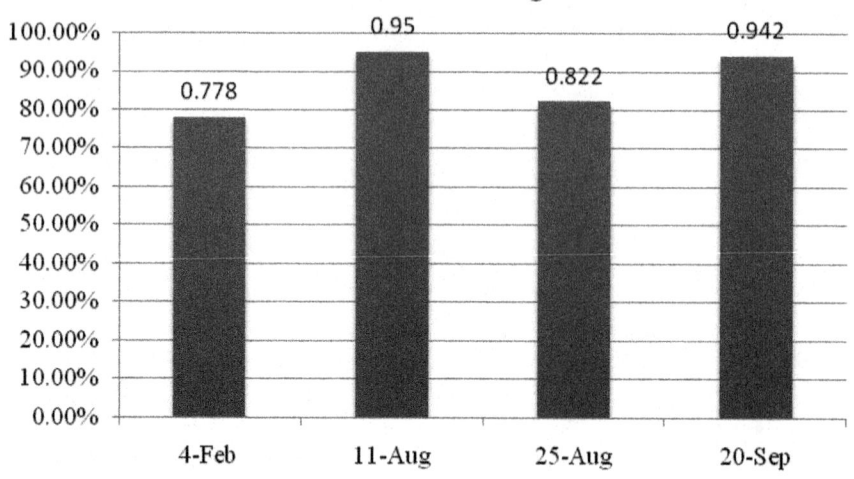

Fig. 3 Reaction to message

Excerpt 8 T3's interacting strategies (1)

Speaker	Utterance
S:	Captain
T:	He is not the captain, jun4yuan2, jun4yuan2, tell me who he is? He is the person who stands in front of the goal, there is a "men (door)" in his name
S:	Oh, I know. "flying door man", "football goal"
T:	It's not "football goal", goal keeper. Together, one, two, three …

Excerpt 9 T3's interacting strategies (2)

Speaker	Utterance
T:	We are at the … football field … play … where else?
S:	At home
T:	Play at home?
S:	Play at home.
T:	Play at home, what will happen?
S:	I know, break our …
T:	Ah, if we play football at home, we will break the glass-made objects
S:	Teacher, I … but teacher …
T:	Can use soft balls, but if you play strongly, the soft ball can also break a vase
S:	I like breaking things. Right!

To sum up this case study, the teacher made certain improvement in terms of the questioning strategies and providing feedback strategies. From the above analysis, we can see that vocabulary teaching and students' familiarity of the topic have impacts on the extent to which the lesson can be communicative. Teaching vocabulary through decontextualized repetition of the words resulted in less authentic communicative interaction between teacher and students. In addition to that, for beginning learners, selection of teaching content is also essential in a CLT lesson. If students are very familiar with the content, there would be minimal information exchange. Therefore, teachers should consider students' background and prior knowledge and select appropriate teaching content accordingly. For professional development, we can see that training has immediate effects on the first lesson. However, the effects do not sustain. This informed us that trainings should be provided based on intervals, and teachers need time to internalize new teaching principles and strategies.

Discussion

Though most teachers were aware that oral lesson is for communicative purpose, their design of oral lessons was tailored for the practice of vocabulary and syntactic structures listed in the textbooks. According to the interviews, repetition and sentence-making were two main strategies. Their feedback on students' oral production was also focused on the grammatical forms. And some teacher even applied the grammar of writing into the teaching of speaking. Besides, there is a lack of learner–learner interaction in oral lessons. On the whole, these teachers commonly believed that vocabulary and syntactic structures were basic resources for students to speak. After the research, teachers gradually realized that grammar of speaking does not equate grammar of writing. They realized their roles as facilitators to promote learners' speaking in class, and provide feedback on content and sustained the topic as possible. In addition, they noticed that learner–learner interaction can be successfully conducted in oral lessons if the structure, given students' roles and task difficulty, were carefully designed.

For professional development, first of all, there are changes in teachers' beliefs and perceptions of speaking ability which play important roles in teaching practice. These changes are caused by observed changes in students' responses, engagement, and class atmosphere. Second, there are changes in teaching practice. However, the change is not immediate and straightforward, but gradually and curly. This informed us that trainings and reflections should be continuously conducted till teachers can sustainably apply the teaching strategies.

The prerequisite and balance between linguistic knowledge and communication skills posed challenges for the implementation of CLT for young beginner learners. Young beginning learners are generally lack of language resources for fluent communication. In order for classes to be communicative, language knowledge should be provided in less communicative classes beforehand. Therefore, we have

Table 2 Recommended framework for designing CLT for young beginning learners

	Topic	Language knowledge	Activities
Language learner	Familiar	Highly demanding	Vocabulary and sentence structure teaching strategies and activities
Language user	Familiar + new information	Lowly demanding	Multiple contexts/scenarios related to the topic Learner–learner interaction

made some adjustments within CLT framework as shown in Table 2. Firstly, the classes should be divided into two groups which differentiate students as either language learners or language users. For language learners, the teacher should focus on teaching language knowledge. The topic has to be familiar to the students so that they can relate and response readily when requested to interact. Vocabulary and sentence structures related to the lesson topics (especially those words that can be used for further communicative purposes) should be carefully selected and taught to students. This type of classes is aimed at delivering language knowledge which provides premises for communication in later classes where learners are treated as language users.

For language users, teachers should design lessons with tasks that require higher communicative skills. Teachers should not introduce much new language knowledge. Instead, teachers should provide multiple contexts/scenarios that relate to the lesson topic so that students could practice the prescribed language knowledge over different circumstances to build their intuition in using those language knowledge. In view of their previously learnt language knowledge, language users can be engaged in structured learner–learner interaction activities, and the content of the topic could be dwell for greater depth based on what students have already knew.

Further research is encouraged on focusing components of CLT individually. Although it is not difficult to adopt and implement the specific strategies of CLT, being able to understand its underlying principles proved to be challenging for teachers. However, we must say that the understanding of the underlying principles of CLT has to be overcome by teachers so as to allow them to adapt the strategies flexibly and appropriately for their students.

Limitations and Suggestions

Like many studies, our study is not without flaws. Firstly, due to time constraint, transcriptions are not fully coded and reported. Therefore, the observations made in this report are restricted to the amount of data we managed to process. Secondly, we noticed that group training sessions for teachers were not sufficient, and it takes time for them to comprehend and internalize the theories and principles. Thus, reflection after each lesson played an important role in the professional development in this study. In future research, stimulus-recall can be employed, in which researchers and teachers watch and analyze classroom videos together. In addition, CLT can be implemented in other grades so as to build a systematic Chinese-speaking curriculum across the primary school years.

References

Canale, M., & Swain, M. (1980). Theoretical bases of communicative approaches to second language teaching and testing. *Applied Linguistics, 1*, 1.
Chinese Language Review Committee, Singapore. (2004). *Report of the Chinese language review committee*. Singapore: Ministry of Education.
Collins, A., Joseph, D., & Bielaczyc, K. (2004). Design research: Theoretical and methodological issues. *The Journal of the Learning Sciences, 13*(1), 15–42.
Ding, A. Q. (2006). Zhuanzhi duiwai hanyu jiaoshi dui ketang huodong kanfa de diaocha. [A study on full-time TCSL teachers attitudes towards classroom activities]. *Yuyan jiaoxue yanjiu*. [Language Teaching and Linguistic Studies], *06*, 57–63.
Doughty, C., & Pica, T. (1986). "Information gap" tasks: Do they facilitate second language acquisition? *TESOL Quarterly, 20*(2), 305–325.
Gao, F. (2015). *Renwu jiaoxuefa zai taiguo qingmai huangjia daxue hanyu zongheke zhong de yingyong anli fenxi*. [The application of cases analysis on task-based approach in comprehensive Chinese class of Chiang Mai Rajabhat University]. Wei fabiao shuoshi lunwen [Unpublished master thesis]. Beijing: Beijing waiguoyu daxue [Beijing: Beijing Foreign Studies University].
Gu, T. (2006). *Renwuxing yuyan jiaoxue zai duiwai hanyu chuji kouyu jiaoxue zhong de yingyong*. [The approach of task-based teaching in oral TCSL]. Wei fabiao shuoshi lunwen [Unpublished master thesis]. Beijing: Beijing yuyan daxue [Beijing: Beijing Language and Culture University].
Ho, W. K., & Wong, R. Y. (Eds.). (2002). *English language teaching in East Asia today: Changing policies and practices*. Eastern Universities Press.
Krashen, S. (1977). The monitor model for adult second language performance. *Viewpoints on English as a Second Language*, 152–161.
Krashen, S. D. (1985). *The input hypothesis: Issues and implications*. Addison-Wesley Longman Ltd.
Littlewood, W. (2004). The task-based approach: Some questions and suggestions. *ELT Journal, 58*(4), 319–326.
Liu, M., & Sim, S. H. (2013). *Developing task-based learning on the iMTL portal to strengthen students' spoken and written interaction proficiency: An exploratory study with upper secondary CLB students*. Internal Report. Singapore: Singapore Centre for Chinese Language.
Long, M. H. (1985). A role for instruction in second language acquisition: Task-based language teaching. *Modelling and Assessing Second Language Acquisition, 18*, 77–99.
Long, M. H. (1998). Focus on form Theory, research, and practice in Michael H. Long Peter Robinson. *Focus on Form in Classroom Second Language Acquisition, 15*, 15–41.
Mother Tongue Review Committee. (2010). *Nurturing active learners and proficient users*. Singapore: Ministry of Education.
Pica, T., & Doughty, C. (1985). The role of group work in classroom second language acquisition. *Studies in Second Language Acquisition, 7*(02), 233–248.
Porter, P. (1986). How learners talk to each other: Input and interaction in task-centered discussions. *Talking to Learn: Conversation in Second Language Acquisition*, 200–222.
Singapore Department of Statistics. (2000). *Singapore census of population*. http://www.singstat.gov.sg/publications/publications-and-papers/cop2000/census_stat_admin.

Spada, N. (2007). Communicative language teaching: Current status and future prospects. In J. Cummins & C. Davison (Eds.), *International handbook of English language teaching*. New York: Springer Science + Business Media LLC.

Spada, N., & Fröhlich, M. (1995). *Colt observation scheme: Communicative orientation of language teaching coding conventions & applications*. NCELTR Publications.

Yang, J. (2003) *Jiaojifa yu duiwai hanyu chuji kouyu jiaoxue-jianping beidaban chuji hanyu kouyu* jiaocai. [Communicative language teaching and teaching elementary Chinese as a foreign language speaking-evaluating Beijing University published *Elementary Chinese Speaking* textbooks]. *Chengdu shifan gaodeng zhuanke xuexiao xuebao*. [Journal of Chengdu Teachers College], *22*(1), 115–117.

Jing Yan (延晶) received Ph.D. from the University of Hong Kong, Hong Kong. She is currently a Lecturer at Singapore Centre for Chinese Language. Her academic interests include Task-Based Language Teaching, Chinese oral development, and learning motivation. She has published journal articles, a teaching toolkit, and several conference presentations. She is currently working on a project exploring Singapore primary and secondary students' Chinese learning motivation.

Hock Huan Goh (吴福焕) received his Ph.D. (NTU, Singapore). He is Chair of Research and Ethics Committee and Research Scientist at SCCL. His academic interests include Chinese Language teaching in multi-/bilingual context, child Mandarin competence, curriculum evaluation, and corpus-based application development. He has compiled and co-compiled a few frequency dictionaries of Singapore Chinese, and published more than 10 co-authored articles, and over 20 paper presentations. He has recently published a book on Mandarin competence of Singaporean Chinese preschoolers.

Hong Xia Zhou (周红霞) received her M.A. (Wuhan University of Technology, China). She is currently Senior Research Associate at Singapore Centre for Chinese Language. Her academic interests include second-language acquisition, Chinese as a Second Language, and Chinese Language pedagogies. Her publications include journal papers, book chapters, and a teaching toolkit.

Oral Interaction: Concept, Competence, and Assessment

Jinghua Fan

Abstract The article delineates the concept of interaction as it derives from language communication and describes the features of interactional competence from the perspective of discourse analysis. With references to categorization of interactional skills, this article proposes that interactional competence can be assessed in terms of the quality observed in a basic interactive unit consisting of responsive turn, turn-switching, and initiative turn.

One of the most conspicuous recent modifications in the objectives of Chinese language teaching in Singapore is the emphasis on interactional competence. The *Active Learners and Proficient Users* (Ministry of Education, Singapore 2011) recognizes the importance of promoting the actual use of Chinese language in the changing landscape of multi-language use in Singapore and adds the dimension of oral and written interactions into the conventional dimensions of language competency in terms of listening, speaking, reading, and writing skills. The rationale of the addition is the division of language skills into three categories, namely the receptive (listening and reading), the productive (speaking and writing), and the interaction skills (e.g., group discussion). To illustrate the framework of targeted skills, the report has also presented a brief description of some proficiency indicators with examples of some situational tasks of communication. The report has since become the guideline for the reform of Singapore's Chinese language education and the development of the new series of textbooks.

However, to many Chinese language teachers who are used to the concept of four traditional skills, interaction competency is a new concept. Interaction has always been functioning in everyday communication and has also been covered as part of teaching in the past. This has resulted in different understanding of the concept of interaction and its forms. This article aims at delineating and defining the concept of interaction and describes the components of interaction competency with examples of interaction activity from Chinese language teaching.

J. Fan (✉)
NUS, Singapore, Singapore
e-mail: Jinghua.fan@sccl.sg

© Springer Nature Singapore Pte Ltd. 2018
K. C. Soh (ed.), *Teaching Chinese Language in Singapore*,
https://doi.org/10.1007/978-981-10-8860-5_6

Language Communication and the Concept of Interaction

The primary purpose of learning a language is to use it for communication, and communication is realized through contextualized use of language forms. Scholars have been dividing the processes in language learning from different perspectives (i), and the most accepted division has been the distinction between *linguistic* competence and *communicative* competence. For a summary of the processes involved in learning a language, refer to Robert M. Dekerser's *Cognitive-Psychological Processes in Second Language Learning* in the *Handbook of Language Teaching* (Long and Doughty 2009).

Three areas of acquirement may be involved in learning a language: the knowledge of the language's linguistic rules and forms, the understanding of the pragmatics, and the abilities to put language forms into use.

By language forms, it is meant the meaningful units of speech, such as a phrase, word, or sentence structure, which can be formally learned or casually picked up. Linguistic forms are functional in communication when they are purposefully contextualized in accordance with the requirements of specific situations. From classroom teaching, language learning is to focus on language forms and functions and apply them to social communicative situations. This is one essential objective of the above-mentioned report entitled *Nurturing Active Learner and Proficient Users*.

Language communication may be one-way or two-way, or linear or interactive. In one-way communication, producers (of speech or texts) are separated from receivers (CEFR 2004: 57). The participants function as either the encoder–sender or decoder–receiver, and there is no feedback channel that allows for response from the receiver. In language learning situations, this one-way communication can be a lecture, a speech, an oral report, or a presentation. In this sense, two-way communication happens when the sender receives feedback from the receiver. In language learning, interaction may be defined as the collaborative exchange of thought, feelings, or ideas between two or more people, resulting in a reciprocal effect on each other, and interaction is the heart of communication (Brown 2001: 165). In interactive activities, such as conversation and correspondence, the participants alternate as producers and receivers, often with several turns (CEFR 2004: 57). In short, interaction takes place when people need to express meaning and exchange information in a way that all the parties involved contribute both as senders and receivers. In other words, interaction is a language action in which two or more language users communicate with or react to each other through language (Wagner 1994: 8).

In real-life situations, there may be synchronic face-to-face oral communication in which the interlocutors' utterances are presented in the real time, or asynchronic written communication in which the messages are presented in deferred relays. Nowadays, communication has been increasingly mediated by information technology, and real-time written communication can also be easily realized. For example, the immediacy of electronic mails has changed time deferment in the traditional mailed exchanges while speech translation devices can now convert the oral utterances in a face-to-face communication into written recording in the virtual reality. Phenomena like this have made it more difficult to define oral and written interaction and distinguish between them. In this article, the analysis of interaction is based on face-to-face spoken communication, although the classroom may have integrated virtual reality.

In the context of Chinese language teaching in Singapore, there is a need to reiterate the difference between *communication* and *interaction*. Although interaction is one aspect of interpersonal communication, there is one fundamental difference between communication and interaction; interaction is two-way communication and can never be one-way. This means that when teachers design oral interaction activities they should have a feedback loop for students to "talk back." For example, one of the oral activities frequently used for lower primary students is *show-and-tell* in which a student speaks before classmates about something while showing the object or its picture. For example, a primary student describes her favorite doll before the class. This activity is presentational rather than interactional, because during the process both the acts to show and tell are one-way, and no interaction is involved. If there is a subsequent session of discussion based on the content, there will be interaction since the presenting student's utterances are not prepared like what has been presented in the *show-and-tell* while the classmates' utterances are made upon both the *show-and-tell* and the utterances by the presenting student and other classmates.

To promote interaction, it is essential to create a situation for the students to react to each other. The participants in such situations should act alternatively as speakers and listeners with one or more interlocutors conjointly through the negotiation of meaning following the cooperative principle of conversational discourse (CEFR 2004: 73). For meaningful learning, the created situation should promote the students' willingness to react to each other. That is, the cooperative principle in conversational discourse should be naturally followed instead of being forced upon. This implies that activities like sentence drills or other pair work exercises where students are assigned the roles of asking and answering without spontaneous role shifting in the session may be called *reactive* but not *interactive*. In the same way, the most common teacher–student conversation type of Initiation–Response–Feedback (IRF) may not be interactive because the teacher almost always initiates with expected responses to which the teacher gives positive, corrective, or negative feedback.

However, in a short conversation like IRF, we can see a prototype of an interactional unit. Speaker A's first turn initiates, and Speaker B's response reacts to the initiation, while Speaker A reacts to Speaker B's response by providing a feedback, thus closing the interactional unit. An interactional unit comprises of at least one initiative turn and one responsive turn. In the IRF model, the responsive turn may function as both a response to the original initiation and an initiation for another response, for example in a conversation between two Chinese language speakers (Table 1).

We should first of all assume that Speaker B responds by following the cooperative principle of conversation, and then it can be understood that Speaker B's

Table 1 A conversation with a question as an answer

Turn 1	A1	Eaten already? (已经吃了?)
Turn 2	B1	You think it isn't the time yet? (你觉得还不是时候?)
Turn 3	A2	So early? (这么早?)
Turn 4	B2	I didn't have breakfast this morning (我没吃早餐。)

response in Turn 2 is intended to be an answer to Speaker A's question (Turn 1) rather than a question to Speaker A. Turn 2 is a rhetoric question, implying that it is a confirmative answer and that Speaker B assumes A actually knows the answer to his own question. Turn 2 functions mainly as a responsive turn, but it also implies an initiation. Hence, in Turn 3, Speaker A response "So early?" implies that Speaker A has grasped Speaker B's implications, and Speaker B in Turn 4 explains the reason for having an early lunch.

It can be seen that a conversational discourse comprises internally connected interactive units, and in each unit there is an initiative turn and a responsive turn, but one turn may be both a response and an initiation to ensure the smooth connection between units and the smooth flow of the discourse. The dual function turn is important in that it both takes up a turn and yields a turn. When a turn is intended and understood to be both responsive and initiative, the producer of the turn takes on the roles of both an initiator and a responder. However, the role shift in an interactional discourse is often seen in a turn which consists of more than one sentence. For example, in the following conversation (Table 2), the role shift takes place in Turns 4 and 6, when the speaker utters two sentences, one being an answer to the previous turn, one being a question initiating a new topic.

In Table 2, the first three turns and the first part of Turn 4 appear to form a question-and-answer session, in which the roles are fixed. This part can be understood to be preliminary interactional communication in which the turn-taking is smooth and natural. When Speaker B in Turn 4 asks Speaker A "*How about*

Table 2 A conversation with turns containing more than one sentence

Turns	Speaker	Utterances (literal translation from Chinese)	Functions
Turn 1	A	Hi, have you eaten?	Asking for information as a greeting
Turn 2	B	Yes.	Responding a greeting
Turn 3	A	What did you eat?	Asking for information
Turn 4	B	Duck noodle. How about you?	(1) Providing information (2) Asking for information as a greeting
Turn 5	A	I've eaten too. With our new colleague. We tried the newly-opened chicken rice stall.	(1) Providing information (2) Complementing (3) Clarifying
Turn 6	B	Oh, so you are his office buddy! Was it good?	(1) Self-clarifying (2) Asking for information

you?", Speaker B's role changes from a responder to an initiator; thus, interaction in its true sense takes place. This interaction may come to an end, if Speaker A in Turn 5 only answers the question with "*I've eaten too.*" However, Speaker A expands the topic by providing two new pieces of information in Turn 5; therefore, the conversation can proceed. Turn 5 appears to be a responsive turn, but the functions of complementation and clarification can imply an invitation for response. Speaker A's addition of information not only expands the topic about the lunch but also introduces a possible new topic about the new colleague. From Turn 5, we can see that the role in an interaction may be slippery, when the response can be an implied initiation and the receiver can be an implied sender. Obviously, Turn 5 is well received, as Speaker B in Turn 6 responds to both topics, and the conversation can be expected to continue.

In sum, an interactional unit consists of a responsive turn, turn-shifting, and an initiative turn, and interactional units are linked to form an interactional chain in which participants take and yield turns by changing their roles as sender and receiver. One turn may perform different functions, which in turn may change the nature of the role based on the turn to the effect that the responder may be both responding and initiating. When different turns are connected based on the cooperative principle, new information is introduced or generated so that the existing topic may be expanded and the conversation is extended.

Components and Descriptors of Interactional Competence

Before analyzing what composes interactional competence, it is necessary to distinguish between oral competence, communicative competence, and interactional competence. Among the different categorizations of oral skills, Martin Bygate's classification in *Speaking* is representative, in which he divides oral skills into two major categories under motor-perceptive skills and the interaction skills. Motor-perceptive skills involve "perceiving, recalling, and articulating in the correct order sounds and structure of the language … and it is the context-free kind of skill" (Bygate 1987: 5). What Bygate puts under interaction skills are categorized into routines and negotiation skills. In routines, information routines are divided into expository and evaluative, and interaction routines are divided into service and social routines. In negotiation skills, there are negotiation of meaning and management of interaction (Table 3).

Routines can be defined as conventional ways of presenting information, and conventionality implies predictability (Bygate 1987: 23), and we can find that most of everyday interactions require routine skills. These conventions predetermine what initiative turns appear to be and what responsive turns are expected to be, and they tend to be characterized in broad terms to include the kinds of turns typically occurring in given situations, and the order in which the components are likely to occur, and to be organized in characteristic ways (Bygate 1987: 25). Bygate gives an example of a restaurant situation, arguing that although we may not know

Table 3 Bygate's classification of oral skills

Motor-perceptive skill			
Interaction skills	Routines	Information routines	Expository
			Evaluative
		Interaction routines	Service
			Social
	Negotiation skills	Negotiation of meaning	
		Management of interaction	

exactly what words or meanings will be communicated, it is still quite easy to predict the kinds of information being asked and giving (Bygate 1987: 26). In this way, language learning can be pre-programmed in the sense that what can be communicated has always been embedded already into different situations.

Bygate separates "routines" from "negotiation" skills, and routines depend less on context. From the perspective of context dependency, it can be argued that the more context-dependent a communication situation is, the more interactional skills are needed, and the higher interaction competence the situation can promote. In a sense, the language forms used in a routine interaction situation are predictable, and therefore they can be prepared. This implies that interaction competence involved in routine situations may not be adequately shown. Therefore, Bygate's classification of oral skills, built around the core concept of routines, may provide an insight for us to look into linguistic features beyond words and meanings.

Based on Bygate's classification of oral skills according to genres (Bygate 1987: 23–41), O'Sullivan et al. (2002: 33–56) develop a checklist of discourse functions as an attempt to design oral tasks to test the language user's performance. They have reorganized Bygate's classification, to put different discourse functions under informational function, interactional function, and managing interaction. For example, under "Interactional Function" there are agreeing, disagreeing, modifying, asking for opinions, persuading, asking for information, conversational repair, and negotiating meaning, while under "Managing Interaction" there are initiating, changing, reciprocating, and deciding (O'Sullivan et al. 2002: 54). As this repertoire of discourse functions in the checklist is easily represented by typical communication situations in which the interaction routines can be functioning well. Therefore, again, if interactional competence is primarily the competence showing in the process and act of interaction instead of the words used to refer to meaning or sentence structure used to organize meaning, what lies in the heart of interactional competence?

In interaction, not only must an interlocutor communicate with the other, but also the interlocutors will react to each other (Wagner 1994: 8). Accordingly, we can examine the skills involved in interaction from two perspectives. One perspective is to examine the skills as needed within a turn, which may be described as intra-turn skills. These skills may not be much different from the ordinary speaking skills, such as how to maintain coherency within the turn, make the turn relevant to the previous turns. In interactional communication, the interlocutor must respond to the previous turn in terms of content. In this sense, in Bygate's classification of oral skills (Table 3), the skills described under interaction, except for negotiation skills, are all intra-turn skills. The other perspective is to examine the skills needed between turns, which may be described as inter-turn skills. These skills are demonstrated as the interlocutor's awareness of the conversational discourse and may be argued to be the interactional skills in the truest sense.

Based on the above analysis, we can argue that interactional competence should focus on the *inter-ness* of communication. And, considering operationality in language teaching, we propose that interactional competence should be examined and described in the following three aspects: (1) turn-taking in a conversational discourse; (2) functions of turns; and, (3) typical language forms. These will be elaborated hereafter.

Turn-Taking in a Conversational Discourse Turn-taking is an important indicator of how interaction flows, and a conversational discourse comprises more than one interactional unit involving role shift between the sender and receiver with the shift automatically realized through turn-taking. In an interactional unit, three aspects may be observed to determine the level of interactional competence: (a) the adequacy of response. This can be understood from the perspective of Grice's (Grice 1989: 26–31) maxim of quantity, which says that a speaker should make his contribution as informative as is required; (b) the smooth and naturalness of turn-taking. This includes whether the speaker has the awareness of turn-yielding, turn-holding, turn-requesting, and turn-taking; and (c) the readiness to initiate an appropriate turn or to terminate a turn. This is to evaluate whether the participant in the interaction has the awareness and ability to contribute to an interaction.

Function of Turns In an interactional unit, a turn can be a short utterance or a sustained one. When a turn comprises of a sustained utterance, the turn itself can be understood as a one-way presentational passage. No matter how long a turn appears to be, it has functions to perform. For example, Turn 4 in Table 2 (*"Duck noodle"*) is a phrase, but it functions perfectly well as an adequate response to the previous question. Turn 5 comprises of three short sentences and performs three functions, and the act of uttering three sentences in one turn may also be seen as a way to hold the turn. O'Sullivan et al. (2002: 47) suggest that the function of the turns may be an aspect of interactional competence, and their checklist can be modified with reference to a notional-functional syllabus developed according to the Chinese Language Syllabus in Singapore to better meet the needs in Singapore's context.

Take the example of an initiative turn. The primary function of an initiative turn is to open an interactional unit with a new topic or to introduce a new element into the existing topic. It can be an exclamation, a statement or a question, to perform the function of greeting, calling for attention, asking for comments, soliciting an opinion, etc. Due to the interrelationship between language functions and forms, the choice of language forms should also be assessed for its appropriateness to perform certain functions. For example, in CERF (2004: 34), the task to "*ask for and provide everyday goods and services*" has been described with different qualifiers across different levels of proficiency. Language functions in interaction can be described and assessed from the perspectives of adequacy, appropriateness, relevance, transparency, and effectiveness. Adequacy refers to the quantity of the utterance, such as ellipsis; appropriateness refers to the register of the chosen language, such as formality or colloquiality; relevance refers to how targeted and direct an utterance is to the previous utterance; transparency refers to how explicit is the meaning of an utterance; and effectiveness refers to the performativity of an utterance, or how the utterance enforces its effect upon the receivers.

Typical Language Forms There are two ways to define the typicality of language forms, but first of all there is the question about whether there is a typical language form. When we talk about typical language forms, we are describing what language forms are most often used in a communication situation, which relies on the assumption that there is an accepted interrelationship between language forms and language functions. The fact is there may be many different language forms to perform one function, and they may appear to be highly colloquial and elliptical or very formal and cumbersome. Different language forms may mean different degrees of difficulty for learners. For example, there are many ways to ask for direction, some of which may not be appropriate in terms of, say, register, formality, or politeness, and obviously appropriateness should be an essential part of interactional competence. Therefore, the final obtainment of the information, e.g., the completion of a communicative task, may not be a valid indicator for interactional competence.

For the same reason, it may also be argued that the *can-do* lists in CERF (2004: 26) may not be adequate to assess language proficiency. For example, the descriptor for the overall spoken interaction of "Independent User" (Level B2) contains the description "Can interact with a degree of fluency and spontaneity that makes regular interaction, and sustained relationships with native speakers quite possible without imposing strain on either party" (CERF 2004: 74). This description can only be a "global scale," and actually it also appears in the "Common Reference Levels: Global Scale" (CERF 2004: 24), and therefore, it can be used as a reference but not a rubric. This may imply that the *can-do* lists are not easily used to indicate interactional competence. The lists have also pointed to typical communication situations that can be used to construct a repertoire of language forms. For example, the descriptor for the overall spoken interaction of "Independent User" (Level B1) contains the description "Can exploit a wide range of simple language to deal with most situations likely to arise whilst travelling" (CERF 2004: 24). Although the situation is given, it is still difficult to generate a set of typical language forms to cover the range of "simple language" so that they may be orchestrated into formal language teaching syllabus.

Given that it is difficult to prescribe a typical language form to represent a typical communication situation, it may be necessary to find an alternative way to describe the indicators of interactional competence in a conversational discourse. In everyday interaction, participants often observe the maxim of economy, which implies that the choice of language forms in an utterance depends more on the context instead of following the linguistic rules. If ambiguity arises, participants will resort to self-monitoring or negotiation of meaning. This leads us to examine the language forms that are less content-related than process-related. This comes to the discourse markers, and we propose that discourse markers can be a good indicator for interactional competence.

The study of discourse markers has long gained attention in the area of linguistics. There are many different definitions of discourse markers, and even discourse markers are referred to with different terms (ii). In this paper, discourse markers are defined as linguistic expressions usually in the form of words or phrases which are commonly used to signal the relationship between an utterance and its immediate context. Discourse markers are "closely related to the non-referential (or interactional) meaning of language rather than referential (or propositional) meaning... of an utterance, but influence the hearer's interpretation of the utterance" (Ogi 2017: 52). Archakis (2001) and Fuller (2003) note from the syntactical and semantic perspective that (1) discourse markers are syntactically separated from the rest of the sentence, (2) they do not add anything to the propositional content of an utterance or affect its truth conditions, and (3) they are used to signal relationships between discourse units in order to create discourse coherence (also cited in Ogi 2017: 12). Discourse markers' close relationship with the process of interaction rather than the content of communication can be a valid indicator of interactional competence.

Just as certain language forms are related to certain functions, which can be seen in Bygate's classification of routines, certain language forms are closely related to certain functions. For example, in negotiation of meaning, when asking for clarification, language forms such as *"Do you mean…?"* will be used, while shifting a topic or introducing a new topic, the interlocutor may use language forms such as *"Speaking of this, I think of…"*. These markers can function to direct the interlocutor's attention to the flow and structure of discourse (Carol Lynn and Martinovic-Zic 2004: 117) and the interaction itself.

Toward a Framework of the Assessment of Interactional Competence

Based on the above analysis, we can now propose a framework of the assessment of interactional competence with reference to the structure of discourse in Chinese language. Chinese discourse focusing on a thematic topic can be divided into four phases, namely the introduction (起 *qi, the opening of a topic*), the development (承 *cheng, the development of a topic*), the transition (to another viewpoint) (转 *zhuan, the inclusion of an alternative viewpoint*), and the conclusion (合 *he, the meeting of minds or conclusion*) (iii). To apply this model into the analysis of a conservational discourse, *qi* is the initiative turn, *cheng* is the taking over and a continuation of a turn, *zhuan* may be understood as the expansion of a turn, and *he* refers to the conclusion or the meeting of mind in the end. These four phases can also be understood as four functions, and this means that there are some expressions and structures closely related to them. For example, some discourse markers in the final phase may include "*to sum up*" and "*in short*".

Interaction is a dynamic system, in which interlocutors are alternatively a speaker and a listener, prepared to take over or yield a turn, and sometimes try to hold a turn or interrupt it, and usually there will be some accompanying prosodic changes (iv). For example, to examine the second phase (*cheng*) of an oral discourse, it should be noted how a turn is taken up without unnatural delay. To examine the third phase (*zhuan*) of an oral discourse, how relevant is the added topic? The following table describes the assessment framework of interactional competence with some examples (Table 4).

The following table (Table 5) exemplifies a sustained conversational discourse with different language functions and discourse markers. The English version is a literal translation of Mandarin Chinese oral interaction, which may appear to the English reader a little unnatural and strained pragmatically. Also, a specific utterance may have different functions according to different interpreters, while there may also be differences between the actual conversation heard and the transcription of a conversation.

This article attempts to expound the essential feature of interaction by distinguishing between communication and interaction. Upon the analysis of turns in a conversational discourse, it puts forward the concept of an interactional unit. The article maintains that the assessment of interactional competence should be based on the process instead of the content of the interaction, and it argues that discourse markers, due to their close relation with interactional meaning of language, may serve as a valid indicator for interactional competence. Finally, the article proposes a framework of assessment of interactional competence which is constructed on the structure of Chinese passage and exemplified with conversational discourse markers.

Notes

(i) For a summary of the processes involved in learning a language, refer to Robert M. Dekerser's "Cognitive-Psychological Processes in Second Language Learning," in The Handbook of Language Teaching, pp. 119-38 (Eds. Michael H. Long and Catherine J. Doughty, 2009).

(ii) For a detailed review of the definitions of and the terms for discourse marker, refer to Naomi Ogi's Involvement and Attitude in Japanese Discourse, especially Sect. 1.2 Chap. 1 (John Benjamins Publishing Co., 2017). In the book, Ogi has also argued for the use of interactive marker to replace the term discourse marker, and I find this argument especially relevant to my preposition for using discourse markers as an indicator for interactional competence.

Table 4 Framework of the assessment of interactional competence

Interaction process	Functions of turn	Language functions	Typical language forms
Introduction (起 qi)	Initiative turn: opening an interactional unit and yield a turn	Asking for information Calling attention Greeting Inviting Offering help, etc.	(1) *Hey, look here* (2) *Today's climate is not bad, isn't it?* (3) *Hi, have you heard of…?*
Development (承 cheng)	Responsive turn: Take over the turn by responding Get prepared to develop and enrich the details	Agreeing Asking for confirmation Elaborating Negotiation of meaning Revising, etc.	(1) *Yeah, I too…* (2) *Actually, I really don't …* (3) *Sorry, I didn't hear clearly* (4) *In another way, you mean…?*
Transition (转 Zhuan)	Adding new perspective to the conversation Introduce new elements into the present topic	Challenging Conceding Opposing Proposing Reviewing Suggesting, etc.	(1) *Do you agree …then?* (2) *Since you've talked about this, I'd like to…* (3) *Oh, yes, I realize…* (4) *Why not just do…?* (5) *Sorry to interrupt, but …*
Conclusion (合 he)	Concluding a conversation Providing feedback Terminating a conversation	Deciding Evaluating Feedback Finding an excuse Summing up, etc.	(1) *Good, let's talk about the details the next time* (2) *You are very right here, but I have to…* (3) *Forget about it, too long a story to tell* (4) *I am very sorry, but I have to go now*
Descriptions for assessment	(1) Smooth shift of turns: timely, politely (2) Adequate understanding of functions of Turns	(1) Adequacy (2) Appropriateness (3) Relevance (4) Transparency (5) Effectiveness	(1) Difficulty and appropriateness of language forms (2) Appropriate discourse markers and contextual references

Table 5 A conversational discourse example

Interaction process	Transcription	Language functions	Discourse markers
Introduction (起 qi)	A1: Hi, are you going back? B1: Oh, sorry, I didn't see you. I am going to Ray Chee's home	Calling attention (A1) Greeting (A1, B1) Asking for information (A1) Explaining (B1) Providing information (B1)	"*Hi*," "*Oh*" and "*Sorry*" as DMs in greetings
Development (承 cheng)	A2: Speaking of him, I haven't seen him for two days B2: Two days? He hurt his knee at Wednesday's football match A3: Is it serious? I didn't watch the game B3: That's just like you. Enough to stay away from the field for three weeks	Disagreeing or Revising by repeating a part of previous utterance (B2) Providing information (B2, B3) Asking for information (A3) Explaining (A3) Confirming (B3)	"*Speaking of sth.*" as a DM to develop a topic
Transition (转 zhuan)	A4: Too sad, but who could tell what will come after a man loses a horse in the wilderness? B4: What? A5: I am saying maybe that is a blessing in disguise for him B5: What on earth do you mean? A6: I mean, maybe that will make his spend more time on his study B6: Are you suggesting he is a poor student? You are too mean by saying this! He was born for sports	Agreeing (A4; A7) Giving opinion (A4; B6) Asking for clarification (B4) Confirmation (A5) Negotiation of meaning (B5) Explanation (A6) Asking for confirmation (B6) Giving an opinion (B6) Opposing (A7)	"*(Yes), but*" (A4; A7) as DMs for transition "*I am saying*" (A5) and "*I mean*" (A6) as DMs for clarification "*On earth*" (B5) as a DM for emphasis "*The fact is*" (A7) as a DM for explanation and defense

(continued)

Table 5 (continued)

Interaction process	Transcription	Language functions	Discourse markers
	A7: No, I am not mean. The fact is, no one could live by playing football in this country if he could not even pass the O-Level exams B7: Well, maybe you are right, but that is not what we can foresee	Defending (A7) Conceding (B7)	*"Well, maybe you are right"* (B7) as a DM for concession
Conclusion (合 he)	A8: Yes, that is too complex a thing B8: True, the future is what yet to come. Now let's hope he gets well soon A9: Good. Say hello to him. Bye B9: Bye	Agreeing (A8; B8) Concluding (B8)	*"Yes"* (A8), *"True"* (B8) and *"Good"* (A9) as DMs for agreeing *"Now let's"* (B8) as a DM for concluding a conversation

Oral Interaction: Concept, Competence, and Assessment

(iii) There are many academic papers and books on the structure of Chinese discourse, and according to Liu Xizai (1813–1881) whose definition in his six-volume *Generalization of Art* (《艺概》) is one of the earliest and most classical, "*qi* means an introduction to what to come, and connecting to what to come is also a method of *qi*; *he* means a convergence with the above, and connecting to what has been written is also a method of he; between qi and he there are *cheng* and *zhuan* which connect in one way to *qi* and in another way to *he*. (起者起下也, 连合亦起在内; 合者合上也, 连起亦合在内; 中间用承用转, 皆兼顾起合也)". For a reflection of the model of a four-phase Chinese discourse, refer to Wan's (2013).

(iv) Given the scope and objectives of the current paper, I will not elaborate on the types and functions of Mandarin Chinese discourse markers and I will only raise some examples to illustrate how they can be used to indicate the different aspects of interactional competence as shown in a Chinese conversational discourse. It also needs to clarify that in Mandarin Chinese conversational discourse, some often used words such as "na (那), na me (那么)" (then) are unstressed and may be heard but often omitted in transcription, as I have done so in the example (Table 5). For a brief review of the functions of Mandarin Chinese discourse markers, refer to Li-Chiung Yang's paper (2006). The paper maintains that "the interactive and communicative nature of the [discourse marker] should be part of the definition, as we view the function of discourse makers as a running commentary on the underlying text that helps to make the text coherent in the context of the particular conversation" (Yang 2006: 268). The paper also suggests that the functions of discourse markers are to signal phrase relationship, interactive relationship, cognitive and emotional relationship which are in turn signaled by discourse context, phrase position, lexical meaning and prosody.

References

Archakis, A. (2001). On discourse markers: Evidence from modern Greek. *Journal of Pragmatics, 33,* 1235–1261.
Brown, D. H. (2001) *Teaching by principles: An interactive approach to language pedagogy.* White Plains, New York: Pearson Education.
Bygate, M. (1987). *Speaking.* Oxford: Oxford University Press.
Carol Lynn, M., & Martinovic-Zic, A. (2004). *Discourse across languages and cultures.* John Benjamins Publishing Company.
Council of Europe. (2004). *The common European framework of reference for languages: Learning, teaching, assessment.* London: Cambridge University Press.
Fuller, J. M. (2003). The influence of speaker roles on discourse marker use. *Journal of Pragmatics, 35,* 23–45.
Grice, P. (1989). *Studies in the way of words.* Cambridge, MA: Harvard University Press.
Long, M. H., & Doughty, C. J. (Eds.). (2009). *The handbook of language teaching.* Oxford: Wiley-Blackwell.

Ministry of Education, Singapore. (2011). *Nurturing active learners and proficient users: 2010 Mother Tongue review committee report.* Singapore: MOE.

Ogi, N. (2017) *Involvement and attitude in Japanese discourse: Interactive markers.* John Benjamins Publishing Company.

O'Sullivan, B., Weir, C. J., & Saville, N. (2002). Using observation checklists to validate speaking-test tasks. *Language Testing, 19,* 33–56.

Wagner, E. D. (1994). In support of a functional definition of interaction. *The American Journal of Distance Education, 8*(2), 6–26.

Wan, Q. (2013) On the structure of Qi-Cheng-Zhuan-He: From poetics to the study of passages. In X. Hu (Ed.), *Views on beauty and Chinese literary theory* (pp. 79–94). Shanghai: East China Normal University Press.

Yang, L. C. (2006). Integrating prosodic and contextual cues in the interpretation of discourse markers. In K. Fischer (Ed.), *Approaches to discourse particles* (pp. 265–297). Amsterdam: Elsevier.

Jinghua Fan (范静哗) received Ph.D. from NUS, Singapore. He is currently a Lecturer at the Singapore Centre for Chinese Language, and he is also a poet and translator. His academic interests include language teaching methodology, language communication, reading difficulty, picture-books, and literary studies. His publications include academic writings of journal articles, chapters, and textbooks and teaching toolkits on language and literature, translated books of poetry and critical theory, and creative books of picture books and poems.

Teaching Oral Narrative Skills to Chinese Children in Singapore

Li Li, Su Yee Au and Geok Hoon Tan

Abstract This article presents an intervention to help Singaporean children in narrative skills in Chinese language to prepare them in coping with the shift. Grade-three children participated in the study. Half of the children were taught through a specifically designed intervention programme, while the other half with the usual programme. Comparisons after a year showed that the experimental group made greater progress than did the control group in oral narrative skills and overall oral skill scores.

Recent studies on enhancing the Singaporean children's oral competence in Chinese language (CL) have shown that oral language teaching, in certain aspects, has positive impact on the children's interest in learning Chinese language and their communicative competence (MOE 2011; Ko et al. 2012; Sun and Fan 2012). Also, some studies found that although Singaporean Chinese children had no trouble using Chinese language in giving short responses during conversation, they faced difficulties in providing longer and more complex sentences in CL (Goh et al. 2008).

The curricular objectives for Singaporean primary school students in the middle grades (i.e. Primary 3 and Primary 4) are shifting from learning to provide conversations on daily topics in CL to conversing over more abstract themes and providing narrations and discourses that are complete and detailed in contents. With this change in the objective, the students need more assistance in narrative skills beyond learning Chinese characters, vocabulary and sentence structures. Narrative skills combine cognitive development, linguistics and social interactive skills. In the classroom context, oral narrative skills refer to students' competence in mastering

---

L. Li (✉) · S. Y. Au
Singapore Centre for Chinese Language, Nanyang Technological University, Singapore, Singapore
e-mail: li.li@sccl.sg

G. H. Tan
Academy of Singapore Teachers, Ministry Of Education, Singapore, Singapore

© Springer Nature Singapore Pte Ltd. 2018
K. C. Soh (ed.), *Teaching Chinese Language in Singapore*,
https://doi.org/10.1007/978-981-10-8860-5_7

the narrative structures, organizing information and textual knowledge, and presenting orally with suitable discourse structure, sentence structure and vocabulary. Narrative skills are often not taught explicitly in CL lessons in Singapore schools where teaching and training focus mainly on enhancing students' reading and writing skills.

The present study is an intervention on narrative skills in CL among Singaporean Primary 3 and Primary 4 students. It is quasi-experimental comparing students' performance in oral language competency, oral narrative skills and reading comprehensions between an experimental group and a control group.

Literature Review

Children's oral narrative skills refer to their skills of processing, organizing and expressing personal experiences and familiar routines (Crais and Lorch 1994). From about the age of two years, monolingual children are exposed to narratives and gradually developing narrative skills along with their cognitive development. They start from naming objects, presenting sequential events, to presenting logically related events and situations. At about seven years of age, monolingual children are able to produce true narratives for a series of events with a clear focus on the theme and being arranged according to their temporal, spatial or logical sequence, or both. (Applebee 1978; Paul et al. 1996)

Except for knowledge about the language, higher-order cognitive skills are also involved in the process of narration (Hudson and Shapiro 1991). Children have to process, reorganize and manipulate knowledge and skills of various aspects, including interpersonal interaction skills, sociocultural knowledge, pragmatic and linguistic knowledge, understanding the sequential and causal relations of events, memory about the past experiences and mastering narrative structural knowledge. Development in oral narrative skills helps with a smooth transit of children's skills in conversations from short and contextualized daily conversation, firstly to the utterance of familiar, decontextualized topics and personal experiences, then to more abstract topics comprising complex relations of events (Hedberg and Westby 1993).

Oral narrative skills are among the essential oral language competence in school. In classrooms, students are constantly required to respond to questions asking about abstract concepts and topics. They have to, for instance, describe the procedure of carrying out a science experiment, tell a story to the class or share experiences with peers. Not only the integration of linguistics knowledge with communication skills is required, students also need to be able to apply their knowledge of narrative structure properly in using language (Applebee 1978; Mccabe and Rollins 1994). Students' knowledge of narrative structure will also help them in reading comprehension in terms of story plot, episodes, theme and event relations (Chi 2004).

Studies on the monolingual children indicate the close associations among children's oral narrative skills, their cognitive development and their language development. For instance, reading comprehension, as a popular indicator of language development, was found to be closely associated with children's narrative skills (Oakhill and Cain 2007). The close relations were similarly found among bilinguals (Westerveld 2013).

From the findings of these summarized studies, we conclude that systematic and explicit instructions in oral narrative skills may enhance children's oral language competence. For bilinguals, this effect may also be observed in their second language. Therefore, the present study developed and implemented an intervention programme among Singaporean bilingual children learning CL as their second language. The programme serves as the transit method helping Primary 3 and Primary 4 students by providing abstract and decontextualized discourse in classrooms. By doing so, the teaching aimed to enhance students' oral competence in Chinese language. Further, with enhanced knowledge of narrative structure, students undergone the intervention programme were expected to perform better in story structure and comprehension of reading materials.

Method

Participants and Procedure

Primary 3 students from two primary schools were invited to this one-year intervention study involving 212 students, assigned to experimental and comparison groups according to their classes. Four classes were assigned to the experimental group and another four classes to the control group. Students in both groups were reported as not having difficulties in cognitive development nor in language development. Students in the experimental group were also reported to be slightly less proficient in CL than those of the control group.

Prior to the intervention, students in both groups were assessed on their CL oral narrative skills individually. Their CL reading comprehension was also evaluated as an important indicator that represents an aspect of children's language development. Students' oral test scores for the first semester were collected.

There was a one-year interval between the pretest and post-test. At the end of the project, the students were retested on oral narrative skills and CL reading comprehension with the same tasks used for pretest. Teachers collected students' oral test scores for the first semester towards the end of the project. A loss of numbers of students was observed at the post-test, because limited time slots could be allocated by the schools for collecting data from all the participants. A final count of the participants who have completed all the tasks in both tests was 126.

The intervention was conducted between the two testing sessions July in one year to April in the following year. The research team worked closely with the CL teachers in designing and implementing the lesson plans and teaching materials. Teachers in the experimental group were trained with the principles of the interventions and introduced to the teaching materials. They were asked about the possible difficulties in the implementation after a trial lesson. Amendments were made after teachers' feedback. Teachers in the control group were briefed to teach in their normal way using their own lesson plans.

Measures

Oral Narrative Skills This study adopted the recount storytelling task as the test of the students' oral narrative skills. Two story topics (*Celebrating Birthday* and *Seeing a Doctor*) which were familiar to Singaporean children and were the most common in their daily lives were selected for the task. Participating students were to choose one from the two topics to tell about their past experience orally in CL.

During the tests, trained researchers provided the students with content-unrelated prompts to keep the conversation going. These prompts are standard across the testers, such as "Then?", "Any more you would like to say?" and words which show affirmation such as "yes", "ok" and "oh".

The student' utterances were recorded for further analysis. Based on Story Grammar (Stein and Glenn 1979), the research team modified a grading rubric (Westerveld and Gillon 2008) and scored students' oral narrative skills. The grading rubric covered five aspects: introduction, theme, conflict and resolution, conclusion and coherence. For each aspect, the researchers used a three-grade rating rubric according to the descriptions for each grade. For the convenience of calculation, one, two and three points were assigned to the three grades, respectively. Two researchers rated all the recordings for the pretests and post-tests ($N = 126$). To avoid rating bias in both pretest and post-test, the recordings of the pretest and post-test were randomized. We calculated the interrater reliability (agreement between the two raters) for the ratings of the pretests and the post-tests. Very good interrater agreement was achieved for the ratings of the pretest (with Cohen's Kappa = 0.80, $p < 0.001$, $N = 126$) and the post-test (Cohen's Kappa = 0.85, $p < 0.001$, $N = 126$). The average scores were taken to represent students' performance in the oral narrative task.

Reading Comprehension Children's CL reading comprehension was tested with two age-appropriate passages with multiple-choice questions. This reading comprehension test was meant to gauge the students' abilities in comprehending CL written texts. The passages were selected and revised with reference to local textbook. Each passage was a story and had less than 300 Chinese characters (237 Chinese characters in Passage 1 and 280 characters in Passage 2). Most of those characters were introduced to the students in their textbooks. Each passage had five multiple-choice questions covering five different aspects, i.e. the theme, the problem and resolution, the feelings of the main character, the reference in the content and the summarization. For instance, the question asking the feelings of the main character in passage is:

How does the red fox feel when he heard the words of the old fox?

(A) Happy,
(B) Afraid,
(C) Disappointed,
(D) Angry.

Two CL teachers with at least 10 years of teaching experience in primary schools were invited to comment on the suitability of the passages and the questions. They confirmed the suitability of the content and the words in the passages for most of the Primary 3 and Primary 4 students, and the estimated completion time was about 30 min. The total scores for this reading comprehension test are 10 points. For the correct answer of each item, one point was given; otherwise, zero point was given to the item. This reading comprehension test was found to have basically acceptable internal consistency (Cronbach's $\alpha = 0.67$ for pretest, $N = 126$; Cronbach's $\alpha = 0.72$ for post-test, $N = 126$) for research purpose.

Intervention Programme

The intervention was conducted in the experimental classes, while control classes went through the usual syllabus without intervention. All the participating teachers were informed to refrain from discussing their teaching practices during the intervention period. During the one-year intervention, the research team closely collaborated with the teachers in the experimental group to revise and develop the intervention procedures: teachers provided valuable feedback on the design of teaching materials and the alignment with the textbook materials; the research team introduced the teaching focus of each lesson and made sure teachers were aware of students' varied CL proficiency and learning needs. There were in total 12 lessons in the programme. The research team provided teaching guide for all lessons. Before the lesson, the research team discussed with the teachers to clarify the lesson objectives and to ensure that the foci were clearly delivered.

The whole set of 12 teaching plans started with an introduction of narrative structures and followed by training on abstracting themes, plot setting and elaboration on details. The training focus was then shifted to the temporal, spatial and logical relationships of events in the stories and the importance of coherence.

The enhancement of the intervention on students' narrative skills can be viewed at three aspects. Firstly, tasks on narrative structure, such as events sequencing, narration from different perspectives and narration upon changing of themes, would help students in the mastering of the narrative structure. Secondly, the training foci on the enrichment of theme abstraction, plot descriptions and details elaboration would enable students to provide more meaningful oral expressions in a variety of ways. Lastly, students would learn about the logical flow of events in a storyline and the coherence of narration, such as causal relations, story plot twist, character referencing. The explicit teaching of the foci in each lesson was emphasized, so that students were clear about the learning objectives, task requirements, prior knowledge and skills, and assessment criteria.

In each lesson, teachers introduced and explained the concept words explicitly and went on with explanation of tasks, including the learning objectives and targeted skills of each task. Learning objectives and skills learnt were then reiterated after the completion of each task.

After the explicit teaching of the programme, the students were expected to demonstrate the following achievement:

1. To be able to narrate a complete and detailed story according to a set of related pictures or a video clip.
2. To be able to narrate an event that they have experienced or heard.
3. To be able to comprehend events and their relationships in passages through listening or reading.

During the process of intervention, we encouraged teachers of the control group to teach with their usual lesson plans, which normally follow the teaching guide provided by the Ministry of Education in Singapore. We have observed two lessons for each of the teachers in the control group during the intervention period (without prior notice to the teachers to avoid special preparation). Some resemblances were found in the content, e.g. teacher using "5WH1" method (by asking questions starting with "who", "when", "where", "what", "why" and "how"), to help students' understanding of a story from the textbook. But none of the lessons exhibited the explicit teaching of narrative structure as used in our intervention programme.

Data Analysis

Students' overall oral test scores, oral narrative skills ratings and reading comprehension test scores were collected before and after the intervention from both the experimental and control groups. Same tasks of reading comprehension and oral narrative skills were deployed to the students in the pre- and post-tests. For the overall oral test ratings, both schools follow the same rating rubrics with scoring range from 1 point to 10 points, but there might exist difference across the teachers who give the ratings.

We did comparison between the experimental group and the control group in students' pretest scores. No obvious difference was found between the two groups in students' overall oral language scores (Cohen's $d = 0.10$) and their oral narrative skill scores (Cohen's $d = 0.24$). But there was difference found between the two groups in their reading comprehension scores (Cohen's $d = 0.43$). Considering that students in both groups may achieve better in the second time of the same tests, and there was group difference among students' pretests, we calculated the gain-scores

Table 1 Comparisons between experimental and control groups

	Experimental group (N = 57)		Control group (N = 69)		Mean difference	Cohen's d
	Mean	SD	Mean	SD		
Overall oral language skills						
Pretest	7.88	1.35	7.74	1.31	0.14	0.10
Post-test	8.06	1.44	7.33	1.55	0.73	0.49
Gain	0.18	1.27	−0.41	1.67	0.59	0.40
Oral narrative skills						
Pretest	9.60	2.76	8.98	2.30	0.62	0.24
Post-test	10.63	2.77	8.97	2.35	1.66	0.65
Gain	1.04	3.44	−0.01	1.92	1.05	0.37
Reading comprehension						
Pretest	5.14	2.41	4.10	2.44	1.04	0.43
Post-test	6.12	2.35	4.80	2.48	1.32	0.55
Gain	0.98	2.24	0.69	2.43	0.29	0.12

of both groups on each measure. Table 1 shows the means and standard deviations of the pretest scores, post-test scores and gain-scores for both groups on each measured task. The difference between the scores of the two groups was calculated with effect sizes for each task.

In the post-tests, students in the experimental group outperformed the control group students in all the three tasks (Cohen's $d = 0.49$ for overall oral language skills; Cohen's $d = 0.65$ for oral narrative skills; Cohen's $d = 0.55$ for reading comprehension task). Descriptive statistics show that the gain-score means of the experimental group in students' overall oral language skills, oral narrative skills and reading comprehension test were slightly higher than those of the control group. In terms of effect sizes, the experimental group improved more in overall oral language skills and oral narrative skills with small to medium effect sizes when compared with the gains of the control group: Cohen's $d = 0.40$ for improvement in overall oral language skills and Cohen's $d = 0.37$ for improvement in oral narrative skills. These indicated that the intervention had observable impact in enhancing students' oral narrative skills and overall oral language skills, and the effect is small but nearly medium. Students in both groups made progress in reading comprehension skills. However, the experimental group made more progress, as shown by the gain-score mean of 0.98 for the experimental group but only 0.69 for the control group. The difference has a corresponding Cohen's $d = 0.12$, which is a trivial effect size. Thus, although there seems to be some impact of the intervention in enhancing students' reading comprehension skills, it cannot be said with certainty in view of the rather small effect size.

Given that the five different aspects in the rubric for scoring students' narrative skills require different levels of cognitive and linguistic knowledge and skills (Westerveld and Gillon 2008), we did further analysis in each of the five aspects.

Table 2 Students' improvement in the different aspects of oral narrative skills

		Pretest		Post-test		Mean difference	Cohen's d
		Mean	SD	Mean	SD		
Low performance group (N = 25)	Introduction	1.56	0.82	2.08	0.91	0.52	0.60
	Theme	1.52	0.59	1.68	0.63	0.16	0.26
	Conflict and resolution	1.76	0.66	2.08	0.76	0.32	0.45
	Conclusion	1.64	0.70	1.96	0.84	0.32	0.41
	Coherence	1.12	0.33	1.48	0.65	0.36	0.70
Average-to-good performance group (N = 32)	Introduction	2.22	0.79	2.50	0.80	0.28	0.35
	Theme	2.19	0.54	2.13	0.70	−0.06	0.10
	Conflict and resolution	2.28	0.81	2.41	0.61	0.13	0.18
	Conclusion	2.38	0.71	2.25	0.76	−0.13	0.18
	Coherence	1.66	0.83	1.97	0.74	0.31	0.39

Ratings of oral narrative skills in both pretests and post-tests from one rater were randomly taken for analyses. Based on students' overall oral language scores in the pretest (*Mean* = 7.88, *SD* = 1.35, *Median* = 8), we selected a group of students from the experimental group with overall oral language scores including and below 7 (*N* = 25) as low-performance group, and the other students were in the average-to-good performance group (*N* = 32). We calculated the effect sizes for each of the five measured aspects to better understand the possible intervention effect on different aspects. Table 2 showed the descriptive statistics and effect sizes.

It was found that students with low performance in overall language skills tended to improve more on narrative structure-related aspects, such as *introduction* (Cohen's $d = 0.60$), *conflict and resolution* (Cohen's $d = 0.45$), *conclusion* (Cohen's $d = 0.41$) and the overall *coherence* of the story (Cohen's $d = 0.70$). Their improvement in the scores of *story theme* seemed not that obvious (Cohen's $d = 0.26$). The improvement of scores in the average-to-good group can be observed, but was not that obvious as the low performance group. Trivial effect sizes were observed in the mastery of *story theme* (Cohen's $d = 0.10$), *conflict and resolution* (Cohen's $d = 0.18$) and *conclusion* (Cohen's $d = 0.18$). And small effect sizes were found in the overall *coherence* of the story (Cohen's $d = 0.39$) and the *introduction* (Cohen's $d = 0.35$).

Teachers of the experimental group also gave positive feedback on the programme. Feedback on the process and the effect of the intervention eight months into the project and at the end of one year was gathered from the teachers of the experimental group. They reflected that their students liked the learning activities and actively participated in these. As for the effect of the intervention, teachers reflected that this programme created more opportunities for students to speak in the classroom. Teachers also mentioned that because the programme trained students in story structure and story construction, it might also help them in composition writing.

Discussion and Conclusion

This article reports on an intervention study aiming to enhance Singaporean primary school students in oral language skills when they were transiting from daily conversation to more complex and abstract talks. The one-year programme comprises twelve teaching plans. Primary 3 and Primary 4 students from two schools participating in the study were trained with explicit and systematic activities for enhancing their oral narrative skills in CL. Small to medium effects were found in students' overall oral language skills and oral narrative skills. The results indicated that the intervention attained the expected outcome of enhancing students' oral narrative skills and their overall oral language skills. However, the intervention was not effective in enhancing students' reading comprehension; this seems to contradict the findings from a study on CL monolingual children (Chi 2004). A possible reason would be that the duration of the intervention is not long enough to have such an effect on students' reading comprehension skills. Another plausible explanation would be that reading comprehension skills are combined competence that was influenced by many reasons. These influential aspects may change along with children's cognitive and language development (Perfetti et al. 2005). And yet another possibility is the short test lengths of only 10 items for two passages, rendering the test not powerful enough to detect the expected group difference.

We also noticed that the intervention might help more on reinforcing the understanding in the narrative structure and coherence of events among students with relatively lower performance in overall oral language skills. For other students, the observed intervention effect was similar across the different aspects of narrative skills examined.

Limitations

The current study has a few limitations. We have only conducted the intervention in two schools. The language ability profiles of the students in these two schools may not be comparable to the national norm. Thus, the observed effect needs to be examined with reference to the students with other language ability profiles. The design of the teaching plans was closely tailored to the current textbooks for the convenience of implementation for the teachers. Possible revision should be considered in the case of curriculum change. Only immediate post-tests were conducted in the study; the long-term effect is worthy of further investigation.

References

Applebee, A. (1978). *The child's concept of story*. Chicago: University of Chicago Press.
Chi, P.-H. (2004). Story grammar abilities in children with poor reading abilities. *Bulletin of Special Education, 26*, 247–269. (in Chinese).
Crais, E. R., & Lorch, N. (1994). Oral narratives in school-age children. *Topics in Language Disorders, 14*(3), 13–28.
Goh, H. H., Liu, Y., & Zhao, C. (2008). *Spoken Mandarin competence of Chinese children from different language-speaking homes: Implications for Mandarin education*. Paper presented at the Annual Meeting of the American Educational Research Association, March 23–26, 2008. New York, NY.
Hedberg, N. L., & Westby, C. E. (1993). *Analyzing storytelling skills: Theory to practice*. Tucson, AZ: Communication Skill Builders.
Hudson, J., & Shapiro, L. (1991). From knowing into telling: The development of children's scripts, stories, and personal narratives. In A. McCabe & C. Peterson (Eds.), *Developing narrative structure* (pp. 89–136). Hillsdale, NJ: Erlbaum.
Ko, G. H., Zhang, H., & Li, J. (2012) *Testing primary school students' communicative competence through questioning*. Paper presented at the International Symposium on Chinese literacy and Chinese educational reform, December 8–11, 2012, Suzhou, China.
McCabe, A., & Rollins, P. R. (1994). Assessment of preschool narrative skills. *American Journal of Speech-Language Pathology, 3*(1), 45–56.
MOE. (2011). Nurturing active learners and proficient users: 2010 mother tongue languages review committee report, retrieved from http://www.moe.gov.sg/media/press/files/2011/mtl-review-report-2010.pdf.
Oakhill, J., & Cain, K. (2007). Issues of causality in children's reading comprehension. In D. S. McNamara (Ed.), *Reading comprehension strategies* (pp. 47–72). New York, NY: Lawrence Erlbaum Associates.
Paul, R., Hernandez, R., Taylor, L., & Johnson, K. (1996). Narrative development in late talkers early school age. *Journal of Speech, Language, and Hearing Research, 39*(6), 1295–1303.
Perfetti, C. A., Landi, N., & Oakhill, J. (2005). The acquisition of reading comprehension skill. In M. J. Snowling & C. Hulme (Eds.), *The science of reading: A handbook* (pp. 227–247). Oxford: Blackwell.
Stein, N. L., & Glenn, C. G. (1979). An analysis of story comprehension in elementary school children. In R. O. Freedle (Ed.), New directions in discourse processing, *Norwood, NJ: Ablex, 2*, 53–120.
Sun, X., & Fan, J. (2012). *Instruction on formulaic sequences to improve fluent expressing in Chinese as a second language*. Paper presented at the International symposium on Chinese literacy and Chinese educational reform, December 8–11, 2012, Suzhou, China. [In Chinese].
Westerveld, M. F. (2013). Emergent literacy performance across two languages: assessing four-year-old bilingual children. *International Journal of Bilingual Education and Bilingualism* (ahead-of-print), http://doi.org/10.1080/13670050.2013.835302, 1–18.
Westerveld, M. F., & Gillon, G. T. (2008). Oral narrative intervention for children with mixed reading disability. *Child Language Teaching and Therapy, 24*(1), 31–54.

Li Li (李丽) received Ph.D. from the Communication University of China, China. She is currently a Senior Research Associate at Singapore Centre for Chinese Language. Her academic interests include second language and bilingual acquisition, Chinese language education in bilingual context and computational linguistics. She has published a number of journal articles, chapters and paper presentations on Chinese language education in Singapore language context.

Su Yee Au (区淑仪) completed M.A. in Chinese Linguistics and Applied Linguistics at the Shanghai Jiao Tong University, China. She is currently a Research Associate at the Singapore Centre for Chinese Language. Her academic interests include Teaching Chinese Language as a second language and Mandarin Chinese in Singapore and Malaysia. Her publications include journal articles and several conference presentations.

Geok Hoon Tan (陈玉云) completed MBA at the Nanjing University, China. She is a Master Teacher of Singapore Ministry of Education and a Lecturer at Singapore Centre for Chinese Language. Her academic interests include critical thinking skills, creative thinking skills, Chinese as a second language, curriculum design and planning. She has co-developed teaching toolkits for schools and co-published journal articles and papers at conferences.

Effective Ways in Teaching Chinese Characters Without Phonetic Clues

Jiaoyang Cui, Hock Huan Goh, Chunsheng Zhao and Kay Cheng Soh

Abstract Learning Chinese characters is a challenge for most English-speaking students. Considering both the learning objective and the learners' ability, we developed the multiple teaching strategies to make learning Chinese characters more enjoyable. Based on the analysis of 947 Chinese characters without phonetic clues, we have devised some relevant teaching strategies in learning different types of Chinese characters and found that the single-component Chinese characters are best learned through the graphic method while the component-based teaching strategy is effective for teaching structural awareness, meaning, and radical position.

Chinese characters are thought to be the most challenging difficulty in learning Chinese. The challenge comes from both the feature of the character, which is a combination of shape, sound, and meaning, with no clear association between the shape and the sound, unlike the alphabetic writing system such as that of English language. On the other hand, recognizing a Chinese character does not mean one can write it correctly as the position of the components must be correct; even a misplaced dot may make a lot of difference in word meanings. Therefore, Chinese characters are believed to be the bottleneck for foreign learners to start Chinese language (Sun 2014; Hui 2015). To solve the challenge, many researchers and educators, especially

J. Cui (✉)
Peking University, Beijing Shi, China
e-mail: Jiaoyang.cui@sccl.sg

J. Cui · K. C. Soh
National University of Singapore, Singapore, Singapore
e-mail: Kaycheng.soh@sccl.sg

H. H. Goh · C. Zhao
Nanyang Technological University, Singapore, Singapore
e-mail: Hockhuan.goh@sccl.sg

in the field of teaching Chinese as a foreign language, have attempted to find effective ways to teach Chinese characters by proposing some innovative approaches (Shen 2005; Lam 2011). In this article, we focus on investigating 947[1] Chinese characters, including 174 simple characters and 773 compound characters which do not provide clues to the pronunciation of the characters.

There is living controversy on the question of how to best teach Chinese characters. Long ago, there has been debates (Lam 2011) focusing on the character-centered approaches (i.e., *Three, Hundred and Thousand; Intensive Learning of Characters; Learning by Components; Learning by Rationales; Wild Association*) and meaning-centered approach (i.e., *Extensive Learning; Using Pinyin; Listening for Learning*). The field of teaching Chinese as a foreign language, some hybrid approaches have been proposed (i.e., *Texts of a Family of Characters; Learning with Information Technology*) to engage learners to learn characters in more attractive ways so as to reduce the difficulties of Chinese character learning.

Jing-Schmidt (2007) tried to reduce the difficulties from meta-knowledge that all humans share the same conceptualization process, namely imaginary. The origin of the pictograms of Chinese characters comes from image, and the compounds with the same radicals (most are pictograms as simple character) can also be attributed to mapping the pictograms. Based on these common cognitive processes, it is necessary to reconstruct the link between images, pictograms, and relevant compounds for learners who are used to the alphabetic writing system. As for the teaching of compound characters, component-based teaching approach has been suggested, as some educators believe that the components are the important unit in recognizing and memorizing Chinese characters. Therefore, it requires more attention in designing the principles of character deconstruction and composition (Zhang 1990; Cui 1997; Taft and Chung 1999). Moreover, the strategy of "Input before output" (or recognition preceding writing) should also be noted in studies relevant to teaching Chinese as a foreign language and has been verified by experiments (Zhou 1999; Jiang 2007). In this article, we adopt the diverse teaching strategies involving both character-centered and meaning-centered approaches according to the characteristics of 947 Chinese characters.

Analysis of Chinese Characters

As mentioned above, there is no phonetic hint in the 947 Chinese characters involved in this study. This means the learners can rely on the form to infer the meaning in the absence of pronunciation clues. In order to obtain more information

---

[1] 947 Chinese characters are classified as the phonetically clueless, and this result is based on the agreement of four researchers who annotated the most frequently 1500 Chinese characters and divided them into characters with or without the component-supported phonetical clue.

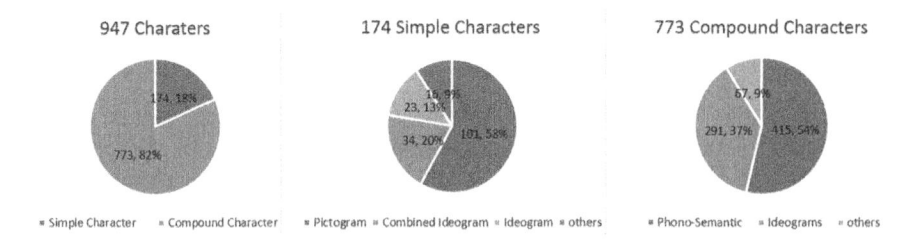

Fig. 1 Percentage of simple character and compound character

between the form and meaning, we first divide these characters into two categories according to simple and compound characters. Five subcategories are listed based on the Liu Shu Theory,[2] and the major constituting part is also calculated. In this way, we learn how many characters within which category we should pay more attention to while teaching. The distributions of the 947 Chinese characters are shown in Fig. 1.

As shown in Fig. 1, the 947 characters are first grouped into simple and compound character, and the latter is 82% of all characters. Furthermore, 58% of the pictograms makes up a major proportion in the simple character, while compound–phono-semantic character is 50% in the compound character. The pictograms derived from pictures are more attractive and accessible to primary students, considering their strong visualization ability. Moreover, those single characters are the components of other compound characters such as the compound–phono-semantic character and therefore require more attention at the beginning stage.

Besides the division by Liu Shu Theory, another perspective is to analyze the Chinese character by components. In this way, teachers are recommended to teach simple characters first and other related compound characters later; for instance, "人 ren2 'man'", "一 yi1 'one'" and "口 kou3 'mouth'" should be taught before "合 he2 'close' or 'together'". Furthermore, this approach would evoke similar leaning process for English-speaking learners as they learn a word based on the previously acquired alphabet, such as learning of the word 'dog' after knowing the three letters 'd, o, g' separately before. Under this assumption, it is necessary to analyzing the 947 Chinese characters by their components. Bearing in mind that the phono-semantic compound is the major constitution in compound characters and there are no phonetic clues for those characters, we have to focus on the link between the semantic component and the compound character. There are 303 compound characters in relation to 56 simple characters. Taking the most

---

[2]*Liu Shu* 'six writings' is the title to stand for six categories of Chinese characters, pictogram, ideogram, combined ideogram, phono-semantic compound, transfer, and phonetic loan. This classification was first described by the scholar Xu Shen in the postface of his dictionary *Shuowen Jiezi* in 100 AD to explain the structure of Chinese characters and the radicals representing the principle of Chinese character formation.

composing function 口 *kou3* 'mouth' for example, there are 40 characters composed with it and some are semantically related, like "哭 *ku1* 'cry', 嘴 *zui3* 'mouth', 吹 *chui1*, 'blow'".

Based on the Chinese Language ability of the students and the features of the 947 Chinese characters, it is essential to consider how to integrate those properties in the teaching of Chinese characters. In the following section, we propose the diverse teaching approaches with the attempt to cover those clueless characters.

Liu Shu-Based Teaching

This approach is in accordance with how the characters were created in ancient Chinese. The direct mimic of the given object's contour makes those characters more accessible and easily memorized. Taking 人 *ren2* 'man', 鸟 *niao3* 'bird', and 水 *shui3* 'water' as examples, Fig. 2 is the evolution chart of each character.

As for those single characters with historical origin meanings, we recommend two teaching materials which have been used by many teachers in classroom, one is video and the other picture book.

Videos The following two videos are strongly recommended while teaching those pictograms, *36 pictograms characters*[3] https://www.youtube.com/watch?v=RxWCAnaKjds and *Chinese Characters*[4] https://www.youtube.com/watch?v=AIeSzxDE_NI. There are 25 characters in total displayed in the two videos with vivid storytelling. This method can also be seen as one of the meaning-centered approaches, more importantly, the constituting elements are Chinese characters by themselves (Figs. 3 and 4).

Picture books Picture books are the most popular form in facilitating early reading of Chinese characters. Similar to the video storytelling, the pictograms can also constitute a storybook where each picture is a character. The following is a picture book called 过河 *'Walk across a river'*[5] with easily understandable sentences to describe the simple story of how a father and his son try to walk across a river in a rainy day. All the pictures are formed according to their pictograms, such as "山" *'mountain'*, "水" *'water'*, "雨" *'rain'* (Fig. 5).

The common features of the above material are context-based; that is, all the characters serve to constitute a whole story. Taking the students' ability into consideration, both the videos and picture books, with sounds, visuals, and even animations as stimulus, have a great attraction in engaging young learners to view

---

[3]The animation of *36 Chinese Characters* is created by the animation director, A Da, in 1983.

[4]The *Chinese Character* is one of the video series for promoting Chinese culture, which was directed by Dong Yuhui in 2011 and later became well-known after being played in New York Times Square.

[5]The picture book is created by the company, 小象汉字 *'Xiaoxiang Hanzi'*, along with relevant 120 flash cards and an animated cartoon.

Fig. 2 Pictographic character of evolution chart

Fig. 3 Image cropped from the video *36 Chinese characters*

Fig. 4 Image cropped from the video *Chinese culture characters*

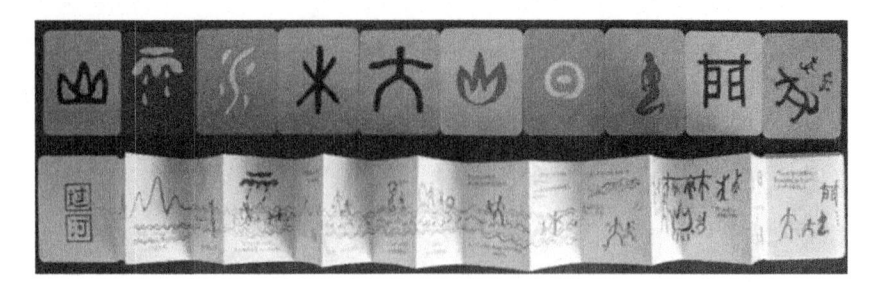

Fig. 5 Chinese character-picture book

Table 1 Pictograms appear in videos and picture book

日	山	水	木	林	鸟	艹	田	竹	马	夫	象	刀	叟	虎	弓	舍	羊	大
舟	鱼	网	燕	云	伞	石	火	龟	鹿	雨	豕	花	门	犬	子	女	月	人

more characters. There are a total of 38 pictogram characters that appear in the material. All the individual characters are shown in Table 1.

It is noticed that some characters are repetitive and good for memorizing while some appear only once and need more effort to remember. More importantly, those simple pictograms are suggested to be taught first for the beginning learners, not only because of their interesting features but also because they can be the building blocks for later learning of the compound characters.

Component-Based Teaching

It is a logical and natural continuation to teach more complex Chinese characters after the previous stage in which the students have mastered some simple characters. For the compound characters, it is essential to use the familiar parts indicating semantic clues to learn the new characters and, moreover, to reinforce the memorization of the single characters learned earlier. For instance, 木 *mu4 'wood'* is a pictogram by itself and can serve to construct other 23 Chinese characters, mostly as the semantic component, like 林 *lin2 'woods'*, 树 *shu4 'tree'*, 森 *sen1 'forest'*. Additionally, applying this approach also requires the teaching of the systematic structure of Chinese character so as to make the student better understand the components as the building blocks. The benefits of explicitly teaching the meaning and function of those components in the compound characters are as follows:

1. To uncover the systematic structure and composition of each individual Chinese character;
2. To highlight the association among characters sharing the same semantic component; and,
3. To reduce the time taken in recognizing and memorizing characters by strokes.

ICT-Assisted Teaching

Pinyin Input Teaching Hanyu Pinyin and Chinese characters with computer are of great help in recognizing Chinese characters. Even in composition lesson, we also found that students preferred typing to handwriting, due to the less effort required and nice presentation of the Chinese characters on the screen. In the field of teaching Chinese as a foreign language, some instructors also use this method as a crutch with which the beginning learners from English-speaking background more easily move up to early reading.

With the computer, Chinese characters can be displayed with shape, sound, and Pinyin; for instance, the following is the Pinyin-input module in *Automated Essay Evaluation System* developed by Singapore Centre for Chinese Language. The aim of this module is to facilitate the students' typing skills so as to enhance their writing ability. By doing so, students can also improve the recognition of Chinese characters by reading and typing with Pinyin as the helper. For example, if the students do not know the Pinyin of some Chinese characters, they just put the mouse to those characters and the correct forms will be shown immediately (Fig. 6).

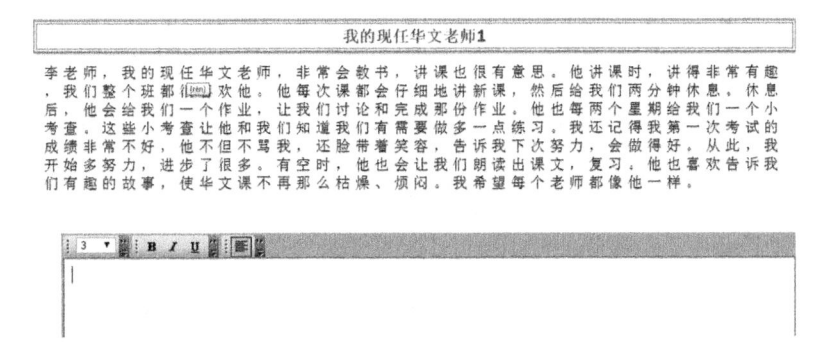

Fig. 6 Pinyin-input typing practice

Conclusions

Considering the sequence of teaching Chinese character, it is suggested to arrange the single characters with less strokes before moving on to the more complex multi-component characters. This can be designed as the complementary exercise to the textbooks practice where the Chinese characters are organized according to the topic, not by the character density.

On the basis of previous studies about the teaching of Chinese characters and the analysis of the 947 Chinese characters, we propose the hybrid teaching approaches including Liu Shu-based method, Component-based method, and ICT-assisted method. Common properties or some principles of these approaches are: (1) simple characters precede compound characters; (2) learning characters in concrete text; (3) using ICT to reinforce the connection among shape, sound, and meaning; and (4) creating more enjoyable atmosphere in leaning Chinese characters. However, experimental studies are needed to verify the proposed teaching approaches; and we will conduct such studies in the near future.

Appendix

Radical	Characters
口	只, 后, 名, 句, 哥, 各, 周, 号, 商, 善, 哭, 嘴, 同, 员, 合, 向, 喜, 品, 告, 司, 命, 古, 台, 器, 吉, 叫, 右, 叶, 君, 呆, 启, 哇, 喊, 含, 唐, 吹, 咖, 唉, 呈, 叹,
木	果, 李, 朵, 某, 条, 杀, 杰, 梁, 林, 检, 梦, 树, 森, 标, 查, 杨, 权, 楚, 杂, 棒, 柔, 染, 槪,
土	在, 塞, 场, 坚, 块, 培, 地, 坐, 坡, 环, 坏, 圣, 墙, 填, 埃, 塑, 域, 坛,
月	有, 朋, 能, 脚, 脑, 服, 肯, 朝, 肥, 胡, 股, 脱, 胖,
日	是, 普, 易, 旦, 旧, 明, 早, 时, 星, 春, 暴, 显, 暗,
贝	赛, 质, 责, 贵, 赢, 负, 赞, 贴, 赚, 赖, 赌, 贤,
心	思, 念, 急, 恩, 意, 感, 总, 惠, 悉, 恶, 患, 恋,
女	姓, 好, 如, 她, 始, 委, 妻, 妇, 威, 娱, 娃,
人	以, 会, 介, 今, 金, 令, 从, 余, 众,
竹	第, 算, 策, 签, 等, 答, 筑, 籍, 篮,
八	公, 共, 美, 兴, 六, 具, 兵, 典,
大	天, 奥, 奇, 套, 夺, 奖, 奏, 奋,
门	闻, 间, 闹, 闪, 闲, 闭, 阅,
又	发, 叔, 反, 爱, 取, 双, 变,
力	劳, 加, 动, 助, 务, 劝, 勤,
车	轻, 辑, 输, 辉, 软, 载,
目	看, 真, 直, 着, 相, 眼,
厂	压, 原, 厚, 厨, 厉, 厌,
十	单, 克, 南, 千, 博, 协,

(continued)

(continued)

Radical	Characters
子	学, 季, 存, 孙, 孔,
立	竟, 竞, 章, 童, 端,
田	画, 番, 留, 男, 略,
工	项, 差, 巧, 左,
火	烦, 灵, 灰, 灾,
雨	需, 雪, 雷, 霞,
一	表, 丽, 丝, 严,
王	珍, 班, 瑞,
虫	虽, 蛋, 蛇,
干	年, 并, 幸,
手	拜, 拿, 拳,
方	族, 施, 旅,
儿	光, 先, 兄,
米	类, 粗,
小	尚, 尝,
几	凭, 凯,
止	步, 武,
鸟	鸡, 鸣,
户	所, 扇,
甘	甚, 甜,
二	井, 些,
示	票, 禁,

References

Cui, Y. H. (1997). Hanzi Bujian he Duiwaihanyu Jiaoxue. *Applied Linguistics, 3*, 51–56.
Hui, L. (2015). *Teaching Chinese literacy in the early years* (1st ed.). Abingdon: Routledge.
Jiang, X. (2007). An experimental study on the effect of the method of 'Teaching the learners to recognize characters more than writing'. *Shijie Hanyu Jiaoxue, 2*, 91–97.
Jing-Schmidt, Z. (2007). Cognitive foundations of the Chinese writing system and their pedagogical implications. *Proceedings of the Cognition, Learning and Teaching of Chinese Characters*, 121–134.
Lam, H. C. (2011). A critical analysis of the various ways of teaching Chinese characters. *Electronic Journal of Foreign Language Teaching, 8*(1), 57–70.
Shen, H. H. (2005). An investigation of Chinese-character learning strategies among non-native speakers of Chinese. *System, 33*(1), 49–68.
Sun, M. (2014). Li-Shu based approach of teaching Chinese character in teaching Chinese as a second language. *Southeast Review of Asian Studies*, 37–57.
Taft, M., & Chung, K. (1999). Using radicals in teaching Chinese characters to second language learners. *Psychologia, 42*(4), 243–251.

Zhang, W. X. (1990). Cong Hanzi Bujian dao Hanzi Jiegou—Tan Duiwaihanzi Jiaoxue. *Shijie Hanyu Jiaoxue, 2,* 112–120.

Zhou, X. B. (1999). Duiwai Hanzi Jiaoxuezhong Duoxiang Fenliu, Jiaoji Lingxian de Yuanze. *Proceedings of Chinese Characters and Characters Teaching,* 237–245.

Websites

http://www.zdic.net/z/15/js/4F11.htm.
http://www.vividict.com/WordInfo.aspx?id=1492.

Jiaoyang Cui (崔娇阳) completed M.A. in Chinese Language and Literature at the Peking University, China, and National University of Singapore, Singapore. She is currently a Research Associate at the Singapore Centre for Chinese Language. Her academic interests include modern Chinese grammar, teaching Chinese as a foreign language, and computer-assisted language learning. She has published journal articles and conference presentations and, currently, is working on a project of Automated Essay Evaluation System.

Hock Huan Goh (吴福焕) received Ph.D. from Nanyang Technological University, Singapore. He is Chair of Research and Ethics Committee and Research Scientist at Singapore Centre for Chinese Language. His academic interests include Chinese language teaching in multi-/bilingual context, child Mandarin competence, curriculum evaluation, and corpus-based application development. He has compiled and co-compiled a few frequency dictionaries of Singapore Chinese and published more than 10 co-authored articles, and over 20 paper presentations. He has recently published a book on Mandarin competence of Singaporean Chinese preschoolers.

Chunsheng Zhao (赵春生) completed M.A. in Applied Linguistics at Nanyang Technological University, Singapore. He is currently a Research Associate at the Singapore Centre for Chinese Language. His academic interests include teaching of Chinese language as a second language, corpus-based language teaching, and Chinese etymology. He has co-compiled three frequency dictionaries of Singapore Chinese words and syntaxes and published journal articles.

Kay Cheng Soh (苏启祯) received Ph.D. from National University of Singapore, Singapore. He is currently Research Consultant at the Singapore Centre for Chinese Language. His academic interests include child bilingualism, creativity, world university rankings, and international achievement comparisons. His publications include books on the psychology of learning Chinese Language and various aspects of education.

Scaffolding Instruction of Chinese Essay Writing with Assessment as Learning

Cheng Gong, Chee Lay Tan and Chee Kuen Chin

Abstract This article shares ideas of how to teach writing through activities based on constructivism and scaffolding. The findings suggested that there is little relation between teacher's feedback and students' writing improvement. Instead, the relation is found between the numbers of communication seeking feedback the students send out.

Since educational reforms took place in 1984, the social linguistic environment in Singapore has been undergoing rapid transformation. The transformation is clearly represented by the percentage figure of ethnic Chinese students whose home language is English, which rose from 28% in 1991 to 59% in 2010 (MOE 2011). Ethnic Chinese Singaporean students' linguistic capability in the Chinese language has been on the decline; most of these students find it a challenge to learn Chinese, especially where the acquisition of writing skills is concerned (Liang 2000; 沈 2008).

Against this socio-linguistic background, there are three conflicts in the teaching of writing.

In the Ministry of Education Chinese Language Syllabus 2011 (MOE 2011), composition writing allocated a higher percentage in exams now than in previous years. Except for Foundation Chinese Language (FCL) and Chinese Language B (CLB) curriculum (these are two courses provided for lower achievers), the percentage for writing in Chinese courses is either 30% (Normal Academic and Express) or even 45% (Higher Chinese). The differentiated requirements show that

---

C. Gong (✉) · C. L. Tan · C. K. Chin
Singapore Centre for Chinese Language, Nanyang Technological
University, Singapore, Singapore
e-mail: Cheng.gong@sccl.sg

C. L. Tan
e-mail: Cheelay.tan@sccl.sg

C. K. Chin
e-mail: Cheekuen.chin@sccl.sg

© Springer Nature Singapore Pte Ltd. 2018
K. C. Soh (ed.), *Teaching Chinese Language in Singapore*,
https://doi.org/10.1007/978-981-10-8860-5_9

writing is not only a compulsory language skill required by MOE, but also extremely important in examinations. On one hand, as mentioned before, the students find it challenging to learn Chinese writing; on the other hand, the curricula set higher requirements in the exams. This is the first conflict.

For many students, composition writing is a challenge. It is especially difficult for many Singaporean students since Chinese is neither the medium of instruction in schools nor the home language. When they were required to write a Chinese composition, they always complained that they had no idea of *what to write and how to write*. The teachers, however, were also reported to have difficulties in teaching compositions. The teachers we interviewed showed concerns on how to teach writing confidently and systematically. They said they did not have a systematic plan on how to teach writing. Instead, they only introduced the writing skills in the reading classes. This makes the teaching of writing skill a by-product of reading.

Nowadays, people communicate using a multitude of methods, such as messaging and emails, rather than conversing in person or via telephones. This requires better written communicative skills among our students, and more effective teaching of writing by our teachers. However, in many places, writing is usually taught by inexperienced and under-prepared teachers (Johns 2009, cited in Lee 2013). Although the skill of writing has always been emphasized, the teaching of writing has received little attention in most teacher education programs (Hall and Grisham-Brown 2011). Hence, the second conflict is: the students have no idea what and how to write, while the teachers mostly just teach them a limited number of writing tips, rather than systematic ways of thinking and writing.

The third conflict comes from the writing process. Students are always trained to write timed essays in class so that they can finish writing in real exams. As a result, they do not have enough chances to improve their writing skills by learning how to revise their writings according to comments and suggestions given by their peers and teachers. When the teachers mark the compositions, they mainly focus on students' language use rather than the content. Teacher's feedback is neither specific nor useful to the students because they may not understand the feedback or may not know how to follow up accordingly. As a result, even if the teachers spent much time on giving feedback, most of the suggestions turned out to be unread or neglected and the same kinds of mistakes were repeated in the students' writings. This problem may be due to the quality of the teachers' feedback or from the students' lack of opportunities and knowledge to revise.

Considering the three conflicts that the students and teachers encounter, we developed an online interactive process writing course. This course combines in-class and out-of-class learning, focusing more on facilitating the students to give feedback to their peers and to do self-revision according to the comments received. Writing assessment, which is to comment on the drafts and to revise according to the rubrics and comments, is the key to the course design.

For this study, the main research questions are as follows:

Question 1: Is the online process writing course effective in enhancing students' performance in narrative essay writing?
Question 2: Do the revision remarks or comments received and generated in the writing process contribute to students' performance?

Scaffolding

Scaffolding instruction as a teaching strategy originates from Lev Vygotsky's sociocultural theory and his concept of the zone of proximal development (ZPD).

The zone of proximal development (ZPD) refers to *"the distance between the actual developmental level as determined by independent problem solving and the level of potential development as determined through problem solving under adult guidance, or in collaboration with more capable peers"* (Vygotsky 1978: 86).

In other words, the zone of proximal development is "the distance between what children can do by themselves and the next learning that they can be helped to achieve with competent assistance" (Raymond 2000). Vygotsky's belief suggests that when a student is in the ZPD doing some tasks, providing appropriate assistance will provide an important boost for the student to achieve the task. This appropriate assistance was mentioned in many literature as "scaffolding instruction." The term "scaffolding" was introduced by Wood et al. (1976). They emphasized that when the scaffolding was appropriately provided, the elements of the task which were initially somewhat beyond the learner's capacity, became within his range of competence. In scaffolding instruction, a more knowledgeable other, be it the teacher or the peer, provides scaffold or support to facilitate the learner's development and performance. Individualized support based on the learner's ZPD can be provided by the scaffolding teaching strategy (Chang et al. 2002). The more capable other provides the scaffold/assistance so that the learner can accomplish the task provided in scaffolding instruction that he or she could otherwise not complete alone, thus helping the learner through the ZPD (Bransford et al. 2000; Olson & Platt 2000).

Information Process Theory and Cognitive Load Theory are also useful in further explaining the necessity of scaffolding instruction. Information Process Theory is a general theory of human cognition. The information processing model consists of three functions: sensory memory, working memory (which significantly overlaps with short-term memory), and long-term memory. Miller (1956) presented the idea that our short-term memory, or working memory, is limited in the number of chunks it can contain simultaneously. This concept of chunking and the limited capacity of short-term memory became a basic element of all subsequent theories of memory. Developed from Information Process Theory, Cognitive Load Theory (CLT) (Sweller 1988, 1999) suggests that learners can absorb and retain information effectively only if the information is provided in such a way that it does not overload their mental capacity. The more information that is delivered at once, the more likely that the students will not actually learn nor call upon the information for later use. John Sweller describes the human cognitive architecture and the need to apply sound instructional design principles based on our knowledge of the brain and memory. It is a major theory providing a framework for investigations into cognitive processes and instructional design because learning happens best under conditions that are aligned with human cognitive architecture (Sweller et al. 1998; Paas et al. 2003, 2004).

Cognitive Load Theory states that the content of long-term memory is a series of sophisticated structures, known as schemas that enable us to perceive, think, and solve problems. They are the cognitive structures that form our knowledge base. Schema directly affects the manner in which information is synthesized in working memory or short-term memory (Sweller 1988). Cognitive Load Theory suggests that learning requires a change in the schematic structures of long-term memory and is demonstrated by performance progress. This performance progress only happens when the learners become increasingly familiar with the cognitive processes associated with the learning material so that it can be handled more efficiently by working memory (Sweller 1988, 1999).

Information contained in instructional material must first be processed by working memory. Hence, from an instructional perspective, in order to help schema acquisition to occur, instruction should be designed to reduce working memory load. Especially when teaching cognitively complex or technically challenging materials, Cognitive Load Theory is concerned with techniques for reducing working memory load in order to facilitate the changes in long-term memory associated with schema acquisition.

Writing is a complex process which involves a lot of cognitive and meta-cognitive activities (Murray 1972). To a large extent, a written product is "the outcome of a set of complicated cognitive operations" (Hedge 2011: 303) that involves planning, drafting, revising, and editing. In the conventional product-oriented writing process, the generation, formulation, and development of ideas seem to be ignored throughout the whole writing process (Zamel 1982). Since Chinese is not the medium of instruction in schools, for Singapore students whose home language is not Chinese, writing is very challenging both cognitively and linguistically. The writing process is recursive in nature whereby revision and writing are integrated, and initial ideas get extended and refined (Zamel 1982). Hence, teachers should guide learners in the writing process in a recursive, interactive, and potentially simultaneous way (Hyland 2003). With teachers' and peers' assistance, the students are more likely to reduce the pressure on their working memory, which in turn will facilitate their short-term memory and further to internalize information into long-term memory.

Assessment as Learning

Three prepositions are sometimes used to relate assessment and learning (Earl 2003). Assessment *of* learning refers to the tradition of judging performance and outcomes. Assessment *for* learning emphasizes the importance of formative feedback during learning process. And, assessment *as* learning expresses that using assessment as a form of learning can develop students' capacity to be self-aware and self-monitoring above and beyond the essential requirements (Davies et al. 2011).

For a long time, assessment has been done after the teaching and learning process. Stiggins (2002) warns that if we wish to maximize student achievement, we must pay far greater attention to the improvement of *summative assessment of learning*. He further stated that the students benefited from assessment *for* learning in several critical ways: They become more confident learners because they get to watch themselves succeeding; and they come to understand what it means to be in charge of their own learning: to monitor their own success and make decisions that bring greater success. In this sense, as Stiggins (2002) suggested, we must balance assessments *of* learning and assessment *for* learning. About assessment *as* learning, Earl and Katz (2006: 54) emphasized that what is assessed is *"each student's thinking about his or her learning, what strategies he or she uses to support or challenge that learning, and the mechanisms he or she uses to adjust and advance his or her learning."*

While assessment *as* learning is the ultimate goal (Earl 2003), the literature on how to achieve this in practice is scarce (Davies et al. 2011). Hatton and Smith (1995) claimed that it can be done through a hierarchy of self-assessment tasks which act as scaffolding for the learner across a curriculum that supports assessment *as le*arning. Marcangelo et al. (2010) argued that achievement of these tasks initially involves the development of strategies for planning, monitoring, checking, and self-testing as well as abilities to analyze what one knows, what one needs to know, and matching these together to achieve the task in hand. To achieve these skills, Davies et al. (2011) suggested the student be exposed to opportunities to practice these skills within different contexts, to self-assess their effectiveness in terms of outcomes achieved, and to receive feedback on their efforts in self-assessment. Kirkwood and Price (2008) believed that the design of assessment influences how the learning content is studied and appropriately designed assessment can change students' approaches to learning.

This article shares the strategies and mechanisms of a hierarchical three-stage scaffolding instruction using scaffolding and assessment *as* learning, and how it helped to construct the students' knowledge and concept of writing.

Method

Students

There were 60 secondary one students who took Express Chinese course in a mainstream school, forming an experimental class ($N = 32$) and a control class ($N = 28$). In the experimental class, there were 15 girls and 17 boys; in the control class, there were 11 girls and 17 boys. They are students in the Express Stream (Chinese course in Singapore is classified into five sub-courses as Foundation Chinese, Chinese Language B Syllabus, Chinese Language (Normal Academic), Chinese Language (Express) and Higher Chinese). Foundation Chinese, Chinese Language B Syllabus, and Chinese Language (Normal Academic) are courses offered for lower achievers, while Higher Chinese is the course offered for higher achievers. Students in the Express Steam make up the majority of the students' population in a neighborhood school.

Procedure

There were five rounds of recursive writing activities for the experimental class in this two-year study, and each activity lasted for about 8 weeks. These five rounds of writing activities were the intervention part. Before and after the intervention, we did the pre-test and post-test. In the control class, the teacher went about her normal teaching but arranged for her students to sit for the same pre-test and post-test.

Each writing activity of the experimental class had nine major steps: pre-writing planning, self-directed learning of the writing skills from online, in-class quiz, in-class writing skill instructions, first draft writing, peer and teacher feedback, in-class teacher review, second draft writing, and student reflection. Before all the activities, there was an orientation training about the writing rubrics. Hence, altogether there were ten steps for the writing activity. In each writing activity, the students wrote the first draft and then did revision and editing, with the feedback from their teachers and peers. After the writing tasks, the students did a reflection. In every step, they needed to write according to the rubrics. Although the core skill that the students need to learn is to assess a piece of writing using the writing rubrics, the teachers should not just throw the rubrics to them and ask them to follow. Without sufficient and appropriate demonstration and guidance, by no means can the students know how to do it. The teacher should divide the learning contents up into smaller "bite-sized" lessons and tasks and encourage the students to accomplish one simpler task before moving on to a harder one. Some examples of gradual and small feasible tasks are: what are the rubrics, how to comment with reference to the rubrics, what is considered good writing, how to transform poor writing into a good one, perform a peer review with reference to the rubrics.

In this process, the teachers "taught" quite little, giving more ownership to the students. The learning materials were on the wiki platform. Students did group presentations in class and taught one another in small groups after class and online. Students assessed their peers' writing and gave feedbacks online, after which they revised their writings on their own. The core part of this project is self-directed learning through the teaching materials and self-editing of the writings according to peer and teacher reviews, and most tasks were completed online.

How did we enable the students to do peer review? How could they comment on each other's writing if they did not know what and how to write? This is the highlight that we would like to share in this paper: the three-stage scaffolding instruction.

By simultaneously considering the structure of the learning content and the cognitive architecture that allows learners to process that content, we have been able to generate a unique instructional design and procedures scaffolding. We call this a three-stage LPA scaffolding. LPA stands for the three stages: learning, practice, and application. The stages and learning goals of each stage are displayed in Table 1.

In order to accomplish the learning goals for these three stages, ten steps of activities must be arranged accordingly. The ten steps are listed in Table 2. At stage one, the learning stage, the students got to learn the form and content of the rubrics. Steps 1–3 belong to this stage. In this stage, the teacher provided a model by demonstrating how students should assess their peer's work and give feedback, using the structure of the writing rubrics and peer assessment guiding questions. The writing rubrics consist of three dimensions: content, organization, and language. Under these three dimensions, ten items of writing, such as theme, choice of materials, plot, emotions, consistency, cohesion, deployment, vocabulary, grammar, and rhetoric techniques were enlisted and described.

Steps 4–9 belong to stage 2, the practice stage. This stage strengthens what the students have learned in stage 1 by providing them more chances to practice. Step 4–6 formed an activity called "Tell me why this is a piece of good writing," and steps 7–9 formed an activity called "Come, let Dr. Woodpecker treat you." These activities guide the students in forming standards firstly on how to appreciate good writing, how to break down/deconstruct texts and then on how to transform poor writings into good ones. All the activities were arranged for students to carry out in

Table 1 Three-stage LPA scaffolding and the corresponding learning goals

Stage	Students' learning goals
1. Learning	Familiarize with the writing rubrics
	Learn how to use the writing rubrics by modelling the examples
2. Practice	Analyze a good piece of writing using the rubrics
	Analyze a piece of poor writing and improve it using the rubrics
3. Application	Comment on peer writings using the rubrics
	Revise own writings using the rubrics

Table 2 Ten steps of activities and the materials used

Steps	Activities	Teaching materials used
Stage 1: Learning		
1	Orientation training to make the students familiarize with the rubrics	Writing rubrics, writing rubrics checklist
2	Group presentation	Same as above
3	Teacher review and demo	A piece of model comments
Stage 2: Practice		
4	Group preparation	A piece of model writing, writing rubrics, guiding questions
5	Group presentation	Same as above
6	Teacher review and demo	Analysis of the model writing
7	Group preparation	A piece of poor writing, writing rubrics, guiding questions
8	Group presentation	Same as above
9	Teacher review and demo	Analysis of the poor writing, improved version of the poor writing
Stage 3: Application		
10	Application of the rubrics	Recursive use of the above mentioned materials as needed

groups to facilitate discussion and collaborative learning. After some preparations, the students did class presentations using the guiding tasks and questions. By group collaborations and presentations, they got to understand how a writing rubrics work on a piece of writing. With this kind of "comprehensible output" activities, the students learned to judge texts critically. They also had the chance to crystallize and consolidate vague ideas of assessment into specific utterances. Teachers were no longer sole knowledge providers but activity guide and supervisors. They only stepped in at steps 3, 6, and 9 to make sure that the students were doing right, and they recapitulated and emphasized what was to be internalized.

Step 10 is actually not a single step job as it shows. However, it requires repeating and recursive works by the students to practice the rubrics on the writings of their peers and their own.

Results

To ascertain whether the experimental and comparison classes were equivalent, we run the independent t test on the pre-test writing scores. As shown in Table 3, there is a mean difference of -2.58 ($t = -1.30$, d.f. 58, $p > 0.05$, two-tailed) indicating that the two classes were equivalent although the experimental class scored somewhat lower than did the comparison class. The Cohen's $d = -0.34$ indicates a small effect size which is non-trivial and deserves some attention.

Table 3 Mean comparisons on writing scores

	Experimental group ($N = 32$)		Comparison group ($N = 28$)		Mean differences	t-value	Cohen's d
	Mean	SD	Mean	SD			
Pre-test	57.44	8.89	60.02	5.96	−2.58	−1.30	−0.34
Post-test	61.17	8.27	58.11	5.40	3.06	1.67	0.44
Gain	3.73	7.69	−1.91	5.10	5.64	3.29	0.86

Note (1) Effect size Cohen's d was calculated using the Web-based effect size calculator of the University of Colorado (http://www.uccs.edu/~lbecker/) which uses the pooled standard deviation as the denominator. For gain scores, SD = $\sqrt{(S1^2 + S2^2 - 2 * S1 * S2 * 0.6)}$, assuming a $r = 0.6$ between the pre-test and post-test scores

In the post-test, the experimental class scored higher than did the comparison class, with a mean difference of 3.06 ($t = 1.67$, d.f. 58. $p < 0.05$, two-tailed). The corresponding Cohen's $d = 0.44$ indicates a small but near medium effect size.

As noted previously, the initial difference favoring the comparison class is not so small that it can be totally dismissed. To offset this, a gain score analysis was attempted. As can be seen in Table 3, the experimental class has improved by 3.73 from the pre-test to the post-test, whereas the comparison class has in fact deteriorated by −1.91. This suggests that, by comparison, the experimental group has gained by 5.64 ($t = 3.29$, d.f. 58, $p < 0.05$, two-tailed) after the intervention. The corresponding Cohen's $d = 0.86$ indicates a large effect size. This leads to an affirmative answer to the first research question: The wiki-based process writing on Chinese narrative essay was effective for lower secondary school CSL students in enhancing their performance.

Effect size is typically used at the conclusion of a research project to ascertain its success or lack thereof (Soh 2010). The obtained Cohen's $d = 0.86$ for the gain scores indicates a large effect size. This compares very favorably with the average effect size of Cohen's $d = 0.40$ recommended by Hattie (1999, 2009) as a benchmark for teaching experiments. Hattie's (2009) study, with a large number of more than 800 meta-analyses covering 165,258 studies, helps us look at the average effect size of similar experiments in the same field. This helps us examine the value of the effect size of our own project in a more objective and comparative perspective without focusing solely on a single value of one experiment.

Correlation

To answer the second research question on whether revision remarks or comments received and generated in the writing process contribute to students' overall performance, Pearson's correlation coefficients between the students' individual scores

Table 4 Correlation coefficients

	Pearson's r
Correlation of remarks only the students gave to their peers with post-test	0.69*
Correlation of all the remarks that the students received from their peers and teachers and gave with post-test	0.49*
Correlation of all the remarks that the students received from their peers and gave with post-test	0.48*
Correlation of remarks the students received only from their teachers with post-test	0.20
Correlation of remarks the students received only from their peers with post-test	0.07
Correlation of remarks the students received from both their teachers and peers with post-test	0.11

Note Asterisked coefficients are statistically significant ($p < 0.05$, d.f. 58, two-tailed)

and the number of remarks that the students gave and received were calculated. The resultant correlation coefficients are displayed in Table 4.

As can be seen from Table 4, three of the six correlation coefficients are statistically significant. The largest $r = 0.69$ ($p < 0.05$, d.f. 58, two-tailed) goes to remarks the students gave to their peers with post-test. This suggests the effectiveness of involving the students in peer review where they had to be able to evaluate their own works first. This is followed by two moderate correlation coefficients of $r = 0.49$ and $r = 0.48$ ($p < 0.05$, d.f. 58, two-tailed) when the students both received and gave comments, where the involvement of teachers made very little difference. The statistically significant correlation coefficients echo some researches that address the effectiveness of peer review for writing (Berg 1999; Rollinson 2005; Villamil and De Guerrero 1998), the effectiveness of teacher review (Zhang 1995; Connor & Asenavage 1994; Paulus 1999), and the combined effectiveness of both teacher review and peer review (Tsui and Ng 2000). It is of interest to note that students benefited the most when they were required to give remarks to their peers' writing using the rubrics; this corroborates with Lundstrom and Baker's (2009) findings.

Conclusion

This study can be considered successful in helping students improve their writing performance. The students get to understand the writing rubrics, assess, and modify their essays through a set of scaffolding activities. *Assessment as learning* played an important role in this course design. We attribute the improvement to the skills and abilities acquired during the five process writing activities, especially the peer review where they mutually engaged with each other in a coordinated effort to raise questions and solve problems together. The three-stage scaffolding teaching activities and materials enable the students and guide them to make feedbacks. Peer review encourages critical reasoning as the students need to consider the validity of the suggestions and make decisions on whether and how to use them.

When the students' critical reasoning ability has been enhanced, it will in turn help students with their writing because writing is an act of discovering meaning. A willingness to engage with students' assertions is crucial, and response is a central means to initiate and guide ideas (Straub 2000). Hence, teachers could focus more on the ideas that our students produce, rather than dwelling on the formal errors (Hyland 1990; Murray 1985). This transformation will liberate the teachers from the time and frustration in picking out every formal error within the students' writings, while maintaining work-life balance.

The finding that the highest relevance with the post-test is the number of feedback sent out, and not the number received, suggested the need to encourage students to generate more feedbacks using the writing rubrics, not necessarily for inviting responses but as a practice in writing with a purpose. James Howell's quote "We learn by teaching" best fits the situation here as the students learn more when they try to "teach" their peers by giving comments and suggestions. When the students need to teach others, it shows that their leaning becomes much more effective.

It is demonstrated in this project that if the teachers incorporated *assessment as learning* and *assessment for learning* into the teaching of writing, *assessment of learning* will likely improve. As the adage goes, *"process is more important than outcome."* When the outcome becomes problematic, the part that we should handle is not the outcome but the process. Our students learn far less from product writing and much more from process writing because the experience of using assessment as a form of learning enables them to construct and internalize the rubrics for writing, which will eventually enable them to see writing from a higher level of perspective.

In the modern days, the teachers cannot teach all that the students need in class. What our students need is the ability for self-directed learning and the desire and ownership for life-long learning. When the teachers step down from the teaching platform, they give more authorities to the students who are supposed to be the real owner of their learning. When the teachers teach LESS, effective learning activities makes the students learn MORE. It requires more profound literacy in teaching writing, better classroom orchestration and activity enactment on the teachers. In order to teach LESS, the teachers need to internalize all the teaching materials and chose wisely what to teach. During the group presentation steps, the teachers need to improvise prompt assessment and remark on the spot, which also requires a lot of teaching skills. This gives the teachers many opportunities and space for their personal professional development.

References

Berg, E. C. (1999). The effects of trained peer response on ESL students' revision types and writing quality. *Journal of Second Language Writing, 8*(3), 215–241.

Bransford, J., Brown, A., & Cocking, R. (2000). *How People Learn: Brain, Mind, and Experience & School.* Washington, DC: National Academy Press.

Chang, K., Sung, Y., & Chen, I. (2002). The effect of concept mapping to enhance text comprehension and summarization. *The Journal of Experimental Education, 71*(1), 5–23.

Connor, U., & Asenavage, K. (1994). Peer response groups in ESL writing classes: How much impact on revision? *Journal of Second Language Writing, 3*(3), 257–276.

Davies, A., Pantzopoulos, K., & Gray, K. (2011). Emphasising assessment 'as' learning by assessing wiki writing assignments collaboratively and publicly online. *Australasian Journal of Educational Technology, 27*(5), 798–812.

Earl, L. (2003). Assessment of learning, for learning and as learning. In *Assessment as learning: Using classroom assessment to maximise student learning.* Thousand oaks, CA: Corwin Press.

Earl, L., & Katz, S. (2006). Rethinking classroom assessment with purpose in mind. Assessment for learning, assessment as learning, assessment of learning. In *Western and Northern Canadian Protocol for Collaboration in Education (WNCP).* Retrieved from https://www.wncp.ca/media/40539/rethink.pdf on March 10, 2015.

Hall, A. H., & Grisham-Brown, J. (2011). Writing development over time: Examining preservice teachers' attitudes and beliefs about writing. *Journal of Early Childhood Teacher Education, 32,* 148–158.

Hattie, J. (1999). *Influence on student learning. Professor of Education Inauguarl Lecture.* New Zealand: University of Auckland.

Hattie, J. (2009). *Visible learning: A synthesis of over 800 meta-analyses relating to achievement.* London, England: Routledge.

Hatton, N., & Smith, D. (1995). Reflection in teacher education: Towards definition and implementation. *Teaching and Teacher Education, 11*(1), 33–49.

Hedge, T. (2011). *Teaching and learning in the language classroom.* Oxford: Oxford University Press.

Hyland, K. (1990). Providing productive feedback. *ELT Journal, 44*(4), 279–285.

Hyland, K. (2003). *Second language writing.* New York: Cambridge University Press.

Johns, A. (2009). *The future of second language instruction.* Paper presented at the symposium on second language writing.

Kirkwood, A., & Price, L. (2008). Assessment and student learning: A fundamental relationship and the role of information and communication technologies. *Open Learning: The Journal of Open and Distance Learning, 23*(1), 5–16.

Lee, I. (2013). Becoming a writing teacher: Using "identity" as an analytic lens to understand EFL writing teachers' development. *Journal of Second Language Writing, 22,* 330–345.

Liang, R. L. (2000). The relationship between Singapore students' Chinese vocabulary and reading ability with their attitudes and Chinese learning achievement. In H. G. Zhang (Ed.), *New trends in teaching Chinese* (pp. 38–52). ILEC: Hong Kong.

Lundstrom, K., & Baker, W. (2009). To give is better than to receive: The benefits of peer review to the reviewer's own writing. *Journal of Second Language Writing, 18,* 30–43.

Marcangelo, C., Cartney, P., & Barnes, C. (2010). The opportunities and challenges of self, peer and group assessment. In M. Hammick & C. Reid (Eds.), *Contemporary issues in assessment in health sciences and practice education.* (pp. 50–69). (Higher Education Academy Assessment Occasional Papers). York: UK Higher Education Academy.

Miller, G. A. (1956). The magical number seven, plus or minus two: Some limits on our capacity for processing information. *Psychological Review, 63,* 81–97.

Ministry of Education. (2011). *Chinese language syllabus 2011, Curriculum planning and development division.* Singapore: Ministry of Education.

Mother Tongue Languages Review Committee. (2011). *Nurturing active learners and proficient users, mother tongue languages review committee report*. Singapore: MOE. Retrieved from http://www.moe.gov.sg/media/press/files/2011/mtl-review-report-2010.pdf on March 7, 2014.
Murray, D. (1972). Teach writing as a process not product. In R. Graves (Ed.), *Rhetoric and composition: A sourcebook for teachers and writers* (pp. 89–92). Upper Montclair, NJ: Boynton/Cook.
Murray, D. (1985). *A writer teaches writing* (2nd ed.). Boston: Houghton Mifflin.
Olson, J., & Platt, J. (2000). *The instructional cycle. Teaching children and adolescents with special needs* (pp. 170–197). Upper Saddle River, NJ: Prentice-Hall, Inc.
Paas, F., Renkl, A., & Sweller, J. (2003). Cognitive load theory and instructional design: Recent developments. *Educational psychologist, 38*(1), 1–4.
Paas, F., Renkl, A., & Sweller, J. (2004). Cognitive load theory: Instructional implications of the interaction between information structures and cognitive architecture. *Instructional Science, 32*(1), 1–8.
Palincsar, A., & Brown, A. (1984). Reciprocal teaching of comprehension-fostering and comprehension-monitoring activities. *Cognition and Instruction, 1*(2), 117–175.
Paulus, T. M. (1999). The effect of peer and teacher feedback on student writing. *Journal of Second Language Writing, 8*(3), 265–289.
Raymond, E. (2000). *Cognitive characteristics. Learners with mild disabilities* (pp. 169–201). Needham Heights, MA: Allyn & Bacon, A Pearson Education Company.
Rollinson, P. (2005). Using peer feedback in the ESL writing class. *ELT Journal, 59*(1), 23–30.
Soh, K. C. (2010). What are the chances of success for my project? and, what if it was already done? Using Meta-Analyzed Effect Sizes to Inform Project Decision-Making. *Educational Research Journal, 25*(1), 13–25.
Straub, R. (2000). The students, the text and the classroom context: a case study of student response. *Assessing Writing, 7*, 23–55.
Stiggins, R. J. (2002). Assessment crisis: The absence of assessment for learning. *Phi Delta Kappan, 83*(10), 758–765.
Sweller, J. (1988). Cognitive load during problem solving: Effects on learning. *Cognitive Science, 12*, 257–285.
Sweller, J. (1999). *Instructional Design in Technical Areas, (Camberwell*. Victoria, Australia: Australian Council for Educational Research.
Sweller, J., Van Merrienboer, J. J., & Paas, F. G. (1998). Cognitive architecture and instructional design. *Educational psychology review, 10*(3), 251–296.
Tsui, A. B. M., & Ng, M. (2000). Do secondary L2 writers benefit from peer comments? *Journal of Second Language Writing, 9*(2), 147–170.
Villamil, O. S., & De Guerrero, M. (1998). Assessing the impact of peer revision on L2 writing. *Applied Linguistics, 19*(4), 491–514.
Vygotsky, L. S. (1978). *Mind in society: The development of higher psychological processes*. Cambridge, MA: Harvard University Press.
Wood, D., Bruner, J., & Ross, G. (1976). The role of tutoring in problem-solving. *Journal of Child Psychology and Psychiatry, 17*(2), 89–100.
Zamel, V. (1982). Writing: The process of discovering meaning. *TESOL Quarterly, 16*, 195–209.
Zhang, S. (1995). Reexamining the affective advantage of peer feedback in the ESL writing class. *Journal of Second Language Writing, 4*(3), 209–222.
沈淑华. (2008). 中文网志写作对提升新加坡中学生写作能力与态度之成效研究. 博士论文, 香港大学,香港.

Cheng Gong (龚成) completed M.A. at the Nanyang Technological University, Singapore. She is currently a Teaching Fellow at the Singapore Centre for Chinese Language, Nanyang Technological University. Her academic interests include teaching of writing with self-directed learning, theories and pedagogies of second language acquisition, and ICT-assisted language teaching. Her publications include one scholarly book, five teaching toolkits, and a number of conference papers and journal articles.

Chee Lay Tan (陈志锐) received Ph.D. from the University of Cambridge, England. He is currently Executive Director (Research and Development) at the SCCL and Associate Professor cum Acting Deputy Head of Asian Languages and Cultures Academic Group of National Institute of Education. He was awarded the Young Artist Award by the National Arts Council in 2004 and the Singapore Youth Award (Culture and the Arts) in 2006. His academic interests include Chinese literature, Chinese as a Second Language, and Drama in education. He has published and edited more than 20 creative writing and academic books. He is a very active Singaporean Chinese poet of the younger generation.

Chee Kuen Chin (陈之权) received Ph.D. from the Central China Normal University, China. He was immediate past-Executive Director and is currently Academic Consultant cum Distinguished Principal Lecturer at SCCL. His academic interests include Chinese as a Second Language, curriculum development, Chinese Language pedagogies, ICT-mediated in teaching and learning of Chinese Language and cultural studies. He has published five scholarly books on Chinese Language research and a university textbook. He has more than 100 journal articles, book chapters, keynote speeches, and conference papers to his credit.

Facilitating Creative Writing Instruction Using iPads in Secondary Schools: A School-Based Research

Chee Lay Tan, Lynn Dee Puah and Hee San Teoh

Abstract Chinese Language creative writing instruction in Singapore has been unable to shake off traditional teaching routines because teachers fear that over-emphasis will cause students to go off-topic in examinations. The Singapore Centre for Chinese Language and Nanyang Girls' High School launched a year-long school-based research project in 2012, using iPads to supplement creative writing. Results indicate that the iPad strengthens the connectivity of knowledge and obtains seamless learning results, beneficial to the teaching of creative writing in the Chinese Language and students' creative thinking abilities.

In Singapore where Chinese Language is considered a Second Language in the school curriculum, writing skills are often harder to nurture than listening and speaking skills. The presence of essay-based examinations makes it harder to do away with the routine of traditional writing instruction which limits students' critical thinking and creativity that are two important skills of students in the twenty-first century (Wong et al. 2010b: 81). In Singapore's teaching environment, most teachers worry that over-emphasizing the teaching of creative writing will cause students to write off-topic in examinations and thereby affecting their performance (Koh 2006: 251), so few teachers carried out experiments with advanced technology (such as tablet computers, applications) to encourage creative writing. However, this research believes that it is exactly through the reintroduction of creative thinking could school teachers break away from the over-emphasis of examination-oriented teaching and learning. The teachers' feedback from this research, to be seen later, also confirms the importance of how and why creative writing will benefit Chinese Language teaching in the Singapore context.

C. L. Tan (✉)
Cambridge University, Cambridge, UK
e-mail: Cheelay.tan@sccl.sg

L. D. Puah
Nanyang Technological University, Singapore, Singapore

H. S. Teoh
National University of Singapore, Singapore, Singapore

© Springer Nature Singapore Pte Ltd. 2018
K. C. Soh (ed.), *Teaching Chinese Language in Singapore*,
https://doi.org/10.1007/978-981-10-8860-5_10

The teaching of essay writing must keep up with the times and be adaptable to our era of an information overflow. The 2010 Mother Tongue Languages Review Committee Report ("Nurturing Active Learners and Proficient Users"; Ministry of Education 2010: 56) mentioned that *"students' passion for learning their mother tongue should be stimulated through students' advantage of being familiar, frequent users of information technology"* because *"using information technology and interactive tools can extend students' learning beyond the classroom, helping them understand concepts more easily"* and *"integrating computers, online resources, and classroom teaching to give teachers and students more opportunities to communicate in real time."* With the premise of using information technology wisely, we notice that the tablet computer invented in the late twentieth century, and especially the iPad, has quickly become students' new toy in recent years. We believe that tablets will be the new trend in technological support of teaching in the future, and multi-sided experiments with them should be conducted in classrooms. From 2010 to 2013, educators from the UK, US, New Zealand, Australia, and other countries also held iPad classroom trials. However, in Singapore, research in using the iPad in Chinese Language teaching is still in its initiating stage.

Thus, the Singapore Centre for Chinese Language and Nanyang Girls' High School collaborated in a year-long school-based project in 2012, carrying out multi-sided experiments in using iPads in teaching creative writing. We designed nine iPad-supported creative writing lesson plans, aiming to develop students' imagination and creativity, and to increase their interest in creative writing by using iPads. This article focuses on sharing design principles behind teaching models that integrate iPads into creative writing lessons and analyses.

Mobile Learning with iPads

In recent decades, because of the integration of information technology, in particular mobile technology (Wong et al. 2011) into classroom teaching, old learning theories gained new definitions, and the role of teachers has changed significantly.

Wong and Chin (2010) organized Chinese Language mobile learning research and the literature of its practical applications, clarifying how Computer-Assisted Language Learning conforms to how language learning theory moved from behaviorism to changes in communicative, situational, and structural learning, integrating with Mobile-Assisted Language Learning to form the "second wave" of learning technology, changing teacher-centered classrooms into student-centered classrooms.

As a mobile technology trend, the tablet computer's recent popularity has a deep impact on teaching. The introduction of the Apple iPad has been more suitable to mobile learning than previous forms of mobile technology, such as cell phones, laptops, iPhones, PDAs. Melhuish and Falloon (2010) note that the iPad has the connectivity and capabilities of a laptop and the portability of a cell phone. Lin and Lien (2012: 248) point out that *"because the iPad can use most of the iPhone's applications, and has a larger visual area and many creative usage methods, it has become the most popular tablet device in recent years.*" The authors believe the popularity of the iPad will give teaching many advantages, and if the iPad can be integrated into teaching, it will "make up for what activities in traditional teaching or teaching that integrates messages cannot do."

In the UK, a report by the National Association of Advisors for Computers in Education (NAACE 2012) confirms the benefits of the iPad in teaching and learning. A study in Longfield Academy (a secondary school) indicated that the iPad had positive effects in both teaching and learning, causing students to have more active learning motivation, research, communication, and writing skills and that the iPad leads to the use of more educational applications. The study indicated that English, Mathematics, and Science were the subjects where the iPad was used most.

The Australian Learning Exchange (2010) also conducted a pilot study in 2010 to understand six situations when the iPad is integrated into the classroom, including the best study settings the iPad can provide, the affordability of learning to students, learners' participation levels, usage by learners with learning disabilities, the educational value of iPad applications, and technical or administrative issues with iPad usage. The results indicated that the iPad provided value-added benefits in all six areas, providing especially positive effects when it came to critical thinking, problem-solving, decision-making, research and information fluency, etc. In particular, the increase in student participation and information literacy strengthened connectivity.

In Singapore, Seah-Tay (2011) conducted an iPad pilot research study to understand student participation levels with iPads. In comparison with a class that did not use iPads, a class that used iPads had more student-centered activities and questions indicating higher-order thinking, showing increased connectivity between students and knowledge.

These studies are pilot studies that did not focus on any subject in particular. Lin and Lien (2012) introduced the iPad applications Idea Sketch, StoryKit/Story Lines, and GoodNotes/Dropbox into creative writing pedagogy in the Chinese Language lessons. Some of these applications are suited to local research, but require systematic research and trials.

As a response to the lack of research on iPads in Chinese Language teaching, we conceptualized iPad-supported Chinese Language creative writing pedagogy because the teaching of creative writing requires the use of various strategies to convert inspiration to thinking, so the classroom must be more student-centered. Moreover, we see many advantages of the iPads to both students and teachers.

Firstly, the personalization and mobility of the iPad can support activities that traditional teaching cannot, and its portability and long battery life overcomes the limitations of traditional desktop PCs or handheld computers that do not allow students to learn outdoors. Secondly, the small size of iPads also allows students to have face-to-face interaction in small-group activities. And, thirdly, the iPad's front and back video heads and microphone can record, store, and share students' language output well. Moreover, the iPad's personalized applications increase students' individualized learning, stimulate their imaginations, and challenge them.

As for teachers, there is a lower threshold for entry compared to traditional computers so teachers can easily download and organize various related applications and iPad teaching activities, and even centralize the use of iPads for lesson preparation, teaching, discussion, homework organization and feedback collection, and so on. So teachers can play the roles of presenters, facilitators, and designers more easily, navigating these three roles more smoothly with a "seamless transition" (Wong et al. 2010b).

Creative Writing Pedagogy

To understand creative writing pedagogy, the definition of "creative" and "creativity" should be understood. US academic Frank E. Williams established the Taxonomy of Creativity in 1970 (quoted in Chen 2008). Williams believed creative learners have four affective levels of creative thinking skills: curiosity, risk-taking, complexity, and imagination. Curiosity is an ability formed by questioning, thought, and confusion, and is the key to asking, pondering, and experimentation. Risk-taking is the courage to guess, attempt, experiment, and take criticism, including the ability to stick to one's beliefs and to take on unknown situations. Complexity is the ability to manage complex problems and unclear opinions, and requires introducing logic to a situation to find out the causes of effects and changes. And, imagination is to conceptualize ideas and make them concrete to surpass the constraints of reality. These four important thinking skills are especially important in the Singapore Chinese lessons, as they break away from the "safe and traditional" approach to examinations where route learning is over-emphasized. Teaching creative writing, which trains these thinking skills, is hence an important way of changing the "safe and traditional" mind-sets of many teachers and students.

Mao et al. (2000, p. 218) note that, firstly, when integrating creative thinking into teaching, creativity must first be the teaching goal. Secondly, activities should be student-centered. Thirdly, the classroom atmosphere should be egalitarian and harmonious. Lastly, teachers should use many strategies to inspire creative thinking. The first and last points are the most important, so teachers should consciously use teaching methods and tools (including information technology) to stimulate student creativity.

Lin (1994) defines three layers of methods for the teaching of creative writing. The first consists of writing genres, such as letters, sentences, essays, stories, and 16 other genres. The second layer consists of teaching methods, including character imagination, sensory usage, essay editing, picture association, and 19 other methods. The third consists of teaching goals, including nurturing the four above-mentioned affective levels of creative thinking skills. Lin also points out that in the creative writing classroom, teachers should be positive, creating a relaxed, harmonious classroom atmosphere. The first and second layers have important implications for curriculum design and teaching methods, while the third layer can be used as the standard for this study, meaning that nurturing the four affective levels of creative thinking skills is its teaching goal for creative writing.

There are also other related creative writing pedagogy studies in China, Hong Kong, and Taiwan. These include Mou (China 2009) use of free association, brainstorming, and sensory stimulation to stimulate elementary school students to write. Zhu (2001) targeted creative writing training for elementary school students that involved representation, association, imagination, and fantasy. Liu's (2005) study with secondary school students, based on mental stimulation, enumeration, image recall and mind-mapping as teaching methods integrated into expository writing, lyric writing, and narrative writing. Lai et al. (2011) study with elementary school students fused mind-map with online writing and showed significant student improvement in writing performance, creativity, and attitude.

The studies reviewed above show that mental stimulation, free association, sensory stimulation are worth referencing, and the research methods and assessment design were especially relevant to our concept of online writing and mobile learning. However, besides Liu's (2005) study, the subjects studied were elementary school students in the monolingual Chinese environments of China, Hong Kong, and Taiwan. For this reason, these studies cannot be fully transported to Singapore's bilingual classroom.

Therefore, the present study aimed to specially design a creative writing pedagogical method for Singaporean secondary schools. Thus, we seek to answer to this research question: Can using the iPad to support the teaching of creative writing enhance the level of creativity in student compositions?

Method

Participants

Two Secondary One classes in Nanyang Girls' High School in Singapore were studied. Nanyang Girls' High School is a Special Assistance Plan and independent school with students of high academic achievement, and possesses complete information technology facilities and a wireless broadband system. The experimental class had 33 students, and the control class had 30. All experimental students had access to a school-provided iPad, making their study and research easy. Before the project commenced, we conducted a survey and found that these two classes of students rarely read Chinese Language books on their own and mainly use English to communicate and think at home and in school. To them, Chinese Language was just an examination subject (even though they study it at the First Language level, as Higher Chinese) and not a language of daily life. In this bilingual environment, these students disliked writing in Chinese and did not know how to write creatively; moreover, they had never used the iPad or any other portable technology product for Chinese composition.

Procedure

A blend of qualitative and quantitative methods were used to collect data and information, including pre- and post-trial interviews with teachers, pre- and post-trial tests with students, classroom observations, and students' pre- and post-trial composition grades (Fig. 1).

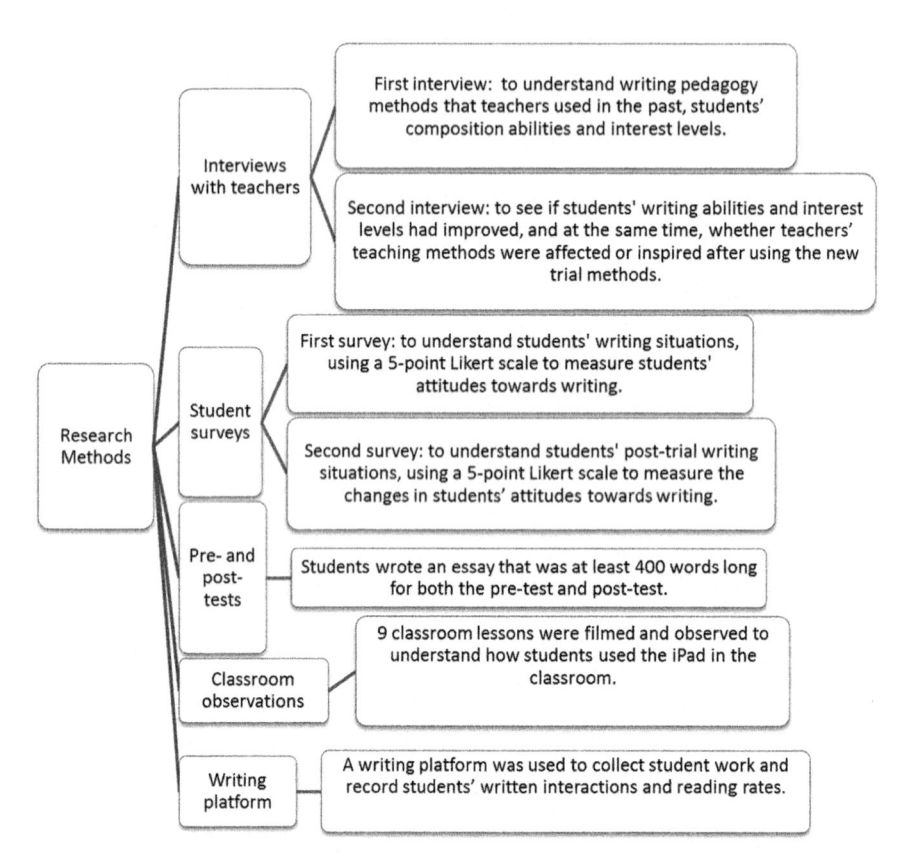

```
Research Methods
├── Interviews with teachers
│   ├── First interview: to understand writing pedagogy methods that teachers used in the past, students' composition abilities and interest levels.
│   └── Second interview: to see if students' writing abilities and interest levels had improved, and at the same time, whether teachers' teaching methods were affected or inspired after using the new trial methods.
├── Student surveys
│   ├── First survey: to understand students' writing situations, using a 5-point Likert scale to measure students' attitudes towards writing.
│   └── Second survey: to understand students' post-trial writing situations, using a 5-point Likert scale to measure the changes in students' attitudes towards writing.
├── Pre- and post-tests
│   └── Students wrote an essay that was at least 400 words long for both the pre-test and post-test.
├── Classroom observations
│   └── 9 classroom lessons were filmed and observed to understand how students used the iPad in the classroom.
└── Writing platform
    └── A writing platform was used to collect student work and record students' written interactions and reading rates.
```

Fig. 1 Research method chart

Teaching Resources

Two categories of teaching resources were consulted for this study: traditional resources (such as Microsoft PowerPoint, paper worksheets, and the usual resources that teachers are familiar with) and iPad resources (such as the camera and video functions, sound recording, cutting and pasting, Wi-fi Internet access) and applications. Besides portability, these all-in-one media functions enabled students to use the iPad indoors and outdoors and allowed them to record sounds, images, and videos to lay the groundwork for creative writing and captioning images. At the same time, many free or cheap applications, such as e-book making applications, were effective in supporting the teaching and learning of creative writing.

In our research, the iPad applications we used included the WordPress blogging application, the Scribble Press application, the SimpleMind+ application, and the iPad Web browser Safari (for usage strategies and their support for student production of creative writing, refer to the lesson plans in 3.5.1). We mainly used the WordPress online blogging application to enable students to directly participate in learning activities on iWrite.sg on the iPad. The seven categories on iWrite.sg included genre introductions, rhetorical introductions, quotes, local writers (where works were displayed with copyright permission), classroom compositions, student writing, and teachers' notes. iWrite.sg was designed and built by the research team, after which teachers participating in the study were consulted for feedback. In the process of the study, researchers and teachers edited and tweaked the content of the platform and students used the iPad to upload their words, images, videos, and audio content to the Web site, rating and providing feedback on each other's work and enriching the platform. The platform was a rich source of reading material, and a space for expression and interaction. Howland et al. (2008, pp. 160–190) point out that the use of a blog in teaching extends student learning beyond the classroom, enabling students to interact with learners and experts outside the classroom, encouraging them to learn actively and to compose texts with goals, promoting critical thinking and reading, and comparing their own writing with their peers. Blogs also accommodate different learning styles, so quieter students have a channel for communication, encouraging meaningful learning. This is the iWrite.sg homepage (Fig. 2).

iWrite.sg can be used on a regular PC, but its use on an iPad with multimedia functions and portability enables students to have seamless learning. Seamless learning is when learners integrate formal and informal learning situations, personal and social learning, and real-life and online learning (Wong et al. 2010a). Through iWrite.sg on the iPad, students can read books, images, and upload text, photographs, sounds, and video, learn and write outdoors, and even upload their creations from different applications (such as their e-books on Scribble Press) onto the iWrite.sg platform—things desktop and handheld PCs cannot do. Hence, a complete "listening, speaking, reading, writing, and commenting" teaching and learning activity can be combined on an iPad, and the process of obtaining and entering knowledge becomes more intuitive, direct, and convenient, helping students

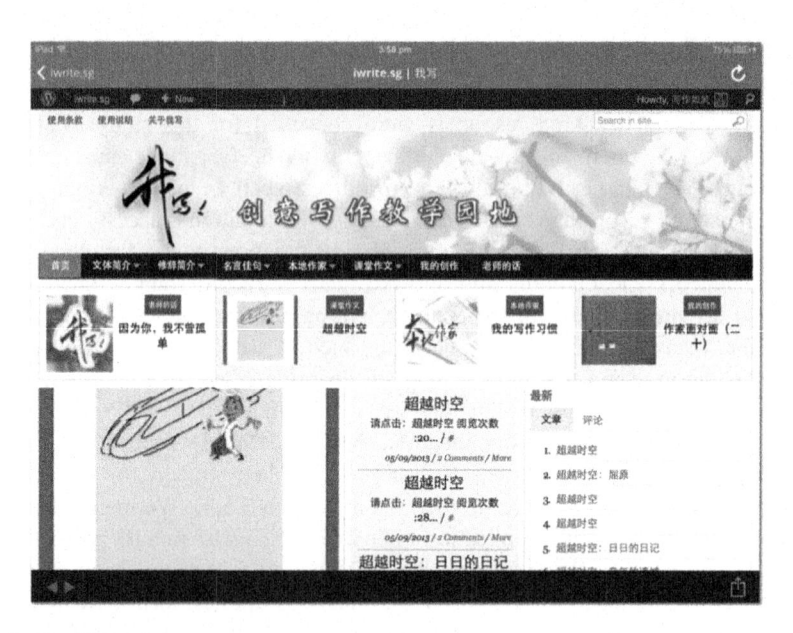

Fig. 2 The iWrite.sg homepage

integrate their knowledge more effectively. So iWrite.sg supports the teaching of creative writing actively, and also provides seamless learning results in students' extracurricular revision, self-directed learning, giving and accepting feedback, and so on.

Lastly, iWrite.sg can be linked to a data analysis tool to help researchers understand students' learning process, enabling us to collect information on hit rates, composition writing, commenting, and rating. These figures and information are very helpful for subsequent qualitative and quantitative analysis. Figure 3 shows the use of Google Analytics in collecting iWrite.sg composition reading rates without double-counting reading rates and visit durations, etc.:

Lesson Plans

This study designed nine iPad-supported lesson plans for creative writing, and a "meet-the-author" session. Through multimodal lesson plans, we hoped to stimulate students' interest in writing and their creativity, and at the same time improve their writing abilities. The "ICT Intervention" section in the teaching design framework chart of Table 1 provides information on iPad-supported teaching activities.

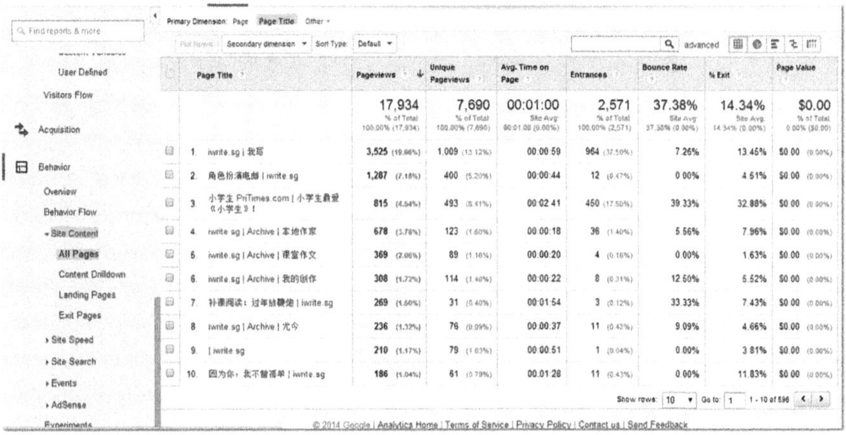

Facilitating Creative Writing Instruction Using iPads in … 143

Fig. 3 An example of Google Analytics Web site data

The chart above shows that the characteristics of the lesson plans of this study are:

1. **The integration of the iPad into the teaching of creative writing**. Each lesson introduced the iPad and iWrite.sg into the classroom, doing away with monotonous, boring teaching and practice styles of traditional writing classes. The multimedia input and output functions of one iPad can make learning more interesting and educational, which is attractive to lower secondary students. iWrite.sg gave each student an opportunity to display their work, and each piece of writing could receive feedback from teachers, students, and students from other classes, stimulating students' desire to express themselves. This went against conventional ways of thinking and was highly beneficial to students' creative writing.

2. **Adherence to the principle of "first explain, next give examples, then practice" in the process of teaching**. Starting with explanations and examples enabled these high-ability Higher Chinese students to get familiar with various creative writing methods (different from how lower-ability students are taught using the "first give examples, next explain, and then practice"). Next, related practice and homework was delivered in the classroom. The iPad was effective in all three steps: First, teachers used iPad slides to explain concepts. Next, students read information on iWrite.sg on the iPad or searched for other examples. And finally, students practiced writing with iPad applications, such as in the creation of e-books.

3. **Using student-centered teaching in which teachers act as guides**. With 1-to-1 computing, the iPad scaffolds and supports learning conveniently, acting as a guide to students' independent and outdoor learning so that learning becomes student-centered with a more open-minded, free atmosphere. This stimulates student creativity and their latent imaginations.

Table 1 Creative writing pedagogy design framework chart

No.	Creative writing unit	Learning goal/main points	Classroom activity	ICT Intervention	Writing production
1	General writing 1	To understand genre types and characteristics. To understand plot and content structures: beginning, rising action, peak, ending	Teachers introduce the basics, raise questions, play games, facilitate small-group discussions and class sharing	Recording small-group discussions with the iPad and sharing later Uploading stories onto iWrite.sg	In class: small-group presentations After class: Each student continues writing on the topic discussed in groups and uploads it to iWrite.sg
2	General writing 2	To understand the importance of beginnings and endings Introducing rhetorical techniques	Teachers introduce the basics, raise questions, facilitate individual writing and feedback	Using the iPad to complete homework on iWrite.sg	In class: completing an introduction and conclusion After class: reading information on iWrite.sg and analyzing relevant sentences
3	Sensory details	Encouraging students to use their five senses and intuition to experience things around them, improving their observation skills	Teachers introduce the basics, raise questions, play games, facilitate small-group discussions and class sharing	Using the iPad to take photographs, record audio or video, etc., and enter text	In class: Each group shares a photograph or video and explains it After class: Each group uses testimonial style and at least one rhetorical technique to write an introduction of at least 30 words, uploads it on iWrite.sg, then votes and conducts a peer review online
4	Creative titles	Understanding requirements and methods of creating titles	Teachers raise questions, explain, facilitate classroom writing and provide feedback	Using the iPad to complete an activity on iWrite.sg	In class: Each student completes a sample creative prompt After class: peer review

(continued)

Facilitating Creative Writing Instruction Using iPads in ...   145

Table 1 (continued)

No.	Creative writing unit	Learning goal/main points	Classroom activity	ICT Intervention	Writing production
5	Image associations	Encouraging student curiosity, observation skills, and appreciation skills. Training students to write in paragraphs	Teachers explain, raise questions, facilitate in-class writing	Using the iPad application Scribble Press to create an e-book	In class: create an e-book. After class: Teachers provide feedback on iWrite.sg, and students vote for their favorite e-book on iWrite.sg and conduct a peer review
6	Character imagination	Improving students' imagination, inspiring curiosity and observation skills. Training students to write e-mails	Teachers explain, raise questions, and facilitate in-class writing	Using the iPad to write character profiles to e-mail to classmates. Uploading to iWrite.sg	In class: Students write a personal letter via e-mail. After class: Students vote for their favorite letter on iWrite.sg and edit their work based on the peer review feedback they receive
7	Essay editing	Improving student imagination. Improving students' dialogue writing and character creation skills	Teachers explain, raise questions, and facilitate role play	Using iPad Voice Memos to record audio. Uploading completed composition and audio memos to iWrite.sg	In class: rewriting a text into a dialogue-based essay. After class: Students conduct peer review and voting on iWrite.sg based on the entertainment level of the rewrite and the interpretation through audio recordings
8	Group writing	Inspiring students' mental association and grouping skills, and originality. Nurturing students' team spirit in group work	Teachers explain, raise questions, and facilitate in-class writing	Using Google Docs on the iPad to write a round-robin essay as a group	In class: small-group round-robin writing. After class: The writing is uploaded to iWrite.sg for teacher feedback. Students vote for the top five most creative works

(continued)

Table 1 (continued)

No.	Creative writing unit	Learning goal/main points	Classroom activity	ICT Intervention	Writing production
9	Time travel	Improving student imagination Improving students' overall writing abilities	Teachers explain, raise questions, and facilitate group discussions and writing	Using the iPad to create courseware	In class: Students make 8–10 PowerPoint slides based on the topic of time travel to the past or to the future in small groups After class: rewriting the text on the slides into 500-word essays
10	Meet-the-author	Meeting a local writer (Dr Tan Chee Lay), understanding his philosophy and thoughts on writing to strengthen students' interest and confidence in writing		Using the iPad to photograph or record in-class writing	After class: Students upload their work to iWrite.sg

4. **Nurturing students' social skills**. In introductions, teaching, practice, conclusions, and extended after-class activities, interactions between the teacher and students, among students, among small groups of students, and between students and the online platform occur. The iPad's portability and interactivity makes human-to-human and human-to-machine interaction easier, inspiring students with each other's minds, the exchange of ideas, and increased interactivity and creativity in their composition process.

Data Analysis

Pre- and Posttest Compositions

As the study stressed creativity in writing, and not the usual essay grades, the pre- and posttests' essay prompts were mostly creativity-based. However, it does not mean that creativity is the only assessment criteria, as writing skills are also reflected in the students' writing, including imagination and use of language, complexity of sentences, etc., which will affect the assessment scores too. Firstly, the research team (including teachers) underwent training together to obtain clearer definitions and examples of the four affective levels of curiosity, risk-taking, complexity, and imagination that were the evaluation criteria. Also, we distinguished some unclear and subjective examples (see Mao et al. 2000: 222–223):

1. **Imagination**: Students redefine reality through words, creating imagistic associations and free associations, then rendering them visually and concretely through precise language use.
2. **Complexity**: Students clarify complicated issues using words and sentences step-by-step and with perseverance.
3. **Curiosity**: Students conduct deep investigations into confusing questions through words, thus raising more issues and getting to their root to thoroughly understand the truth.
4. **Risk-taking**: Students raise bold conjectures or stick to their beliefs through words, and have the courage and spirit to conduct experiments and receive criticism.

Secondly, student work would be anonymous and graded during the pre- and posttests in the first grading round, after which researchers would conduct a second round of grading and cross-checking. Creativity points were calculated, which is different from the grading system for regular compositions: If there was an example of one affective level, it would be counted as one point out of the maximum of four. In the end, the research leader would conduct a third round of grading and checking

Table 2 Comparison of the composition creativity levels

		Pretest	Posttest	Gain
Experimental class	Mean (SD)	1.00 (0.95)	2.88 (1.10)	1.88 (1.29)
Control class	Mean (SD)	1.61 (0.96)	2.14 (1.01)	0.54 (1.40)
Cohen's d		0.64	0.70	1.00

because the definitions of the four affective levels of curiosity may lead to overlapping or vagueness, so defining them is difficult. The pre- and posttest graders were the same, and to ensure a high level of grading reliability, a comparison would be carried out only after triangulation across the three stages. As some students were absent during the tests, the scores come from just 32 students of the experimental class and 28 of the control class.

As shown in Table 2, initially, control class scored higher than did experimental with a medium effect size in terms of Cohen's $d = 0.64$. However, this was turned around at the posttest with the experimental class scoring higher, and the corresponding effect size is Cohen's $d = 0.70$. This reversal in means resulted in a gain in creativity in favor of the experimental, with an effect size of Cohen's $d = 1.00$. In sum, when the initial difference was offset, the experimental class gained much from the lessons in creative writing using iPads.

The results showed that both experimental class and control class improved after a year of training in writing. However, experimental class had greater improvement. Control class outperformed experimental class in the pretest, while experimental class outperformed control class in the posttest. This has shown that the intervention has a positive impact on experimental class students as compared with control class students who received traditional training in writing composition.

Qualitative analysis was carried out with pre- and posttest student compositions. Student 7 wrote a composition on the topic *If I had magical powers* in the pretest and a composition on the topic *If I were a small drop of water* in the posttest. Both pre- and posttest compositions had a child protagonist who was in unfortunate situations, and her writing performance and creativity in the posttest far outshined her pretest. Comparing her first and last paragraphs: In her pretest, the student just used a simple comparative technique in her introduction, but in her posttest, she used lively personification in her introduction, with descriptions that were more diverse and accurate, making her essay more imaginative and engaging—a clear sign of greater creativity, as well as much enhanced writing skills. Her teacher was glad to see the changes in her last paragraphs. In her pretest's last paragraph, a string of questions brought her essay to a close as her speaker asked herself what else she could do for children and for society, which was simpler and more direct, like her classmates' writing styles. But in her posttest's last paragraph, this student was more immersed in the role of being "a drop of water" and wrote with imagination and emotion, "I closed my eyes with determination and rushed towards those pale lips." This student was writing from the point of view of a drop of water which had to fall to the ground in a storm, and when it saw a child in a drought yearning for water, it decided to sacrifice itself to quench the child's thirst. The ending was full of empathy and made an artistic gesture (see Appendix 1).

Student 18 wrote an average essay in her pretest that was mainly clichés, but in her posttest, her writing improved vastly. Her posttest topic was "If you were the earth" and its theme was environmentalism, which was rather creative. The whole essay used parallelisms to begin every paragraph, and used questions to conclude each paragraph, which was a big structural and linguistic improvement. Also, she used many unique phrases and advertising language free of clichés, and finally used an appeal with pathos to the reader: if you were the earth and were sad, don't let Mother Earth cry any more (see Appendix 2). The essay had feeling and philosophical thinking.

There are many similar examples, showing that after a year of creative writing training, the experimental class' creativity was stimulated. Since they were previously trained in the Primary Six Primary School Leaving Examination (PSLE) composition format, they lacked opportunities to delve into their creativity. iPad supported the experimental class in referring to resources such as iWrite.sg's rhetorical techniques and model essays, epitomizing mobile and seamless learning concepts, in the details of learning tasks (e.g., teachers would set up homework instructions and guidance on iWrite.sg), in multimedia stimulation and support for sensory descriptions in writing, in creating more learning nodes and strengthening connections between nodes, and in increasing the breadth and depth of writing output. These teaching strategies for creative writing enabled the experimental class' students to effectively use the iPad to scaffold their writing, expand their thinking, leading their essays' creativity level to exceed the control class significantly.

Teacher Feedback

The feedback shows that this year-long study of the teaching creative writing stimulates student thought and that students dare to think about and design content from different angles and that in the area of conceptualization, there was more flexibility. It is especially important as, with creative writing, the mind-sets of teachers and students are challenged to be more open and receptive to changes. Not only did the content become more creative, the creative use of language and structure also reflect better writing skills and overall performances. In addition, the teacher agrees that the study was successful mainly because with the iPad-supported teaching of creative writing, the teacher speaks less in class and students have more opportunities to participate in class. Students actively participated in class activities and welcomed the creative writing content. More concrete observations of the iPad by teachers were that even though the iPad applications are complex with many functions, students adapt to using them quickly, and it is portable and can be used for outdoor learning, in which students can record whatever inspires [them] and search for information online to enrich their essay content. An example of the latter is that if a discussion of a character requires knowledge of ancient figures or famous people, students can do a search of that person's background on the iPad and share their findings, seamlessly linking real-life and online learning. Teachers also believed students would have a new form of stimulation from searching for pictures for picture association: "more colourful pictures, text, and design [enabled students to] express their imaginations." Students were familiar with the iPad and adapted to using it as a learning tool quickly, getting into learning mode.

The teacher who taught the control class found that writing lessons were not exciting enough and were unable to stimulate student interest. Students did acceptably; they probably listened attentively in order to prepare for examinations. This shows that the support of an iPad and matching creative writing teaching strategies can make a class more exciting, stimulate student interest, and improve student performance.

Classroom Observations

Nine iPad-supported creative writing lessons positively affected student creativity in essay writing. Compared to lesson observations prior to iPad use, the integration of the iPad gave students an outdoor learning tool, more face-to-face interaction opportunities, a platform for more intuitive input and output, making students more engaged in discussions, and creating a more active atmosphere.

Taking the lesson plan for editing an essay as an example, this lesson's goal was to improve students' imagination, dialogue writing, and character creation skills. Teachers suggested that students select a familiar text and discuss it in small groups, rewriting it into a dialogue-based text or a text in another genre using the iPad's text editing application, using the iPad to record audio, then uploading both text and audio on iWrite.sg.

Whenever students participated in this lesson in small groups, they would actively seek assistance from the teacher whenever they had technical issues or questions about how to edit content. They also actively asked teachers questions, making the participation rate much higher than that in non-iPad composition classes. Classroom production was also of higher quality (see Appendix 1). For example, a group of students adventurously went beyond the teacher's requirements and boldly rewrote the text as a game, different from any other group, and also tried to rewrite it as a poem, displaying their creativity by going beyond the rules. In addition, the text they chose, *The Hunger Games*, was originally a popular computer game for youths with intense and violent elements, but this group of students changed the focus by converting the complex game rules and content into a sorrowful, lonely short lyric poem. They were inspired by the rules of the online text and their gaming background but did not just view the tasks as a game, but rather to make the reader (or the player) create associations with the fragility of human life, connecting nodes of knowledge, and exercising a rich sense of innovation.

Conclusion

From a year-long pilot study, we found that using the iPad in the teaching of creative writing had a measurable positive impact on students' creativity, as well as their overall writing performances. When evaluating students' pre- and posttest compositions, we found a large gain in creativity and writing skills in the experimental class.

Teacher feedback indicated that iPad support changed the classroom from a teacher-centered to student-centered, stimulating students' active classroom participation and group participation. Teachers affirmed that the iPad was a new tool for composition learning and teaching, and stressed that the iPad enabled students to understand that its use could make writing interesting and entertaining, overturning their impressions of language classes, and adding new possibilities to teaching processes by providing space for them to express their creativity. Teachers' responses indicated that the iPad enabled them to move away from being a traditional "lecturer" into becoming an organizer and manager of classroom activities, and to consciously value classroom activity design, giving students a sense of ownership.

Compared to the traditional teaching method of the control class, iPad support for creative writing was better at making the classroom active, enabling students to be more proactive and involved in discussions. Besides, teachers were not just teaching to students, but acting as guides, participants, respondents, classroom observers, with multiple roles.

Student-produced writing, teacher feedback, and researcher observations show that the iPad provided more opportunities for students to express their creativity, compose boldly, explore resources and opportunities independently, and created mobile and seamless learning effects. The positive and productive connotations that the iPad has for creative writing are worth future popularization.

152　C. L. Tan et al.

Appendix 1: Excerpts from Student 7's Pre- and Posttest Compositions

Paragraph 1 from the pretest:

> 假如我会变魔法
> 魔法
> 假如我会变，我会飞到世界各地的孤儿院，去探望那儿的小孤儿们，给他们变出一点糖果让他们开开心。我会像哈里波特一样，变出一把魔法扫帚，让孩子们在天上快乐地飞，忘掉所有的烦恼……

"If I had magical powers

If I had magical powers, I would fly to orphanages all across the world to visit the little orphans in them, and create sweets to make them happy. I would create a magical broom like in Harry Potter so the children can fly happily in the sky and forget all their worries…"

Paragraph 1 from the posttest:

> 假如我是一个小水滴
> 狂风呼啸，我和其它的小水滴紧拥在一起，躺在草地上。呼，呼——风吹得越来越大，突然，我被凭空卷起，在空中翻腾着。树叶在我身旁飞舞着……再见了，弟弟妹妹哥哥姐姐爸爸妈妈外婆外公祖父祖母水滴们！

"If I were a small drop of water

The strong wind blew. I hugged other drops of water, and lay on the field. Wooo, wooo – the wind blew stronger and stronger, suddenly, I was blown away by the wind and tossed in the air. The leaves flew past me... good bye, brother, sister, father, mother, grandfather, and grandmother droplets!"

Last paragraph from the pretest:

假如我会变魔法......我还能做些什么事？

"If I had magical powers... what else would I do?"

Last paragraph from the posttest:

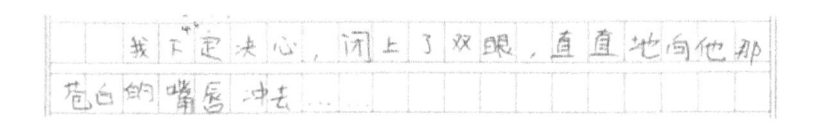

我下定决心，闭上了双眼，直直地向他那苍白的嘴唇冲去......

"I closed my eyes with determination and rushed towards those pale lips."

Appendix 2: Student 18's Posttest Composition

《假如你是地球》

人们总是为了一时的方便而对地球妈妈造成永久的伤害。但是你是否想过地球妈妈的感受呢？

假如你是地球，看着大家对"小草对你笑一笑，请你绕一绕"的提示牌视若无睹，依然踩踏草坪，把你的一部分狠狠地踩在脚下，毫无愧疚之感。你不觉得心痛吗？

假如你是地球，看着大家对"节能减排，低碳生活"的宣传视而不见，仍然开着私家车到处旅游，不断地排放尾气，熏得你喘不过气来，毫无停止之意。你不觉得难过吗？

假如你是地球，看着大家对"保护环境，人人有责"的温馨提醒无动于衷，仍然乱扔垃圾，随地吐痰，在你脸上、身体上留下狰狞的疤痕，还听不到你的哭泣，毫无悔过之意，你不觉得伤心吗？

假如你是地球，看着大家对"随手关灯"、"拔除电源"的标签毫不关心，还是让日光灯

> 亮了整个黑夜后，继续点缀白昼，让电视、电脑等一切电器处于休眠状态，即使是没用时还不让它们休息，你不觉得心疼吗？
>
> 假如你是地球，看着大家对"自带购物袋，一起保护地球"的活动毫无热情，宁愿拥有付费的便利，也不愿伸出双手对你好一点，四处仍是白色垃圾遍地，毫无羞愧之感，你不觉得绝望吗？
>
> 假如你是地球，看着大家……
>
> 如果，你对以上这些问题的答案都是肯定的，那就不要让地球妈妈再流泪了，好吗？

学生《文章改写》课产出之样例
Adaptation of The Hunger Games: Catching Fire (translated from Chinese)

Cold glass
separates two close hearts.
A familiar temperature
with a fresh memory
but unable to be touched.
Is a call of help from afar

the arrival of dawn
or an eternal sleep?

改写《饥饿游戏》：抓把火

冰冷的玻璃，

隔开了两颗紧靠的心。

熟悉的温度，

记忆犹新，

却触碰不到。

远处的呼救，

是黎明的到来，

还是永远的沉睡？

References

Chen, L. (2008). *Chuang yi si kao jiao xue de li lun yu shi ji [The theory and practice of creative thinking pedagogy]* 《创造思考教学的理论与实际》 (pp. 32–34). Taipei: Psychological Publishing Co., Ltd.

Howland, J. L., Jonassen, D. H., & Marra, R. M. (2008). *Meaningful learning with technology* (pp. 160–190). Upper Saddle River: Pearson.

Koh, H. K. (2006). Xie zuo jiao cheng yu duo yuan zhi neng [Writing course and multiple intelligence] 写作教程与多元智能. In Chinese Language Society (Singapore) (Ed.), *Xin jia po hua wen jiao xue lun wen si ji [Teaching and learning of Chinese language series: Volume 4]* 《新加坡华文教学论文四集》 (pp. 247–268). Singapore: Raffles Editions.

Lai, A., Chen, M., & Lan, Y. (2011). Xin zhi yu tu ce lve jie he xian shang xie zuo jiao xue fang an dui guo xiao wu nian ji xue tong xie zuo neng li, chuang zao neng li ji xie zuo tai du zhi ying xiang [Integrating mind-map strategy and web-based writing website to improve the writing ability, creativity and attitude of fifth graders] 心智舆图策略结合线上写作教学方案对国小五年级学童写作能力、创造力及写作态度之影响. *Hua wen xue kan [Journal of Chinese Language Education]* 《华文学刊》, 9(2), 23–39.

Learning Exchange. (2010). *iPads in schools: Use testing*. Retrieved from http://www.learningexchange.nsw.edu.au/research—development/support-material/support-material.aspx/technology/ipads-in-schools—use-testing.aspx.

Lin, J. (1994). *Chuang yi xie zuo jiao shi [Creative writing classroom]* 《创意的写作教室》 (pp. 49–60). Taipei: Psychological Publishing Co., Ltd.

Lin, C.-H., & Lien, Y.-J. (2012). Li yong iPad jin xing zhong wen jiao yu xue [Teaching and learning Chinese with and iPad] "利用iPad进行中文教与学". In J. Da, S. Jiang, & S. Liu (Eds.), *The 7th International Conference & Workshops on Technology & Chinese Language Teaching: Conference Proceedings 2012* (pp. 248–260). University of Hawaii at Mānoa: National Foreign Language Resource Center.

Liu, M. (2005). Chuang si ji fa rong ru zuo wen jiao xue mo shi yu xing dong yan jiu [The integration of creativity techniques into teaching model and action research] 创思技法融入作文教学模式与行动研究. In K. Wang & L. Chen (Eds.), *Guo wen zuo wen jiao xue de li lun yu* shi wu [*The theory and practice of Chinese writing teaching*] 《国文作文教学的理论与实务》 (pp. 191–220). Taipei: Psychological Publishing Co., Ltd.

Mao, L., Guo, Y., Chen, L., & Lin, H. (2000). *Chuang zao li yan jiu [The research of creativity]* 《创造力研究》 (pp. 218–223). Taipei: Psychological Publishing Co., Ltd.

Melhuish, K., & Falloon, G. (2010). Looking to the future: M-learning with the iPad. *Computers in New Zealand Schools: Learning, Leading, Technology, 22*(3). Retrieved from http://researchcommons.waikato.ac.nz/bitstream/handle/10289/5050/Looking%20to%20the%20future.pdf?sequence=1.

Mou, R. (2009). Chuang yi xie zuo huo dong de jiao xue ce lve [The teaching strategies of creative writing activities] 创意写作活动的教学策略. *Shanghai jiao yu ke yan [Shanghai Education Science Academy]* 《上海教育科研》, *9*, 69–71.

Naace. (2012). *The iPad as a tools for education—A study of the introduction of iPads at Longfield Academy, Kent*. Retrieved from http://www.naace.co.uk/publications/longfieldipadresearch.

Seah-Tay, H. Y. (2011). Student engagement in iPad pilot classes. *NYGH Research Journal*. Parts of this paper were presented at the Apple Educators Workshop in Hong Kong on 11–15 July and at Apple Leaders Conference at Nanyang Girls' High School on 10 October 2011. Retrieved from http://nyrj.pbworks.com/w/page/47264902/2011.

The Mother Tongue Languages Review Committee Report (2010) Nurturing active learners and proficient users (pp. 16, 56). Singapore: Ministry of Education, Singapore.

Wong, L. H., & Chin, C. K. (2010). Liu dong ke ji wei hua yu wen xue xi kai tuo xin fang xiang [Expanding horizons: Mobile technology in Chinese language learning] 流动科技为华语文学习开拓新方向. *Hua wen xue kan [Journal of Chinese Language Education]* 《华文学刊》, *8*(2), 69–84.

Wong, L.-H., Chin, C.-K., Tan, C.-L., & Liu, M. (2010a). Students' personal and social meaning making in a Chinese idiom mobile learning environment. *Educational Technology & Society, 13*(4), 15–26.

Wong, A. F. L., Divaharan, S., & Choy, D. (2010b). Planning for effective lessons. In C. S. Chai & Q. Wang (Eds.), *ICT for self-directed and collaborative learning* (pp. 81–106). Singapore: Pearson.

Wong, L. H., Liu, M., Chin, C. K., Tan, C. L., & Gong, C. (2011). Liu dong ke ji ba cheng yu xue xi cong ke tang yan shen dao sheng hu-xian dao yan jiu de jing yan [Mobile technology extends the learning of idioms from classroom to real life] 流动科技把成语学习从课堂延伸到生活——先导研究的经验. In C. L. Tan (Ed.), *Xing dong yu fan si:hua wen zuo wei di er yu yan zhi jiao yu xue [From practice to practical: Teaching and learning of Chinese as a second language* 《行动与反思:华文作为第二语言之教与学》 (pp. 247–263). Nanjing: Nanjing University Press.

Zhu, Z. (2001). Xiang gang chuang yi xie zuo jiao xue [The teaching of creative writing teaching in Hong Kong] 香港创意写作教学. *Xiao xue qing nian jiao shi [《Primary Schools' Young Teachers], 261*, 49–50.

Chee Lay Tan (陈志锐) received Ph.D. from the University of Cambridge, England. He is currently Executive Director (Research and Development) at the SCCL, and Associate Professor cum Acting Deputy Head of Asian Languages and Cultures Academic Group of National Institute of Education. He was awarded the Young Artist Award by the National Arts Council in 2004 and the Singapore Youth Award (Culture and the Arts) in 2006. His academic interests include Chinese literature, Chinese as a Second Language, and drama in education. He has published and edited more than 20 creative writing and academic books. He is a very active Singaporean Chinese poet of the younger generation.

Lynn Dee Puah completed M.A. at the Nanyang Technological University, Singapore. She is formerly Research Associate at the Singapore Centre for Chinese Language and was involved in several school-based experimental projects and large-scale surveys. Her research interests include child language development, bilingual acquisition, and sociolinguistics.

Hee San Teoh (张曦姗) completed M.A. at the National University of Singapore, Singapore. She is currently a Master Teacher (Chinese Language) at the Academy of Singapore Teachers, Ministry of Education, and Lecturer at Singapore Centre for Chinese Language. She specializes in Chinese Language and Chinese literature curriculum. Her research interests include Chinese literature pedagogies and design of Chinese Language teaching materials. Her publications include journal articles, chapters, and a teaching toolkit.

Effect of Phonological and Semantic Radicals on the Identification of Chinese Characters: Instructional and Research Possibilities

Limei Zhang and Suan Fong Foo

Abstract Phonological and semantic radicals are important clues to the learning and remembering of Chinese characters. This chapter reviews relevant studies in this regard and suggests that Chinese Language teachers use the phonological and semantic radicals as a framework to organize teaching materials for effective teaching.

Singapore is a multilingual country with four official languages, namely English, Chinese, Malay, and Tamil (Chua, 2011; Shepherd, 2005). Chinese is spoken by the largest ethnic group which accounts for 74% of the whole population (Department of Statistics, 2016). Under the bilingual education policy of Singapore, students of all ethnic groups are required to learn English plus their respective ethnic language while English is the medium of instruction of all other subjects. The teaching of Chinese has become a keen concern among educators, parents, and students (Soh, 2016). A survey by Singapore Centre for Chinese Language shows Chinese Language teachers are facing various challenges. It was noted that the teaching and learning of Chinese characters is the greatest difficulty. Among the primary school teachers, 39.2% mentioned that word recognition is most challenging for their students. Actually, inadequacy in Chinese character identification has become a barrier to students' improvement of reading and writing ability in Singapore (e.g., Soh, 2016; Zhang et al., 2016). Therefore, it is imperative to find effective methods to help students and teachers in the learning and teaching of Chinese characters.

To read successfully in a language, information about orthography, phonology, and semantics of the words encountered should be processed effectively (Taft & Graan, 1998). Orthographic units are technically called graphemes. In other words,

L. Zhang (✉) · S. F. Foo
Singapore Centre for Chinese Language,
Nanyang Technological University, Singapore, Singapore
e-mail: limei.zhang@sccl.sg

© Springer Nature Singapore Pte Ltd. 2018
K. C. Soh (ed.), *Teaching Chinese Language in Singapore*,
https://doi.org/10.1007/978-981-10-8860-5_11

graphemic, phonological and semantic constituents are characteristic of any language. Graphemic information provides the visual basis for lexical processing. Phonological information is necessary if the word is to be read aloud (or silently in the mind), whereas semantic information is important for the meaning of the word. While reading in a language, the reader needs to bind the three constituents successfully. This seems to be the universal rule of grapheme–phoneme correspondence (GPC) (Pritchard et al., 2016) in the reading process.

Structure of Chinese Characters

In the case of alphabetical system such as English, the phonemes are associated with graphic units closely, which is termed the grapheme–phoneme connection (Perfetti & Zhang, 1995). That is, words can be broken into phonemes describing their pronunciation (Hagiwara, 2016). While reading in alphabetical writing system, the conversion from graphemes to phonemes is necessary for semantic access (Hung et al., 2014). For logographic system like Chinese, word meaning is mainly associated with visual units (Perfetti & Zhang, 1995). Chinese characters, which represent words or morphemes (Taylor & Taylor, 1983), mostly cannot be broken into phonemes which give a description of pronunciation. This gives rise to the argument about the role phonology plays in processing Chinese.

Modern Chinese characters can be divided into four major categories: pictographs, self-explanatory characters, associative compounds, and phonograms (Chen & Yeh, 2017; Tan et al., 1995). Pictographs normally have an etymology related to the picture of the symbol. For example, 月 (*noon*) is a pictographic character representing the shape of a crescent. Self-explanatory characters are normally based on pictographs. For example, adding a symbol in the root part of 木 (*tree*) would produce a new character 本 (*root*). Associative compounds are also produced on the basis of pictographs. For example, 休 (*rest*) is composed of a 亻 (*person*) and a 木 (*tree*), indicating that a person leans on a tree to have a rest.

Phonograms, made up of phonetic radicals and semantic radicals, constitute 80–90% of all modern Chinese characters (Chen & Yeh, 2017; Tan et al., 1995; see Fig. 1 for an example). Phonetic radicals may provide clues to the pronunciation of phonograms, while semantic radicals are supposed to provide clues to the meaning of characters (Hagiwara, 2016). Take the phonogram 液 (*liquid*) for example. The character consists of two radicals at different positions: 氵 (*water*) on the left and 夜 (*night*) on the right. As shown in Fig. 1, the two radicals have different functions. The radical 氵 provides a semantic clue whereas the radical 夜 indicates its phonological clue. Furthermore, the semantic radical 氵 helps form new phonograms 沐 (*taking a bath*) and 湖 (*lake*) while the phonetic radical 夜 is connected to two other phonograms 掖 (*tucking in*) and 腋 (*armpit*) which share the same pronunciation with 液 and 夜. Therefore, in spite of the lack of grapheme–phoneme connection, it is possible to predict the pronunciation of the phonograms (Hagiwara, 2016).

Fig. 1 An example of phonogram "液"

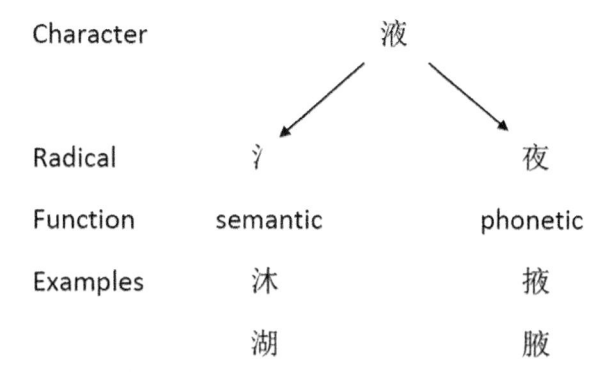

```
Character            液
                    ╱    ╲
Radical            氵      夜

Function        semantic   phonetic

Examples          沐        掖
                  湖        腋
```

When armed with knowledge of pronunciation and word meaning presented by phonetic and semantic radicals, readers of Chinese characters are likely to learn more effectively (Shu et al., 2003). The current chapter aims to review the relevant literature of the effect of phonetic and semantic radicals on the identification of Chinese phonograms. Based on the review, possible approaches to and necessary research on the learning and teaching of Chinese characters in Singapore schools will be discussed.

Chinese Processing Models in L1

How Chinese is processed among first language (L1) readers has attracted many researchers' attention during the past two decades (e.g., Chen & Yeh, 2015; Perfetti & Liu, 2005; Wong & Chen, 1991). Regarding the retrieval of appropriate word meaning, different theories have been proposed. Some researchers argued that the meaning of a word can be accessed directly through its orthographic information (e.g., Hino et al., 2012; Jared & Seidenberg, 1991; Taft & Graan, 1998). Often referred to as the Direct Route Model, this involves the direct activation of the semantic information correspondent to its orthographic representation (Hino et al., 2012). For example, Taft and Graan (1998) conducted a study to investigate whether it is possible to read a word for meaning without phonological mediation. On the basis of their semantic categorization tasks, they concluded that the direct route plays the main role in retrieving meanings of words.

An alternative route involves the activation of phonological information. In other words, the phonological information is activated when a word is read, followed by the activation of its semantic information which is similar to how meaning is retrieved when listening to the word. This route is termed phonological-mediated route (Perfetti & Liu, 2005). In the past two decades, considerable research has shown that phonological encoding is an indispensable processing strategy in reading, be it the alphabetical or logographic writing system (Perfetti & Liu, 2005; Perfetti et al., 1992). This is known as the Universal Phonological Principle (e.g., Perfetti & Liu, 2005; Perfetti & Zhang, 1995; Tan et al., 1995 etc.). For example, Perfetti and Zhang (1995) investigated whether phonology is a part of word identification in Chinese reading using two experiments of Chinese synonym and homophone tasks. Their results provide support for the principle.

On the basis of the direct route model and the phonological-mediated route, Coltheart (2005) proposed a dual route view, which holds that reading involves two separate cognitive mechanisms: a lexical route and a sub-lexical route (Pritchard et al., 2016). Whole words carrying meaning are processed through spelling alone while unknown words are decoded via phonological knowledge. In other words, according to the dual route model, there are two pathways to meaning: one is the O → S (orthography → semantics) pathway and the other is the O → P → S (orthography → phonology → semantics) pathway. Recent research findings confirmed that both orthographical and phonological routes are used for word identification (e.g., Chi et al., 2014; Pritchard et al., 2016; Spinks et al., 2000). For example, Chi and associates (2014) investigated whether phonological information of the phonetic radicals is important in the processing of phonograms. Results indicate that the phonetic radicals play an important role in identifying Chinese phonograms in both naming tasks and normal reading. Their study provides support for the dual route model.

By way of summary, the review of Chinese processing models indicates that in the course of word identification in L1 reading, phonological and orthographical information are all activated to gain access to meaning. In other words, both phonological and visual decoding are involved in Chinese character identification (Chen & Yeh, 2015; Perfetti & Liu, 2005; Perfetti & Zhang, 1995; Spinks et al., 2000 etc.). On this basis, in the case of identification of the phonograms which constitutes the majority of Chinese characters, phonological radicals should be attached more importance. In the following section, implications for the instruction of Chinese characters in Singapore are provided.

Implications for Teaching Chinese Characters in Singapore Schools

As mentioned in the previous sections, phonetic radicals play an important role in the identification of Chinese characters. In spite of the imperfect grapheme–phoneme connection among Chinese characters, teachers can help raise students' awareness of phonetic radicals, especially the role of phonetic radicals in the identification of Chinese characters (Chi et al., 2014). It might be interesting if teachers can practice new methods of Chinese character instruction under teacher trainers and researchers' guidance and help.

For example, it might be helpful for Chinese Language teachers to select all the phonograms from among the textbooks and categorize them into different types based on the connection between the phonetic radicals of the characters and their respective pronunciation. This way, the teaching of Chinese characters would be more directed toward the connection between phonetic radicals and Chinese characters. Meanwhile, students might find it is easier to draw the link between the character, its phonetic radical and semantic radical, thus leading to more effective memorization of the character. It is hoped that with more practice from teachers and students, the findings about the effect of phonetic radicals on the identification of Chinese phonograms can provide more effective methods for learning and teaching of Chinese characters in Singapore.

Conclusions

This chapter reviews the relevant literature about the effect of phonological and semantic radicals on the identification of Chinese characters. It provides an illustration of the structure of Chinese characters, especially phonograms, which constitutes the major part of modern Chinese characters. Chinese processing models in L1 were reviewed, followed by the implication of research findings in this area for teaching Chinese characters in Singapore schools. As suggested, Chinese teachers are encouraged to teach characters making full use of the research findings. Meanwhile, their practice in classrooms provides useful data for further research which benefits teaching and learning of Chinese characters in the long run.

References

Chen, Y.-C., & Yeh, S.-L. (2015). Binding radicals in Chinese character recognition: Evidence from repetition blindness. *Journal of Memory and Language, 78*, 47–63.
Chen, Y.-C., & Yeh, S.-L. (2017). Examining radical position and function in Chinese character recognition using the repetition blindness paradigm. *Language, Cognition and Neuroscience, 32*(1), 37–54.
Chi, H., Yan, G., Xu, X., Xia, Y., Cui, L., & Bai, X. (2014). The effect of phonetic radicals on identification of Chinese phonograms: Evidence from eye movement. *Acta Psychologica Sinica, 46*(9), 1242–1260.
Chua, S. K. C. (2011). Singapore's language policy and its globalised concept of bi(tri) lingualism. *Journal of Current Issues in Language Planning, 11*(4), 413–429.
Coltheart, M. (2005). Modeling reading: The dual-route approach. In M. Snowling & C. Hulme (Eds.), *The science of reading: A handbook* (pp. 6–23). Malden, MA: Wiley-Blackwell.
Department of Statistics. (2016). *Population trends 2016*. Accessed December 28, 2017 at www.library/publications/publications_and_papers/population_and_population_structure/population2016.pdf.
Hagiwara, A. (2016). The role of phonology and phonetics in L2 Kanji learning. *The Modern Language Journal, 100*(4), 880–897.
Hino, Y., Lupker, S. J., & Taylor, T. E. (2012). The role of orthography in the semantic activation of neighbors. *Journal of Experimental Psychology. Learning, Memory, and Cognition, 38*(5), 1259–1273.

Hung, Y., Hung, D. L., Tzeng, O. J., & Wu, D. H. (2014). Tracking the temporal dynamics of the processing of phonetic and semantic radicals in Chinese character recognition by MEG. *Journal of Neurolinguistics, 29,* 42–65.

Jared, D., & Seidenberg, M. S. (1991). Does word identification proceed from spelling to sound to meaning? *Journal of Experimental Psychology: General, 120*(4), 358–394.

Perfetti, C. A., & Liu, Y. (2005). Orthography to phonology and meaning: Comparisons across and within writing systems. *Reading and Writing, 18*(3), 193–210.

Perfetti, C. A., & Zhang, S. (1995). Very early phonological activation in Chinese reading. *Journal of Experimental Psychology. Learning, Memory, and Cognition, 21*(1), 24–33.

Perfetti, C. A., Zhang, S., & Berent, I. (1992). Reading in English and Chinese: Evidence for a "universal" phonological principle. In R. Frost & L. Katz (Eds.), *Orthography, phonology, morphology, and meaning* (pp. 227–248). Amsterdam: North-Holland.

Pritchard, S. C., Coltheart, M., Marinus, E., & Castles, A. (2016). Modelling the acquisition of grapheme–phoneme correspondences within the dual-route cascaded model of reading aloud. *Scientific Studies of Reading, 20*(1), 49–63.

Shepherd, J. (2005). *Striking a balance: The management of language in Singapore*. Frankfurt, Germany: Peter Lang.

Shu, H., Bi., X. M., & Wu, N. N. (2003). The role of partial information a phonetic provides in learning and memorizing new characters. *Acta Psychologica Sinica, 35*(1), 9–16.

Soh, K. (2016). Chinese language teachers' perceptions of training needs and perceived student difficulties. In K. C. Soh (Ed.), *Teaching Chinese language in Singapore—Retrospect and challenge* (pp. 65–84). Singapore, Singapore: Springer.

Soh, K. (2017). Strategies of rectifying improper use of Chinese characters. *TCSOL Studies*.

Spinks, J., Liu, Y., Perfetti, C., & Tan, L. (2000). Reading Chinese characters for meaning: The role of phonological information. *Cognition, 76,* B1–B11.

Taft, M., & Graan, F. V. (1998). Lack of phonological mediation in semantic categorization task. *Journal of Memory and Language, 38,* 203–224.

Tan, L. H., Hoosain, R., & Peng, D. L. (1995). Role of early presemantic phonological code in Chinese character identification. *Journal of Experimental Psychology. Learning, Memory, and Cognition, 21*(1), 43–54.

Taylor, I., & Taylor, M. (1983). *The psychology of reading*. New York: Academic Press.

Wong, K., & Chen, H. (1991). Orthographic and phonological processing in reading Chinese text: Evidence from eye fixations. *Language and Cognitive Processes, 14,* 461–480.

Zhang, L. M., Chin, C. K., Gong, C., Min, Y., & Tay, B. P. (2016). Investigating the relationship between Singapore lower secondary students' strategy use and Chinese writing performance: A mixed method approach. *Journal of Chinese Language Education, 14*(1), 19–32.

Limei Zhang (张丽妹) received her Ph.D. from Nanyang Technological University, Singapore. She is currently lecturer at Singapore Centre for Chinese Language, Nanyang Technological University. Her academic interests include language assessment literacy, reading and writing assessment, and learner metacognition. She has published a number of articles and book chapters on language assessment and reading and writing issues. Her most recent work is a book on the relationship between learners' metacognition and reading comprehension.

Suan Fong Foo (符传丰) received his Ph.D. from Fudan University, China. He is currently Executive Director of Singapore Centre for Chinese Language, Nanyang Technological University. Previously, Dr. Foo was the Principal of Nan Hua High School and Dunman High School, both of which are reputed Special Assistance Plan schools in Singapore. His research interests include school leadership and management, curriculum development, Chinese language and modern Chinese literature. He has published books and papers in these areas.

Part III
Assessment Literacy

Investigating the Training Needs of Assessment Literacy among Singapore Primary Chinese Language Teachers

Limei Zhang

Abstract This study gathers empirical data from primary Chinese Language teachers to examine their learning needs in language testing and assessment. Primary Chinese Language teachers ($N = 103$) responded to a survey on language assessment literacy (Fulcher, 2012). Results from the study reveal teachers' needs in language testing and relevant issues. The findings provide guidance for the design of training materials and development of programs for enhancing teachers' assessment literacy.

Language assessment literacy refers to teachers' knowledge about measurement practices and its application to classroom teaching (Inbar-Lourie, 2008; Malone, 2008, 2013; Taylor, 2009). With more details, Fulcher (2012, p. 125) defines it as *"knowledge, skills and abilities required to design, develop, maintain or evaluate large-scale standardized and/or class based tests, familiarity with test processes, and awareness of principles and concepts that guide and underpin practice."* Due to its importance in language education and teaching training, researchers have paid growing attention to the investigation of assessment literacy among language teachers.

The term *assessment literacy* was first introduced by Stiggins (1991) who defined it as the ability to know and understand key principles of sound assessment. According to Stiggins, assessment literacy helps teachers evaluate students' achievement outcomes effectively. Inbar-Lourie (2008) argued that assessment literates should have the knowledge and ability to give answers to important questions about the purposes of assessment, the appropriateness of measurement tools, testing conditions and the effects of the assessment on students. More recently, assessment literacy is defined as teachers' knowledge, skills, and abilities in designing, developing, or evaluating assessments, competencies about test

L. Zhang (✉)
Singapore Centre for Chinese Language, Nanyang Technological University, Singapore, Singapore
e-mail: limei.zhang@sccl.sg

processes as well as the application of the knowledge to classroom practices (Fulcher, 2012; Malone, 2013).

However, to date, few studies have been conducted to investigate Chinese Language teachers' assessment literacy, although learning Chinese has attracted global interests. This study was therefore designed to examine Singapore primary Chinese Language teachers' training needs in assessment literacy through questionnaire data. The purpose of the study was to provide information about Singapore primary Chinese Language teachers' training needs in assessment knowledge and to inform the design of training materials and development programs.

Relevant Studies

Researchers have conducted studies investigating classroom teachers' assessment literacy and provided solutions to existing problems. For example, based on her study on foreign language education in the USA, Boyles (2005) examined teachers' professional development in assessment in districts experienced in this practice, aiming to provide examples for other districts. Boyles (2005) recommended that a universal understanding of assessment literacy and criteria of good assessments should be reached and further suggested that professional development about assessment literacy should be organized through online training, workshops, and programs at national and regional levels.

Based on a review of components of language assessment literacy knowledge in general education and research on language testing and assessment courses, Inbar-Lourie (2008) proposed that a framework of core language assessment knowledge is established. According to Inbar-Lourie (2008, p. 396), this framework includes "*a body of knowledge and research grounded in theory and epistemological beliefs, and connected to other bodies of knowledge in education, linguistics and applied linguistics*."

Koh (2011) investigated the effects of professional development on Singapore primary teachers' assessment literacy over two school years. The participating teachers were randomly assigned to two groups: one group receiving ongoing and sustained professional development about assessment, the other group attending a one-day professional development workshop. Results showed that teachers' assessment literacy in the former group improved significantly.

Fulcher (2012) conducted a survey study examining language teachers' training needs. Participants were 287 ESL/EFL teachers from seven countries or regions. In addition to informing the design of teaching materials and development of online resources for teaching training, the study developed and piloted an instrument used to elicit language teachers' training needs in assessment literacy. More importantly, it provided new and expanded contents of assessment literacy based on empirical data.

Zhang and Soh (2016) reported on Singapore primary and secondary Chinese Language teachers' knowledge of language assessment. The study involved 323 primary and secondary teachers who responded to the Assessment Literacy Scale prepared by the researchers. Results indicate that the participating teachers' shortfalls in assessment literacy and their training needs. The respondents were able to answer general questions of commonsensical nature correctly but were weak where specific technical knowledge is concerned. Findings from this study have useful implications for primary and secondary Chinese Language teachers' training in assessment literacy.

More recently, Soh and Zhang (2017) developed a questionnaire of Teacher Assessment Literacy Scale which covers four essential aspects of educational measurement including nature and function of assessment, design and use of test items, interpretation of test results, and concepts of reliability and validity. Both classical and Rasch analyses were conducted with encouraging psychometric qualities. It is hoped that Teacher Assessment Literacy Scale can help gauge teachers' understanding and skills in assessment literacy.

As gathered from the above, while studies on teachers' assessment literacy are gaining momentum, there is a dearth of such studies in Singapore, especially concerning Chinese Language teachers. This study will therefore address the following two research questions:

1. What are Singapore primary Chinese Language teachers' specific training needs in assessment literacy, especially in terms of test design and development, large-scale testing, classroom testing and test validity and reliability?
2. Are there any differences in assessment training needs among Singapore primary school teachers of different genders, ages, educational backgrounds, and levels of assessment knowledge?

Method

Participants

The participants in this study were 126 Chinese Language teachers from Singapore primary schools. Among these teachers, 14.3% were males and 85.7% were females. The information of their age, academic qualifications, and self-evaluated assessment knowledge levels is presented in Table 1. Their assessment knowledge was measured through a five-point Likert scale ranging from 1 for "very poor" to 5 for "very good." As shown in Table 1, the participating teachers' assessment knowledge varies in terms of its adequacy. 62.4% of participating teachers had average knowledge in assessment, while 33.3% teachers had good assessment knowledge and the rest 4.3% possessed poor knowledge in assessment.

Table 1 Demographic information of the participating teachers

Items	Variables	Percentage (%)
Age	21–30	32.3
	31–40	36.3
	41–50	24.2
	Above 50	7.20
Academic qualifications	Below bachelor's	6.4
	Bachelor'	72.4
	Master's	16.3
	Others	4.9
Assessment knowledge	Poor	4.3
	Average	62.4
	Good	33.3

Instruments

A survey which elicits language teachers' assessment training needs was adopted in this study (Fulcher, 2012). There are 23 closed-response designed to evaluate language teachers' knowledge need in assessment. They are categorized into four subscales: six items measuring test design and development, eight items measuring large-scale standardized testing, seven items measuring classroom testing and washback, and two items about validity and reliability. Teachers were required to provide their response on a five-point Likert scale ranging from 1 "unimportant" to 5 "essential." The survey is shown in the Appendix.

Data Collection and Analysis

The survey was first translated into Chinese, followed by a back-translation procedure to ensure the accuracy of the translated version. A group of primary school teachers attending in-service training courses and seminars was invited to participate in this study voluntarily.

To analyze the data, confirmatory factor analysis (CFA) was conducted first. Since Fulcher (2012) examined the underlying structure of the questionnaire using exploring factor analysis (EFA), CFA was used in this study to verify the structure of the questionnaire.

Multiple fit indices were used to examine the model fit. The value of chi-square to degree of freedom ratio (χ^2/df) should be less than three for a well-fitting model (Hu & Bentler, 1999). The comparative fit index (CFI) is to evaluate the relative fit improvement of the hypothesized model compared with the null model. A value greater than 0.90 is considered a good model fit (Kline, 2011). The absolute fit index root mean square error of approximation (RMSEA) indicates how well a model fits the population and should be less than 0.10 to indicate good model fit

(Kline, 2011). The narrow interval of the RMSEA 95% confidence interval shows better model fit.

A series of independent *t* tests and ANOVAs were then conducted, examining the relationship among teachers' training in assessment literacy and their different gender, age, levels of educational background, and assessment knowledge.

Results

Descriptive Statistics

Descriptive statistics of each item and subscales of the questionnaire were calculated first (See Tables 2 and 3). The values of skewness and kurtosis of all the items were within an accepted range of normal distribution (Bachman, 2004). In addition, it was found that the average scores of the four subscales ranged from 4.16 ($SD = 0.81$) to 3.45 ($SD = 0.54$), with the highest being validity and reliability ($M = 4.16$, $SD = 0.81$), followed by test design and development ($M = 3.99$, $SD = 0.67$), large-scale standardized testing ($M = 3.66$, $SD = 0.55$), and classroom testing and washback ($M = 3.45$, $SD = 0.54$). The reliability of the questionnaire was also estimated. The Cronbach's alphas for all items and each subscale were 0.91, 0.84, 0.81, 0.74, and 0.96, as shown in Table 3.

Confirmatory Factor Analysis (CFA)

On the basis of the structure of the questionnaire, the CFA model was hypothesized and tested. The fit indices are shown in Table 4. The value of chi-square to degree of freedom ratio is 1.55, which is less than 3. CFI is 0.93, greater than 0.90; RMSEA is 0.066, less than 0.10. RMSEA 95% confidence interval is narrow (0.051–0.080). The fit indices showed that the CFA model is a well-fitting model, which provides supportive evidence that the questionnaire is a valid instrument used among Singapore primary Chinese Language teachers.

ANOVA and t Test

An independent sample *t* test was conducted to examine male and female teachers' differences in assessment training needs. Results showed that the differences were not statistically significant with $t(118) = 0.32$, $p > 0.05$; $t(118) = 1.23$, $p > 0.05$; $t(116) = 0.94$, $p > 0.05$; and $t(122) = 0.05$, $p > 0.05$. On average, male teachers reported greater needs than female teachers in terms of test design and development

Table 2 Item level analysis of the questionnaire

	Items	Mean (SD)	Skewness	Kurtosis	Response (%) Important	Response (%) Essential
Test design and development	Item 5 Writing test tasks and items	4.21 (0.84)	−1.23	1.90	42.1	42.1
	Item 3 Deciding what to test	4.17 (0.86)	−1.19	1.90	43.7	39.7
	Item 6 Evaluating language tests	4.07 (0.84)	−0.97	1.62	47.5	32.0
	Item 13 Rating performance tests	3.95 (0.78)	−0.53	0.67	50.4	24.0
	Item 4 Writing test specifications	3.94 (0.98)	−0.93	0.86	39.5	32.3
	Item 2 Procedures in test design	3.58 (1.06)	−0.48	−0.27	34.4	20.8
Large-scale standardized testing	Item 8 Test analysis	4.17 (0.78)	−0.34	0.04	48.4	35.7
	Item 7 Interpreting scores	3.90 (0.91)	−0.45	−0.29	37.6	29.6
	Item 17 Standard testing	3.90 (0.77)	−0.49	0.74	52.0	20.8
	Item 12 Use of statistics	3.75 (0.88)	−0.51	0.02	47.6	18.5
	Item 16 Large-scale testing	3.62 (0.82)	−0.30	0.12	45.5	12.2
	Item 14 Scoring close-related items	3.48 (0.93)	−0.63	0.49	43.7	10.3
	Item 23 Principles of measurement	3.41 (0.88)	−0.27	−0.14	39.7	8.7
	Item 22 The uses of tests in society	3.01 (0.91)	−0.12	−0.32	23.8	4.8
Classroom testing and washback	Item 18 Preparing learners	3.97 (0.92)	−0.63	−0.10	38.9	32.5
	Item 15 Classroom assessment	4.09 (0.75)	−0.61	0.96	50.0	30.2
	Item 9 Selecting tests for use	3.90 (0.82)	−0.34	0.04	43.7	24.6
	Item 19 Washback	3.55 (0.87)	−0.46	0.21	45.5	10.7
	Item 21 Ethical considerations	3.17 (0.92)	−0.28	−0.24	33.3	4.8
	Item 20 Test administration	3.20 (0.85)	−0.24	−0.07	33.3	4.1
	Item 1 History of language testing	2.29 (0.88)	0.38	−0.15	8.1	0.80
Validity and reliability	Item 10 Reliability	4.15 (0.86)	−0.76	0.23	35.7	41.3
	Item 11 Validation	4.15 (0.82)	−0.75	0.52	40.3	38.7

Table 3 Reliability and descriptives of the subscales of the survey

Subscale	Cronbach's α	M	SD
Test design and development	0.84	3.99	0.67
Large-scale standardized testing	0.81	3.66	0.55
Classroom testing and washback	0.74	3.45	0.54
Validity and reliability	0.96	4.16	0.81

Table 4 CFA model confirming the structure of the questionnaire

Model	χ^2	df	χ^2/df	CFI	RMSEA	RMSEA 95% confidence interval
CFA model	306.58*	198	1.55	0.93	0.066	0.051–0.080

*$p < 0.05$

(male: $M = 4.04$, $SD = 0.68$; female: $M = 3.98$, $SD = 0.67$), large-scale standardized testing (male: $M = 3.81$, $SD = 0.47$; female: $M = 3.63$, $SD = 0.57$), classroom testing and washback (male: $M = 3.56$, $SD = 0.53$; female: $M = 3.43$, $SD = 0.54$), and validity and reliability (male: $M = 4.17$, $SD = 0.69$; female: $M = 4.16$, $SD = 0.83$).

One-way ANOVA was run to evaluate the assessment training needs of teachers of different ages, education levels, and levels of assessment knowledge.

Results showed that there were no significant differences among teachers of different ages ($F(9, 108) = 0.66$, $p > 0.05$; $F(9, 108) = 0.35$, $p > 0.05$; $F(9, 107) = 0.90$, $p > 0.05$; and $F(9, 112) = 0.82$, $p > 0.05$). In spite of this, an examination of the mean differences indicates that for test design and development, large-scale testing and classroom testing, those aged between 21 and 25 have the strongest training needs, while for validity and reliability issues, those aged between 51 and 55 need training the most.

For the differences in assessment training needs among teachers of different education levels, analysis results showed that there were no significant differences among the groups ($F(3, 107) = 1.86$, $p > 0.05$; $F(3, 108) = 0.87$, $p > 0.05$; $F(3, 106) = 1.98$, $p > 0.05$; and $F(3,111) = 0.47$, $p > 0.05$). An examination of the mean differences indicates that the teachers with diplomas had the strongest training needs in all four aspects, followed by those with master degrees.

Finally, regarding assessment training needs of those with different assessment knowledge, there were no significant differences among teachers with different levels of assessment knowledge ($F(3, 107) = 0.93$, $p > 0.05$; $F(3, 108) = 0.22$, $p > 0.05$; $F(3, 108) = 1.11$, $p > 0.05$; and $F(3, 111) = 0.60$, $p > 0.05$). In spite of the non-significance, the mean differences among the groups are obvious. It is interesting to find that those with poor assessment knowledge have stronger training needs in test design and development and validity and reliability, while those with average and good assessment knowledge are more interested in training in terms of large-scale testing and classroom testing and washback. This finding has important implications for the design of training courses in assessment literacy for Singapore primary Chinese Language teachers.

Discussion

This study examined Singapore primary Chinese Language teachers' training needs in assessment literacy. Results revealed the Chinese Language teachers' needs and interest in learning about all four aspects of assessment literacy: test design and development, large-scale testing, classroom testing and test validity and reliability. As indicated in the mean scores of the four subscales, Singapore primary Chinese Language teachers showed strong training need in knowledge regarding validity, reliability, test design and development, but relatively weaker need in large-scale standardized testing and classroom testing and washback. Answers to the research questions are presented below:

Research question 1: What are Singapore primary Chinese Language teachers' specific training needs in terms of test design and development, large-scale testing, classroom testing and test validity and reliability?

Singapore primary Chinese Language teachers' training needs are categorized into four types, i.e., test design and development, large-scale testing, classroom testing and test validity and reliability. In terms of test design and development, teachers reported to have the greatest need to know about writing test tasks and items (Item 5), followed by deciding what to test (Item 3), and how to evaluate language tests (Item 6).

For large-scale testing, their top training needs were to learn how to do test analysis (Item 8), interpret test scores (Item 7), standard testing (Item 17), and use of statistics. Regarding classroom test and washback, teachers were most interested in classroom assessment (Item 15), how to prepare learners to take tests (Item 18) and selecting tests for their own use (Item 9). In addition, they think that it is necessary to know more about the issue of validity and reliability (Item 10 and 11). Of all the listed items of training needs, the participating teachers were most interested in wring test tasks and items (Item 5), deciding what to test (Item 2), test analysis (Item 8), reliability (Item 10), validity (Item 11), and classroom assessment (Item 15).

On the whole, the teachers had the greatest need in receiving training in writing test tasks and items, test analysis and deciding what to test. In other words, hands-on, practical knowledge, and key issues of validity and reliability in language assessment attracted teachers' attention and interest the most. The findings are consistent with Fulcher's (2012) conclusion that the practice of language testing is the core component in assessment literacy framework.

Research question 2: Are there any differences in assessment training needs among Singapore primary school teachers of different genders, ages, educational backgrounds, and levels of assessment knowledge?

The results of analysis showed that there were no significant differences in assessment training needs among teachers of different genders, ages, and educational backgrounds and assessment knowledge.

In addition, it was found that the topics of test design and development, large-scale standardized testing, and classroom testing were more interesting to younger teachers while validity and reliability attracted more interest from teachers of older age. The possible explanation for this tentative finding might be that younger teachers, who are not experienced in teaching and assessment, intended to know more about fundamental knowledge in language assessment. Older teachers, who have more experience in teaching, are more likely to be interested in the deeper level of assessment knowledge such as validity and reliability (Malone, 2013).

Regarding the relationship between teachers' academic qualification and training needs in assessment, those with diplomas and masters' degree seem to have more interest in learning assessment knowledge than those with bachelors' degree and below bachelors' degree. The explanation might be that the diplomas holders are more likely to be newly recruited teachers, so they are the group who need training in assessment knowledge the most. For those master degree holders, it might be that the higher academic qualification the teachers achieved, the more important they feel it to learn knowledge about language assessment literacy. Also, the teachers with higher academic qualifications might have better chances to get to know the importance of assessment literacy in language teaching. However, due to the limitation of the sample size, this conclusion should be subject to further examination.

As indicated previously, those who self-reported to have poor assessment knowledge have stronger training needs in test design and development and validity and reliability, while those with average and good assessment knowledge are more interested in topics of large-scale testing and classroom testing and washback. This might be due to the common understanding that former topics are the fundamental ones while the latter ones are more advanced in assessment knowledge.

Conclusions and Implications

This study examined Singapore primary Chinese Language teachers' training needs in assessment literacy. Results indicated that the participants were interested in practical, hands-on knowledge of language assessment. Those with poor assessment knowledge seemed to have greater training needs in fundamental topics in assessment knowledge, while those with good knowledge in assessment showed greater training needs in more advanced topics.

Expectations are that the findings from this study can provide useful information for the preparation of relevant training materials and courses for primary Chinese Language teachers in Singapore.

Future research is suggested to be conducted with a larger and more representative sample. It is hoped that studies carried out in this way will provide more revealing and comprehensive findings of Singapore Chinese Language teachers' assessment literacy and their related training needs.

The present study used self-report questionnaire data, which are understandably open to acquiescence and faking biases. It is therefore useful to conduct studies using actual tests of knowledge (Kunnan & Zhang, 2015), for instance, asking the teachers to interpret reliability indices such as the Cronbach's alpha coefficient. However, it is readily appreciated that this approach will entail much more testing time and may even be psychological threatening to the teachers.

Appendix: The Questionnaire

For each one please decide whether you think this is a topic that should be included in a course on language testing.

Indicate your response as follows:

5 = essential; 4 = important; 3 = fairly important; 2 = not very important; 1 = unimportant

1	语言测试的历史 History of language testing	1	2	3	4	5
2	语言测试的设计程序 Procedures in language test design	1	2	3	4	5
3	确定应测试的内容 Deciding what to test	1	2	3	4	5
4	编写测试规范 Writing test specifications	1	2	3	4	5
5	编写测试题目 Writing test tasks and items	1	2	3	4	5
6	评价语言测试 Evaluating language tests	1	2	3	4	5
7	解释测试分数 Interpreting scores	1	2	3	4	5
8	试题分析 Test analysis	1	2	3	4	5
9	选择合适的测试题目为我所用 Selecting tests for your own use	1	2	3	4	5
10	测试的信度 Reliability	1	2	3	4	5
11	测试的效度 Validation	1	2	3	4	5
12	统计分析的使用 Use of statistics	1	2	3	4	5
13	评估绩效测试(如口语/书面表达) Rating performance tests	1	2	3	4	5
14	如何给封闭式试题打分(如MCQ) Scoring closed-response items	1	2	3	4	5
15	课堂评估 Classroom assessment	1	2	3	4	5
16	大规模测试 Large-scale testing	1	2	3	4	5
17	标准化测试 Standard setting	1	2	3	4	5
18	如何帮助学习者备考 Preparing learners to take tests	1	2	3	4	5
19	考试对于课堂教学的反拨作用 Washback on the classroom	1	2	3	4	5

(continued)

(continued)

20	考试管理 Test administration	1	2	3	4	5
21	考试中的伦理考量 Ethical considerations in testing	1	2	3	4	5
22	考试在社会中的使用 The uses of tests in society	1	2	3	4	5
23	教育评量的原则 Principles of educational measurement	1	2	3	4	5

References

Bachman, L. (2004). *Statistical analyses for language assessment*. Cambridge: Cambridge University Press.
Boyles, P. (2005). Assessment literacy. In M. Rosenbusch (Ed.), *National assessment summit papers* (pp. 11–15). Ames, IA: Iowa State University.
Fulcher, G. (2012). Language literacy for the language classroom. *Language Assessment Quarterly, 9,* 113–132.
Hu, L., & Bentler, P. M. (1999). Cutoff criteria for fit indexes in covariance structure analysis: Conventional criteria versus new alternative. *Structural Equation Modeling, 6,* 1–55.
Inbar-Lourie, O. (2008). Constructing a language assessment knowledge base: A focus on language course. *Language Testing, 25,* 385–402.
Kline, R. B. (2011). *Principles and practices of structural equation modeling* (2nd ed.). New York, NY: Guilford.
Koh, K. H. (2011). Improving teachers' assessment literacy through professional development. *Teaching Education, 22*(2), 255–276.
Kunnan, A. J., & Zhang, L. M. (2015). Responsibility in language assessment. In H. Yang (Ed.), *The sociology of language testing* (pp. 211–231). Shanghai: Shanghai Foreign Language Press.
Malone, M. (2008). Training in language assessment. In E. Shohamy & N. H. Hornberger (Eds.), *Encyclopedia of language and education* (Vol. 7, pp. 273–284)., Language testing and assessment New York, NY: Springer.
Malone, M. (2013). The essentials of assessment literacy: Contrasts between testers and users. *Language Testing, 30,* 329–344.
Soh, K. C., & Zhang, L. M. (2017). The development and validation of teacher assessment literacy Scale: A trial report. *Journal of Linguistics and Language Teaching, 8*(1), 91–116.
Stiggins, R. (1991). Assessment literacy. *The Phi Delta Kappan, 72,* 534–539.
Taylor, L. (2009). Developing assessment literacy. *Annual Review of Applied Linguistics, 29,* 21–36.
Zhang, L. M., & Soh, K. C. (2016). Assessment literacy of Singapore Chinese language teachers in primary and secondary schools. In Soh, K. C. (Ed.), *Teaching chinese language in Singapore—Retrospect and challenge* (pp. 85–103). Springer.

Limei Zhang (张丽妹) received her Ph.D. from Nanyang Technological University, Singapore. She is currently lecturer at Singapore Centre for Chinese Language, Nanyang Technological University. Her academic interests include language assessment literacy, reading and writing assessment, and learner metacognition. She has published a number of articles and book chapters on language assessment and reading and writing issues. Her most recent work is a book on the relationship between learners' metacognition and reading comprehension.

Teacher Assessment Literacy Scale: Design and Validation

Kay Cheng Soh and Limei Zhang

Abstract With the increased use of language assessment, language teachers are required to develop assessment literacy and take the testing and assessment responsibilities. This article reports the processes and outcomes of the development and validation of the Teacher Assessment Literacy Scale for use with Singapore's Chinese Language teachers.

In the past, patients were passive recipients of medical treatments. The present-day patients are involved in the healing process; they are informed and they are engaged. Analogously, in the past, student assessment tools were crafted by test specialists while teachers were passive users; this is true at least in the American context where standardized tests are the regular fixture of the school. Nowadays, with the emphasis on assessment *for* learning (or *formative* assessment) in contrast with assessment *of* learning (or *summative* assessment), teachers, in America and elsewhere, are expected to use assessment in a more engaged manner to help students learn. Teachers are therefore expected to use test information not only for assessment *of* learning but also, perhaps more importantly, assessment *for* learning. This shift all the more underlines the importance of teachers' assessment literacy if they were to complete this crucial aspect of their job with professionalism. Popham (2006) brought up his very apt analogy between educational and healthcare professions where proper use of test information is crucial. Not only do teachers need assessment literacy but everyone else who has an interest in education and *everyone* includes teachers, school leaders, policy-makers, and parents.

Due to the change in the emphasis on formative assessment and its contribution to learning (Fulcher 2012), the notion of assessment literacy has changed contingently. Traditionally, assessment emphasizes objectivity and accuracy (Spolsky

K. C. Soh (✉) · L. Zhang
Nanyang Technological University, Singapore, Singapore
e-mail: Kaycheng.soh@sccl.sg

L. Zhang
e-mail: Limei.zhang@sccl.sg

1978, 1995), due to the influence of the psychometric and positivistic paradigms, and testing activities normally are carried out at the end of learning periods (Gipps 1994; Wolf et al. 1991). In that context, only measurement specialists were expected to have specialized knowledge of test development, score interpretation, and theoretical concepts of measurement. In contrast, assessment is now perceived as an integral part of teaching and learning to provide timely information as feedback to guide further instruction and learning. This requires teachers to design assessment, make use of test results to promote teaching and learning, and be aware of inherent technical problems and limitation of educational measurement (Fulcher 2012; Malone 2008). Thus, it is important that teachers have sufficient practical skills as well as theoretical understanding.

Assessment Literacy Measures

Over the years, efforts have been made to measure teacher assessment literacy. Gotch and French (2014) systematically reviewed teacher assessment literacy measures within the context of contemporary teacher evaluation policy. The authors collected objective tests of assessment knowledge, teacher self-reports, and rubrics to evaluate teachers' work in assessment literacy studies from 1991 to 2012. They then evaluated the psychometric work from these measures against a set of claims related to score interpretation and use. Across the 36 measures reviewed, they found weak support for these claims. This highlights the need for increased work on assessment literacy measures in the educational measurement field.

DeLuca et al. (2016) emphasized that assessment literacy is a core professional requirement across educational systems and that measuring and supporting teachers' assessment literacy have been a primary focus over the past two decades. At present, according to the authors, there is a multitude of assessment standards across the world and numerous assessment literacy measures representing different conceptions of assessment literacy. The authors analyzed assessment literacy standards from five English-speaking countries (i.e., Australia, Canada, New Zealand, the UK, and the USA) and Europe to understand shifts in the assessment developed after 1990. Through a thematic analysis of 15 assessment standards and an examination of eight assessment literacy measures, the authors noticed shifts in standards over time though the majority of the measures continue being based on early conceptions of assessment literacy.

Stiggins (1991) first coined the term *assessment literacy* to refer to teachers' understanding of the differences between sound and unsound assessment procedures and the use of assessment outcomes. Teachers who are assessment literates should have a clear understanding of the purposes and targets of assessment, the competence in choosing appropriate assessment procedures, the capability of conducting assessment effectively and of avoiding pitfalls in the process of assessment practices and interpretation of results.

This sounds simple but can be a tall order in actuality. For example, the by now classic textbook of educational measurement by Linn and Miller (2005) has altogether 19 chapters in three parts. The five chapters in Part I cover such topics on the role of assessment, instructional goals of assessment, concepts of reliability and validity, and issues and trends. These may not be of immediate relevance to the classroom teachers' work but provide necessary conceptual backgrounds for teachers to be informed assessors. Part II has ten chapters of a technical or procedural nature, which equip teachers with the necessary practical skills in test design using a wide range of item formats. The ending Part III has four chapters, dealing with selecting and using published tests as well as the interpretation of scores involving basic statistical concepts. The three parts that made up the essential domains of assessment literacy expected of classroom teachers are typical of many education measurement texts supporting teacher training programs.

According to Popham (2009), increasing numbers of professional development programs have dealt with assessment literacy for teachers and administrators. Popham then asked the question of whether assessment literacy is merely a fashionable focus or whether it should be regarded as a significant area of professional development for years to come. Popham first divided educators' measurement-related concerns into either classroom assessments or accountability assessments and then argued that educators' inadequate knowledge about either of these can cripple the quality of education. He concluded that assessment literacy is a *condicio sine qua non* for today's competent educator and must be a pivotal content area for current and future staff development.

The above review of the pertinent literature on assessment literacy and its measurement has implications for the present study. First, in recent years, the Singapore Ministry of Education has launched the initiatives emphasizing higher-order thinking skills and deep understanding in teaching, such as 'Teach Less, Learn More' (TLLM) and 'Thinking Schools, Learning Nations' (TSLN). Consequently, school teachers are required to make changes to their assessment practice and to equip themselves with sufficient assessment literacy. In spite of the importance of assessment literacy, few studies have been conducted to examine their assessment knowledge and skills. Among the very few local studies, Koh (2011) investigated the effects of professional development on Primary 4 and 5 teachers of English, Science, and Mathematics. She found that ongoing professional development of assessment literacy is especially effective in improving teachers' assessment literacy, when compared with teachers who participated in workshops training them to design assessment rubrics. The findings suggest that to successfully develop teachers' assessment literacy, the training needs be broad enough in the topics covered, and the training has to be extended over a reasonable period of time.

In a more recent study, Zhang & Chin (under review) examined the learning needs in language assessment among 103 primary school Chinese Language teachers using an assessment literacy survey developed by Fulcher (2012). Results provide an understanding of teachers' interest and knowledge in test design and development, large-scale testing, classroom testing, and test validity and reliability. With these very limited number of studies in the Singapore context, there is a need for more studies to be carried out for a better understanding of Singapore school teachers' assessment literacy. For carrying out such studies, it is necessary to develop an assessment literacy scale which is broad enough and yet concise to measure the teachers' assessment competence properly and accurately.

Secondly, in systems like that of the USA where standardized tests are designed by test specialists through a long and arduous process of test development, applying sophisticated psychometric concepts and principles (with regular intermittent revisions), it is reasonable to assume that the resultant assessment tools made available for teachers are of a high psychometric quality. In such a case, the most critical aspect of assessment literacy that teachers need is the ability to properly interpret the results they obtain through the tests. Measurement knowledge beyond this is good to have but not really needed. However, in a system like that of Singapore where standardized tests are *not* an omnipresent fixture, teacher-made tests are almost the only assessment tool available. This indicates the teachers' need for assessment literacy of a much broader range, going beyond the interpretation of test results. Therefore, this study aims to develop an instrument for assessment literacy to measure teachers' assessment literacy in the Singapore context.

Thirdly, previous studies have provided the framework for the present writers to follow in designing an assessment literacy scale. As one of the most influential studies in language assessment literacy, Fulcher (2012) has expanded the definition of assessment literacy. According to him, assessment literacy comprises three levels' knowledge:

- Level 1 concerns the knowledge, skills, and abilities in the practice of assessment, especially in terms of test design. Specifically, this type of knowledge includes how to decide what to test, writing test items and tasks, developing writing test specifications, and developing rating scales.
- Level 2 refers to the processes, principles, and concepts of assessment, which are more relevant to quality standards and research. This type of knowledge includes validity, reliability, fairness, accommodation, washback/consequences as well as ethics and justice of assessment.
- Level 3 is about historical, social, political, philosophical, and ethical frameworks of assessment, which is concerned with such issues as the historical, social, and political as well as the philosophical and ethical bases for assessment practice.

Following Fulcher's (2012) framework, we aim to measure teachers' assessment knowledge of two aspects, i.e., (1) the knowledge, skills, and abilities in assessment practice as well as the fundamental principles and (2) concepts of language assessment. This does not mean that we did not value the third domain (Level 3) but that we considered this as not being so urgently needed by teachers in Singapore and as not being so critical to their day-to-day use of assessment in the classroom context.

Method

Design

In the development of the *Teacher Assessment Literacy Scale*, consultation was made to two classics of educational measurement (Hopkins 1998; Linn and Miller 2005). The first decision to be made was to identify and delimit the domains to be covered in the scale, and it was decided that four key domains needed to be represented in the new measure:

1. Understanding of the nature and functions of assessment.
2. Practical skills to design and use a variety of item formats to meet the instructional needs.
3. Ability to properly interpret these to inform further teaching and guide student learning.
4. Ability to evaluate the qualities of the test results, involving basic knowledge of statistics.

Against the background of the above considerations, it was decided that ten items be written for each domain as a sample representing the possible items of the domain. Four domains having been delimited, the whole scale thus comprises 40 items. It was further decided that the items would take the form of four-option multiple choice to ensure objectivity in scoring and keep the testing time within a reasonable limit of about 30 min.

Due to space constrain, the actual items are not presented in this article. However, interested researchers may contact the first author for a copy of the items via sohkaycheng@hotmail.com.

Trial Sample

The scale thus crafted was then administered to 323 Chinese Language teachers, 170 from primary schools, and 153 from secondary schools and junior colleges. There is a female preponderance of 83%. Of the teachers, 52% have more than ten years of teaching experience. In terms of qualification, 93% hold a university degree and 95% have completed professional training. However, only 48% reported that they had elected to study assessment in their pre-service training, and 78% acknowledged that they felt the need for more training in assessment.

Teachers attended various in-service courses at the Singapore Centre for Chinese Language from January to March 2015. The participants can be considered mature in the teaching profession as more than half of them having ten or more years of teaching experience. Moreover, the female preponderance is typical of the teaching profession in Singapore. Thus, bearing in mind some limitations in these regards, the participating Chinese Language teachers can be deemed sufficiently representative of Chinese Language teachers in Singapore.

Analysis

Confirmatory factor analysis was performed to examine whether the collected data support the proposed model of four specified dimensions. Next, the classical item analysis was performed to obtain item difficulty (p) and item discrimination (r). Then, the Rasch analysis was conducted to estimate item locations to indicate item difficulty within the context of the whole set of items analyzed, with a positive index indicating the *difficulty to answer correctly* and vice versa.

Results

Results of statistical analysis are highlighted below, and details can be found in Soh and Zhang (2017).

Descriptive Statistics

As Table 1 shows, the means for the subscales vary between 5.52 and 2.97, out of 10. The highest mean is for the first subscale (nature and function of assessment) while the lowest is for the fourth subscale (concepts of reliability, validity, etc). Generally, the means show that teachers were able to answer correctly about half of the 30 questions in subscales 1–3, but they were able to answer correctly only about three of the 10 questions in subscale 4. If a criterion-referenced approach requiring 90% of the teachers to be able to answer correctly 90% of the questions, thus expecting approximately 80% of correct responses, the results obtained are far from being satisfactory, being 45% on average.

Table 1 Descriptive statistics

Subscale	Mean	Standard deviation
Nature and function of assessment	5.53	1.23
Design and use of test items	4.87	1.38
Interpretation of test results	4.50	1.58
Concepts of reliability, validity, etc.	2.97	1.50

Confirmatory Factor Analysis

When confirmatory factor analysis was run, the results show that the incremental fit index CFI = 1.00 is greater than 0.95, while the absolute fit index RMSEA = 0.001 is less than 0.06. The RMSEA 95% confidence interval is narrow. $X^2/df = 0.57$ is less than 3.00.

Table 2 shows the path coefficients of assessment literacy range from 0.21 (concepts of reliability, validity, etc) to 0.49 (nature and function of assessment), all significant at the 0.05 level, and the average is 0.39, indicating that the latent variable is well-defined by the four variables. However, of the four path coefficients, those for the first three subscales are sizable, varying from 0.41 to 0.49, but that for the fourth subscale (statistical and measurement concepts) is rather low at 0.21, indicating that the other three subscales are better measures of assessment literacy.

Classical Item Analysis

Subtest 1: Nature and Functions of Assessment
Subtest 1 deals with understanding the functions assessment has in teaching and learning, and concepts related to the norm- and criterion-referenced interpretation of test scores. For this subtest, the facility indices (p) vary from a very low 0.07 to a very high 0.94, with a mean of 0.55 and a median of 0.56. In short, the items of Subtest 1 vary widely in difficulty although the average facility suggests that this subtest as a whole is moderately difficult. At the same time, the discrimination indices (r) vary from 0.13 to 0.33, with a mean discrimination of 0.23 and a median of 0.22. These figures indicate that the items have a low but acceptable discriminatory power.

Subtest 2: Design and Use of Test Items
The items of Subtest 2 deal with the understanding of the suitability of various item formats and their appropriate uses. The p's vary from a low 0.13 to a very high 0.96, with a mean of 0.49 and a median of 0.44. In short, these items vary widely in

Table 2 Path coefficients

Subscale	Path coefficient	Error
Nature and function of assessment	0.49	0.24
Design and use of test items	0.41	0.17
Interpretation of test results	0.47	0.22
Concepts of reliability, validity, etc.	0.21	0.64

difficulty although the mean suggests that this subtest is moderately difficult as a whole. At the same time, the r's vary from 0.11 to 0.30, with a mean of 0.21 and a median of 0.22. These results indicate that the items have a low but.

Subtest 3: Interpretation of Test Results
The items of Subtest 3 pertain to knowledge of item indices and meanings of test scores. The p's vary from a very low 0.03 to a high 0.78, with a mean of 0.45 (median 0.51). These figures indicate that the items vary widely in difficulty although the mean suggests that this subtest is of moderate difficulty. At the same time, the r's vary from 0.05 to 0.47, with a mean of 0.24 (median 0.23). These results indicate that the subtest as a whole has acceptable discrimination.

Subtest 4: Concepts of Reliability, Validity, and Basic Statistics
Subtest 4 deals with abstract concepts of test score qualities and knowledge of simple statistics essential to understand test results. The p's vary from a low 0.11 to a high 0.64, with a mean of 0.30 (median 0.25). These figures indicate that the items are difficult ones when compared with those of the other three subtests. The r's vary from 0.05 to 0.36, with a mean of 0.19 (median 0.17). These results indicate that the subtest as a whole has low discrimination.

By way of summary, the 40 items generally have an acceptable level of facility for the teachers involved in this study, although the facilities and discrimination vary widely, reflecting probably the wide heterogeneity of the teachers' assessment literacy. Moreover, the items tend to be have low discrimination power, partly due to the constrains of low facilities of some items. These findings could at least partly account for the fact that the teachers taking part in this study have discernible deficits in their assessment literacy, with an overall mean of 18 for the 40 items (i.e., 45%).

Rasch Analysis

For the Rasch analysis (Rasch 1993) performed on the 40 items, item estimates vary from −3.664 to +3.245, with a mean of 0.000 (median 0.260). These show that the items cover a wide range of difficulty, and the median indicates that the items as a set are somewhat on the difficult side of the scale. For the 40 items, the Infit MSQs vary between 0.690 and 1.146, with a mean of 0.965 and a median 0.999. At the same time, the Outfit MSQs vary between 0.859 and 1.068 (with a mean of 0.970 and a median of 0.978). These indicate that the item fit statistics all fall within the recommended range of 0.7–1.3, and therefore, all 40 items of the scale fit the Rasch model well.

Based on the item estimates, the 40 items can be classified into three groups in terms of item difficulty. The 11 items of the 'difficult' group have facilities (p's) less than 0.2. These items are separated from the rest by a natural gap in Rasch difficulties between 14.17 and 1.125. Most of these difficult items deal with some quantitative aspects of test. The remaining items deal with diagnosis, functions, assessing written expression, and above-level assessment. Generally, answering these questions correctly requires more specific training in assessment many of the teachers do not have, especially for items which are quantitative in nature.

At the other end, there are seven items in the 'easy' group, with facilities greater than 0.80 indicating that 80% or more of the teachers answered them correctly. These items are separated by a natural gap in Rasch difficulties, between −1.579 and −2.009. These items deal with concepts which can be gained through experience in assessment and are therefore commonsensical in nature; no specific training may be needed to answer such questions correctly.

In between the 'difficulty' and 'easy' groups, there are 22 items of 'appropriate' facilities, between $p = 0.20$ and less than $p = 0.80$. Their Rasch difficulties span from +1.125 to −1.579. In terms of item content, only three are from Subtest 1 (Nature and Function). There are six items from Subtest 2 (Design and Use of Test Items), seven items from Subtest 3 (Interpretation of Test Results), and six items from Subtest 4 (Reliability, Validity, and Basic Statistics). These clearly show the location of the teachers' deficits in assessment literacy.

Correlations Between Classical Facilities and Rasch Estimates

A question that has often been asked is whether the two approaches (classical and Rasch) to item analysis yield comparable results. It is therefore interesting to note that the correlation between the classical p's and the Rasch estimates is $r = |0.99|$, indicating that the two approaches of item calibration yielded almost identical results. This corroborates with many recent studies (e.g., Fan 1998; Magno 2009; Preito et al. 2003).

Discussion

Reliability

The conventional method of assessing score reliability is Cronbach's alpha coefficient, which indicates the degree of internal consistency among the items, with the assumption that the items are homogeneous. The 40 items of the scale are scored 1 (right) or 0 (wrong), and therefore, the Kuder–Richardson Formula 20 (KR20), which is a special case of Cronbach's alpha for dichotomous items, was calculated. The reliability coefficients vary from KR20 = 0.18–0.40, with a median of 0.36. Moreover, for the scale as a whole and the total sample of combined primary and secondary teachers, Cronbach's internal consistency coefficient is $\alpha = 0.471$. These indices are generally low, compared with the conventional expectation of a minimum of 0.7. This definitely leads to the question of trustworthiness.

However, there have been criticisms on Cronbach's alpha as a measure of item homogeneity or unidimensionality (Bademci 2006). One condition which might have led to the low reliabilities is the heterogeneous nature of item content among the 40 items since they cover many different aspects of educational measurement, some being qualitative and others quantitative in nature, even within a particular subtest. This renders suspect of the conventional reliability measures which assume item homogeneity. Participant homogeneity could be another factor contributing to low score reliability. Pike and Hudson (1998: 149) discussed the limitations of using Cronbach's alpha (and its equivalent KR20) to estimate reliability when using a sample with homogeneous responses in the measured construct and described the risk of drawing the wrong conclusion that a new instrument may appear to have poor reliability. They demonstrated the use of an alternate statistic that may serve as a cushion against such situation and recommended the calculation of the Relative Alpha by considering the ratio between the standard error of measurement (SEM) which itself involves the reliability as shown in the formula, thus,

$$SEM = SD * SQRT\,(1 - \text{reliability})$$

Pike and Hudson's Relative Alpha can take a value between 0.0 and 1.0 and uses an alternative way to evaluate score reliability. Their formula is,

$$\text{Relative Alpha} = 1 - SEM^2/(\text{Range}/6)^2$$

In this formula, SEM is the usual indicator of the lack of trustworthiness of the obtained scores and, under normal circumstances, the scores for a scale will theoretically span over six standard deviations. Thus, the second term on the right is an indication of the proportion of test variance that is unreliable. Relative Alpha indicates the proportion of test-variance offset for its unreliable portion, i.e., the proportion of test variance that is trustworthy.

In the present study, the maximum possible score is 40, and the theoretically possible standard deviation is 6.67 (=40/6). However, the actual data yields standard deviations of 4.24 (primary) and 4.66 (secondary) for the scale as a whole, which are 0.64 and 0.70, respectively, of the theoretical standard deviations. In other words, the two groups are found to be more homogeneous than theoretically expected.

The Relative Alphas for the primary teachers vary from 0.94 to 0.98, with a mean of 0.97. For the secondary teachers, the Relative Alphas vary from 0.93 to 0.97, with a mean of 0.97. Thus, in both cases, the statistics suggest that much of the test variance has been captured by the 40-item scale, and the scores can therefore be trusted.

Validity Evidence

Regarding content-referenced evidence, the scale was developed based on a model resulting from an analysis of empirical data and a survey of relevant literature. In addition, content analysis was conducted on the scale for a better content representation. The Rasch analysis provides further content-referenced evidence. Substantive validity evidence refers to the relationship between the construct and the data observed (Wolfe and Smith 2007a, b). In the current study, the Rasch analysis, Infit and Outfit as well as the confirmatory factor analysis provide substantive referenced evidence. Also, the alignment of the analysis based on classical test theory and the Rasch analysis supported the validity argument further.

Conclusion

This article presents preliminary evidence of the psychometric quality, the content-referenced and substantive validity of the newly developed scale. As pointed out by Popham (2006), there is a similarity between the healthcare and teaching professions in that the practitioners need to be able to properly read information about the people they serve as a prerequisite to what they intend and need to do. Thus, the importance of teachers' assessment literacy cannot be over-emphasized. There is therefore a need for an instrument that can help gauge this crucial understanding and skills of teachers. However, interest in this regard has rather a short history, and there are less than a handful of such measurement tools at our disposal at the moment.

The new scale reported here is an attempt to fill the vacuum. It covers essential conceptual skills of educational measurement which are a need-to-know for teachers if they are to perform this aspect of their profession adequately. The new scale is found to be on the 'difficult' side, partly due to a lack of relevant training among the teachers who provided the data. However, it is encouraging that its items have also been found to fit the measurement model reasonably well. What needs be done from here on is to apply the scale to larger and more representative samples of teachers in varied contexts and subjects for its consolidation. In short, the current study is the alpha, far from being the omega.

References

American Federation of Teachers, National Council on Measurement in Education, & National Education Association. (1990). *The standards for competence in the educational assessment of students.* Retrieved July 22, 2003, from http://www.unl.edu/buros/article3.html.

Bademci, V. (2006). *Cronbach's alpha is not a measure of unidimensionality or homogeneity*. Paper presented at the conference Paradigm shift: Tests are not reliable at Gazi University, 28 April 2006.

DeLuca, C., laPointe-McEwan, D., & Luhange, U. (2016). Teacher assessment literacy: A review of international standards and measures. *Educational Assessment, Evaluation and Accountability, 28*(3), 251–272.

Fan, X. (1998). Item response theory and classical test theory: An empirical comparison of their item/person statistics. *Educational and Psychological Measurement, 58*(3), 357–373.

Fulcher, G. (2012). Language literacy for the language classroom. *Language Assessment Quarterly, 9*, 113–132.

Gipps, C. (1994). *Beyond testing: towards a theory of educational assessment*. London: Falmer Press.

Gotch, C. M., & French, B. F. (2014). A systematic review of assessment literacy measures. *Educational Measurement: Issues and practice, 33*(2), 14–18.

Hopkins, K. D. (1998). *Educational and psychological measurement and evaluation*. Needham Heights, MA: Allyn & Bacon.

Koh, K. H. (2011). Improving teachers' assessment literacy through professional development. *Teaching Education, 22*(2), 255–276.

Linn, R. L., & Miller, M. D. (2005). *Measurement and assessment in teaching* (9th ed.). Upper Saddle River, New Jersey: Pearson, Merrill, Prentice Hall.

Magno, C. (2009). Demonstrating the difference between classical test theory and item response theory using derived test data. *The International Journal of Educational and Psychological Assessment, 1*(1), 1–11.

Malone, M. (2008). Training in language assessment. In E. Shohamy & N. H. Hornberger (Eds.), *Encyclopedia of language and education* (Vol. 7, pp. 273–284)., Language testing and assessment New York, NY: Springer.

Pike, C. K., & Hudson, W. W. (1998). Reliability and measurement error in the presence of homogeneity. *Journal of Social Service Research, 24*(1/2), 149–163.

Popham, J. (2006). All about accountability/needed: A dose of assessment literacy. *Educational Leadership, 63*(6), 84–85. http://www.ascd.org/publications/educational-leadership/mar06/vol63/num06/Needed@-A-Dose-of-Assessment-Literacy.aspx.

Popham, W. J. (2009). Assessment literacy for teachers: Faddish or fundamental? Theory Into. *Practice, 48*, 4–11. https://doi.org/10.1080/00405840802577536.

Preito, L., Alonso, J., & Lamarca, R. (2003). Classical test theory versus Rasch analysis for quality of life questionnaire reduction. *Health and Quality of Life Outcomes, 1:27*. 10.186/1477-7525-1-27.

Rasch, G (1993). *Probabilistic models for some intelligence and attainment tests*. Chicago: Mesa Press.

Soh, K. C., & Zhang, L. (2017). The development and validation of a teacher assessment literacy scale: A trail report. *Journal of Linguistics and Language Teaching, 8*(1), 91–116.

Spolsky, B. (1978). Introduction: Linguists and language testers. In B. Spolsky (Ed.), *Approaches to language testing: Advances in language testing series* (Vol. 2, pp. V–X). Arlington, VA: Center for Applied Linguistics.

Spolsky, B. (1995). *Measured words: The development of objective language testing*. Oxford: Oxford University Press.

Stiggins, R. J. (1991). Assessment literacy. *Phi Delta Kappan, 72*(7), 534–539.

Wolf, D., Bixby, J., Glenn, J., & Gardner, H. (1991). To use their minds well: Investigating new forms of student assessment. *Review of Research in Education, 17*, 31–125.

Wolfe, E. W., & Smith, E. V., Jr. (2007a). Instrument development tools and activities for measure validation using rasch models: Part I—instrument development tools. *Journal of Applied Measurement, 8,* 97–123.

Wolfe, E. W., & Smith, E. V., Jr. (2007b). Instrument development tools and activities for measure validation using Rasch models: Part II—validation activities. *Journal of Applied Measurement, 8,* 204–233.

Author Biographies

Kay Cheng Soh (苏启祯) received Ph.D. from NUS, Singapore. He is currently Research Consultant at the Singapore Centre for Chinese Language. His academic interests include child bilingualism, creativity, world university rankings, and international achievement comparisons. His publications include books on the psychology of learning Chinese Language and various aspects of education.

Limei Zhang (张丽妹) received Ph.D. from NTU, Singapore. She is currently Lecturer at the SCCL. Her academic interests include language assessment literacy, reading and writing assessment, and learner metacognition. She has published a number of articles and book chapters on language assessment and reading and writing issues. Her most recent work is a book on the relationship between learners' metacognition and reading comprehension.

Epilogue

Having compiled and edited this monograph, I realized that it was not as easy a task as I first thought it would be. Like climbing a tall hill for morning exercise, you panted only when you have stopped. This is because the chapters cover so many different topics, although all pertaining to effective teaching of a difficult language, Chinese Language of course.

Admittedly, my training in educational psychology, especially in research and statistics, does not prepare me sufficiently for the task in the field of language and linguistic research. Nonetheless, the understanding and enthusiasm of the authors have made the task much easier and pleasant and I have to trust their expertise in their specialized fields.

My engagement as the Research Consultant at the Centre has taught me much about Chinese Language and its linguistics, and I hope, in return, my colleagues have benefitted from my sharing with them in educational measurement, experimental designs, and statistical analysis. I strongly believe that an interaction of the two disciplines (educational psychology and Chinese linguistics) will help to unravel some of the essential instructional problems of how to teach and learn Chinese Language more efficiently. And the chapters collected here attest to this conviction.

I am grateful to all the authors who have contributed generously their time and efforts to make this monograph possible. In the course of editing, I learned.

Kay Cheng Soh